D0345895

19 СЕНТ. 1982

CONTEMPORARY SOCIAL RESEARCH SERIES

General Editor: MARTIN BULMER

3

The Uses of Social Research

CONTEMPORARY SOCIAL RESEARCH SERIES
Series Editor: MARTIN BULMER

1   SOCIAL MEASUREMENT AND SOCIAL INDICATORS
    Issues of Policy and Theory
    by Michael Carley

2   MODELLING SOCIETY
    An Introduction to Loglinear Analysis for Social Researchers
    by G. Nigel Gilbert

BOOKS EDITED BY MARTIN BULMER:

Working Class Images of Society (1975)
Sociological Research Methods (1977)
Mining and Social Change: Durham County in the Twentieth Century
(1977)
Social Policy Research (1978)
Censuses, Surveys and Privacy (1979)
Social Research and Royal Commissions (Allen & Unwin, 1980)
Social Research Ethics (1982)

The Uses of Social Research

Social Investigation in Public Policy-Making

MARTIN BULMER

London
GEORGE ALLEN & UNWIN
Boston   Sydney

© Martin Bulmer, 1982
This book is copyright under the Berne Convention. No reproduction
without permission. All rights reserved.

George Allen & Unwin (Publishers) Ltd,
40 Museum Street, London WC1A 1LU, UK

George Allen & Unwin (Publishers) Ltd,
Park Lane, Hemel Hempstead, Herts HP2 4TE, UK

Allen & Unwin, Inc.,
9 Winchester Terrace, Winchester, Mass. 01890, USA

George Allen & Unwin Australia Pty Ltd,
8 Napier Street, North Sydney, NSW 2060, Australia

First published in 1982

British Library Cataloguing in Publication Data

Bulmer, Martin
    The uses of social research: social investigation in public
    policy-making.
1. Decision making   2. Great Britain –
Social policy
I. Title
361.6′1′0941   HN390
ISBN 0–04–312011–3
ISBN 0–04–312012–1 Pbk

Library of Congress Cataloging in Publication Data

Bulmer, Martin.
    The uses of social research.
(Contemporary social research series; 3)
Bibliography: p.
Includes index.
1. Policy sciences – Research.   2. Social Sciences – Research.
I. Title.   II. Series.
H97.B84   361.6′1′072   81-20580
ISBN 0–04–312011–3   AACR2
ISBN 0–04–312012–1 (pbk.)

Set in 10 on 11 point Times by Rowland Phototypesetting Ltd,
Bury St Edmunds, Suffolk
and printed in Great Britain by Billings and Sons Ltd,
Guildford, London and Worcester

Contents

To Joan

Preface

This book appears as part of the *Contemporary Social Research* series, which I edit. The series is concerned with topics in the methodology of social research, with the principles and practice whereby the structure of the social sciences is kept standing. This structure combines two separate elements, theory and empirical evidence. That one without the other is barren and that both are necessary for successful social understanding is one of the central themes of this book, as of the series as a whole.

The series is intended to provide concise introductions to significant methodological topics. Broadly conceived, research methodology deals with the general grounds for the validity of social scientific propositions. How do we know what we do know about the social world? More narrowly, it deals with the questions: how do we actually acquire new knowledge about the world in which we live? What are the strategies and techniques by means of which social science data are collected and analysed? The series will seek to answer such questions through the examination of specific areas of methodology. Titles in the series focus upon specific topics, procedures, methods of analysis and methodological problems to provide a readable introduction to its subject. The intended audience includes the advanced undergraduate, the graduate student, the working social researcher seeking to familiarise himself with new areas, and the non-specialist who wishes to enlarge his knowledge of social research. Research methodology need not be remote and inaccessible. The series is concerned above all to demonstrate the general importance and centrality of research methodology to social science.

The Uses of Social Research deals with the ways in which empirical social research gets used in the policy-making process. There has been a growing interest in the potential usefulness of social science, particularly during the last twenty years, though the roots of this interest are much older. The growth and relative health of the social sciences owes a good deal to the belief that they offer useful knowledge to policy-makers, who are therefore willing to finance both teaching and research on a large scale. What, however, does one mean by 'research', since it is not a unitary term and may mean different things to different people? What is meant by 'use' and 'utilisation'? What models of the relationship between research and policy are most convincing?

Questions of this kind have interested me ever since I spent a short period working in the British civil service in the mid-1970s. The gulf which tends to separate the British academic social scientist (particularly in sociology, political science and psychology) from the world of the politician and administrator is a broad one which needs to be bridged more often than it is at present. 'Social research' inside government tends to be identified with descriptive studies and information-gathering, uninformed by any type of social science theory. A good deal of social science theory on the other hand, particularly in sociology, shows little familiarity with the empirical world, while subjects like social administration which study the policy process are still to a considerable extent wedded to outmoded empiricist conceptions of the nature of social scientific knowledge. One purpose of this book is to criticise such empiricist views of knowledge as failing to gain a proper purchase upon the nature of social phenomena. This discussion draws on examples such as deprivation, handicap and health from the social policy field.

The need for a critical discussion of the uses of social research is apparent if one simply considers the term 'research'. One familiar distinction is that between 'basic' and 'applied' social research. Although this book is concerned with applied social research the distinction is not really a very satisfactory one. The history of the natural sciences demonstrates that many of the most important and far-reaching applications of research have stemmed from basic research findings which have revolutionised or changed the way in which the world is perceived and understood. Among the social sciences, economics and economists enjoy the high esteem that they do (relative to other social scientists, if not absolutely) in part because in Britain the relevance of economics to policy was demonstrated above all through the influence of Keynes and his *General Theory* (1936). Logically there is no reason why basic research may not be used and have practical consequences for policy-making, any more than why applied research may not throw light on more basic theoretical issues and problems.

It is more satisfactory to think of a range of different kinds of 'research', rather than a simple dichotomy between 'basic' and 'applied'. The range of meanings of the term is wide. It may refer to statistical data collection and monitoring of a purely descriptive kind or, at the other extreme, to basic academic social science research to test and refine theory. In between it may have tactical objectives, to help in the administration of a service, for example, or its aims may be strategic understanding of the context of a particular policy, drawing on social science theory as well as empirical studies of the field. Another mode is action research, where intervention and diagnosis proceed side by side. A more ambitious form, so far mainly confined to the United States, is the social experiment which involves both intervention by the study team and a controlled investigation of the effects of such intervention.

'Applied' social science and 'applied' social research are not homogeneous. Social scientists themselves conceive of them in various ways. Policy-makers expect different things from social science, often different in nature. In addition, the contexts in which research is carried on affect its character. Research done 'in-house' in government is likely to be more factual and descriptive; that done in university departments perhaps more theoretical, though the evidence on this suggests that the contrast may be overdrawn. One part of the book looks specifically at the use of social research by governmental commissions, a manageable area for an in-depth study of 'use' and 'effectiveness' and one in which I became interested earlier when editing a collection of case-studies on the subject (Bulmer, 1980b).

The patterns of influence of empirical social inquiry are many and various, not homogeneous. Those who carry out research for policy-makers often have clear ideas of what 'use' their research will be and are then nonplussed, dismayed, enraged or embittered when it is not given the treatment which they considered it deserved. A principal argument of this book is that the applied social scientist does not really work in ways analogous to the engineer or doctor, designing better social mechanisms or structures, means of trying to cure society's ills. Social research and social science rather provide enlightenment and understanding, an angle of vision upon the problems of the world which may influence decision-makers and the policy process but does not provide neat technical solutions that can be applied in any simple manner.

A wide range of literature on social science and the applications of research is referred to in the course of this book. There is a large and increasing volume of literature in this field, spanning several social sciences and the academic and non-academic worlds. No attempt has been made to provide a comprehensive bibliography, but those interested may consult three recent guides to the literature, by myself (Bulmer, 1978, pp. 313–26), by Charles Lindblom and David Cohen (1979, pp. 102–26) and by Carol Weiss (1980a, pp. 289–325).

It remains to thank those who helped in various ways while the book was being prepared. Valerie Campling typed the manuscript and deciphered my handwriting, not only with patience but with exemplary clarity and efficiency. I am indebted to Mildred Blaxter, Nicky Hart and Geoffrey Hawthorn who gave permission for material to be reproduced in Chapters 3 and 4. Part of Chapter 5 previously appeared in the *Journal of Public Policy*. The staff of the London School of Economics and Political Science Geography Department Drawing Office under Mrs E. Wilson drew a number of the figures to their usual very high standards. Stuart S. Blume, Robert F. Boruch, Morris Janowitz and Carol Weiss have at various times discussed with me issues in the application of social science research. I alone, however, am responsible for the interpretation and line of argument put forward in this book.

MARTIN BULMER
London

1

A Historical Perspective upon Applied Social Research in Britain

There is in the development of applied social research in Britain a marked historical continuity. We begin with a discussion of this long tradition of the use of research in policy-making, since it continues to exercise a major influence upon the utilisation of social research in the present day. It is particularly important to realise that this tradition is considerably older and to some extent apart from the history of academic disciplines such as psychology, sociology or political science. The distinction between social *research* and social *science* which runs all through this book has deep historical roots which the present chapter aims to clarify. The emphasis here is upon the historical development of British applied social research, without paying too close attention to what is meant by terms such as 'use' or 'applied research'. These conceptual problems are discussed in Chapter 2 once the scene has been set historically.

Where does the story begin? Any starting point is to a considerable degree arbitrary. Some would argue that it lies in the seventeenth century with the early population statisticians John Graunt and William Petty (G. N. Clark, 1948). Others would point to the beginnings of modern census-taking (1790 in the United States, 1801 in Britain) as signalling the start of modern social inquiry. Others would point to English vital registration and the establishment of the General Register Office in 1837. It can be questioned, however, whether birth, marriage and death registration is 'social research'. The history with which we are concerned, it can be argued, begins later in the nineteenth century when adequate scientific methods for social inquiry were first developed.

These arguments about starting data are to a large extent academic. There is clearly a close connection between the scientific study of social conditions, industrialisation and intensified urbanisation. So the discussion will begin around 1830 and sketch some main developments during the nineteenth century. This is not to ignore developments in the eighteenth century and earlier (see Lecuyer and Oberschall, 1968), which must be part of an adequate history of empirical social research. The history of British census-taking and vital registration will also only be mentioned briefly (Glass, 1973; Susser and Adelstein, 1975).

The Royal Commission on the Poor Law, 1832–4

The influence of English social investigation upon policy-making perhaps became most dramatically obvious with the Report of the Royal Commission on the Poor Law of 1834. This was the first occasion on which extensive first-hand inquiries were undertaken as part of a government commission of investigation. The commission was set up to review the workings of the Elizabethan Poor Law and to make recommendations to the government for its reform. To do its work, it determined to inquire into the operation of the Poor Law in different areas of the country, for there was very considerable variation in the administration of poor relief. Thus the commission drew up three questionnaires which were sent to all districts which administered relief. This was not a great success – only one in ten of parishes replied – so as a second step twenty-six assistant commissioners were sent out to 'ascertain the state of the poor by personal inquiry among them, and the administration of the Poor Law by being present at the vestries and at the sessions of the magistrates'. Since not all parishes could be visited, the assistant commissioners were told to select which areas they would visit. The investigators were unpaid, philanthropically minded amateurs, who nevertheless managed to cover 3,000 places, about one in five of Poor Law authorities. Their reports were published in thirteen volumes of appendices (totalling 8,000 pages) to the Report of the commission in 1834. The commissioners believed that when they reported they tendered to His Majesty 'the most extensive and at the same time the most consistent body of evidence that was ever brought to bear on a single subject', evidence moreover which seemed to support the recommendations of the report.

The Report itself – 'one of the classic documents of western social history' (Checkland and Checkland, 1974, p. 9) – had of course a most significant influence upon social welfare policy, turning it in a direction which it was to hold until the mid-twentieth century. By the Poor Law Report and particularly through the work of one commissioner – Edwin Chadwick (1800–90) (see Finer, 1952) – social inquiry became recognised as a part of policy-making within government.

The demonstration effect of the Report has been greater than its real value as social research. Indeed later scholars have not shared the commissioners' high opinion of their own work. They have pointed to the fact that much of the Report was written before all the evidence had been collected; that the whole process was carried on in great haste in a matter of months; that much of the evidence collected by the assistant commissioners was impressionistic and tinged with moralism; and the degree of local variation and the complexity of the problems (for example, the relation between local wage levels, unemployment levels and poor relief) was much greater than the commission realised (see Blaug, 1963 and 1964). 'Of all the empirical investigations before the [eighteen-] fifties, that which preceded the Act of 1834 was the least open-minded, the most concerned to validate the dogmatic presuppositions of political economy' (McGregor, 1957, p. 148). Far from making a dispassionate scientific study of social conditions, the commissioners and assistant commissioners tended to select evidence in terms of their preconceptions about the nature of the problems and the kinds of reforms which were desirable. The Report demonstrated that social inquiry had an important role, but it has not been judged by posterity to be a good example of such inquiry.

This is not surprising. The state of social investigation in the 1830s was primitive, and this resulted in the grave deficiencies in the use of evidence by the commissioners. Nevertheless the 1834 Report served to distinguish social inquiry from policy-making, or political propaganda, or pressure group representations. The idea of objective scientific inquiry into social conditions was given an impetus within the sphere of government which was soon followed up.

The Influence of Chadwick

One of those who was instrumental in this was Chadwick, who in 1834 became secretary to the Poor Law Commissioners. He was a remarkable and extremely forceful public servant, a man of tireless energy and persuasiveness, if not with a personally agreeable temperament. Chadwick was concerned about the effects of insanitary conditions upon the state of the population. He saw a connection between sanitary problems, illness, poverty and the cost of the Poor Law. If there was a link between them, then a way to reduce the cost of poor relief would be to improve sanitary conditions. In 1839, with that objective in mind, he began work which culminated in 1842 in the *Report on the Sanitary Condition of the Labouring Population*. This, unlike the Poor Law Commission Report, was a more scientific and objective inquiry. The degree of objectivity is attested by the shock with which it was received by the more well-to-do sections of the population, most of whom existed in ignorance of how the working classes lived. Chadwick himself noted the astonishment with which his account of social conditions was received 'by persons of the wealthier classes living in the immediate vicinity, to whom the facts were as strange as if they related to foreigners or the natives of an unknown country'.

The purpose of the 1842 Report was threefold: it described graphically the appalling social and health conditions in expanding towns; it demonstrated that these conditions were proportionately worse in towns than in rural areas; and it demonstrated the inability of the central and local administration to deal with the problems which they faced. The first two of these achievements were solidly based on social inquiry. For example, the Report showed that in industrial areas the number of deaths for all classes of the population was greater for the under-20 age group than for the 20- to 60-year-old age group. Only among labourers was this true in rural areas, but whereas in those areas the proportion was 2:1, in industrial areas it was 3:1. Another analysis showed that deaths of adults attributed to epidemic disease were twice as great among the industrial population as among the gentry and professional classes, while the average life expectancy was eight to ten years lower among industrial workers. The deaths of heads of families before the age of 45 placed (it was estimated) 43,000 widows and 112,000 orphans upon the Poor Laws. The Report observed that 'the annual loss of life from filth and bad ventilation is greater than the loss from death or wounds in any wars in modern times'. The 1842 Report had a wide effect, partly because it was well written and presented and partly due to Chadwick's appeal to the economies which sanitary improvement could bring.

Chadwick was not alone in exercising a reforming influence upon mid-Victorian Britain. Others such as Kay-Shuttleworth, Southwood Smith and Sir John Simon (see Lambert, 1963) made important contributions to social and medical investigation and reform. With Chadwick, they were concerned with social improvement, combating the perceived evils of industrialism and urbanism. Few men in the early or mid-nineteenth century luxuriated in knowledge for its own sake; social inquiry had a purpose and an end, the understanding of current social conditions with a view (usually) to some sort of intervention. Some inquiries were undertaken by private individuals, some by and for governments, but generally the same individuals were prominent in government-sponsored inquiries.

Mid-Victorian Social Inquiry

Backing up the work of these individuals was the work of the statistical societies (particularly those of London and Manchester), founded by citizens active in social reform.

> The rapidly expanding urban environment of industrialism deman-
> ded the measurement of human as well as natural resources . . . the
> stench of urban poverty drove thoughtful, vigorous, unsentimental
> middle-class people – doctors, bankers, those experienced in insur-
> ance and the like – to the study of social pathology . . . [They]
> organised themselves up and down the country in statistical and
> philosophical societies for the investigation of the accumulating
> consequences of urban and technological growth. (McGregor, 1957,
> p. 147)

Members of such societies

were united in a common sense of the usefulness of quantitative social information. Many privately enjoyed a confidence, springing directly from the logic of political economy, that facts when discovered would speak with a single unequivocal voice to indicate practical conclusions. (P. Abrams, 1968, p. 13).

By generating social facts, their members aimed to demonstrate the condition of Britain and influence social policy. Though local societies were important, the Statistical Society of London became a major forum for the presentation of the results of nineteenth-century statistical social investigation. It can be debated to what extent the members were primarily concerned with the 'ideology of improvement' rather than objective inquiry for its own sake (Cullen, 1975), but the significant feature is the close connection which was seen between quantitative inquiry and social improvement.

Moreover, although such inquiries were primarily statistical, fact-gathering exercises, there was some interest in the analysis of causes, particularly the causes of disease. William Farr, statistician at the General Register Office for forty years from 1839, exercised a most significant influence, pioneering medical statistics and population studies, providing statistical backing for much of the later work of Chadwick and Sir John Simon, and himself making many original contributions (Susser and Adelstein, 1975). As early as 1839 he wrote to the Registrar-General that

diseases are more easily prevented than cured, and the first step of their prevention is the discovery of their exciting causes . . . The deaths and causes of death are scientific facts which admit of numerical analysis; and science has nothing to offer more inviting in speculation than the laws of vitality, the variations of those laws in the two sexes at different ages, and the influence of civilisation, occupation, locality, seasons and other physical agencies, either in generating diseases and inducing death, or in improving the public health. (Farr, 1885, p. 213)

His own investigations included work on the causes of cholera and on the relationship between mortality and density of population, for which he produced a multifactorial explanation.

By 1850, then, several distinct types of social investigation had developed which had not existed a quarter of a century earlier.

(a) Royal Commissions were likely, in some cases at least, to undertake inquiries of their own into social conditions.

(*b*) Parliamentary committees investigating social conditions would call witnesses before them to provide evidence of the situation in different parts of the country.

(*c*) Reports were compiled by government departments, influenced by (and often written by) reforming civil servants such as Chadwick and Simon.

(*d*) Reports were compiled by government inspectors who were increasingly appointed to carry out supervision of certain legislation, for example, factory inspectors to enforce the Factory Acts.

(*e*) The statistical work of the General Register Office, set up in 1837, consisted in conducting the decennial census and compiling mortality data. (In the early years birth and marriage statistics were less satisfactory.)

(*f*) Statistical investigations were carried out by private individuals, most of whom were members of and reported their findings to one of the Statistical Societies.

Collectively, all but the last came to be known in time as 'blue-book sociology', after the distinctive blue covers in which many government reports were and are published. Applied social research had a practical policy-oriented slant before the emergence of the academic social science disciplines which are so dominant nowadays. Indeed the empirical measurement of phenomena which are now the preserve of those disciplines was often pioneered by nineteenth-century practical men little concerned with developing social theory. The evolution of 'social class' is an excellent example (see Leete and Fox, 1977). Moreover the materials so collected formed the basis of the analysis of the degraded, cruel and exploited working and living conditions of the Victorian working class produced by Karl Marx, notably in *Das Kapital*, published in 1867. In the introduction Marx commented favourably on the English practice of appointing commissions of inquiry, 'armed with plenary powers to get at the truth', and praised

men as competent, as free from partisanship and respect of persons as are the English factory inspectors, her medical reporters in public health, her commissioners of inquiry into the exploitation of women and children, into housing and food. (Marx, 1959, p. 9)

Most of those who undertook such inquiries were Victorian gentlemen not only far removed from Marx's perspective but committed to Victorian values such as absolute economy in public spending and a minimal role for government. 'Social research and social policy derived essentially from professional middle-class anxieties to maintain the stability of institutions by correcting the measured costs of inefficiencies of social wastage' (McGregor, 1957, p. 154). Associated with a redefinition of the functions of government in the decades after 1832, men such as Chadwick and Simon were the architects of the new, industrial civilisation, professional public servants who formulated the social and administrative principles on which it was to develop. By and large they were hostile to what a later generation came to call 'collectivism' (Dicey, 1905). Yet their social objectives led them to greater and greater extensions of state activity to modify social conditions, albeit reluctantly and hesitantly. (For alternative interpretations see MacDonagh, 1977, and Corrigan, 1982.)

Many of the leading public servants played an important role in the statistical societies, particularly the London society (which became the Royal Statistical Society after 1887). The work of the societies illustrates two features characteristic of early social investigations. One was the belief that it was the facts that were needed, and nothing more. The task was to collect these facts (most often from the administrators of institutions, not from members of the public directly), analyse them and present them. The second characteristic was the direct connection made between social research and social reform. Lord Shaftesbury, for example, was a president of the London Statistical Society. Social reformers often believed that all that had to be done to bring about reform was to publicise the shocking social and environmental conditions which led to bad health, housing or whatever. Strong implicit moral assumptions were built into the reliance upon social research as a method of inquiry.

These twin tendencies became more accentuated in the 1850s, with the foundation in 1857 of the National Association for the Promotion of Social Science (NAPSS), which flourished until the 1880s as a forum for people from all sorts of backgrounds interested in social research *and* social reform. Clergymen and doctors were the commonest occupations among the general membership, but it included prominent politicians, lawyers, clergy and other members of the elite. It saw its role as the promotion of legislation – a kind of social experimentation through action and practice, in which social science was quite secondary. The influence and impact of the NAPSS declined and then disappeared in the 1880s, largely because it could not reconcile real conflicts between different interests – for example, between advocates of temperance and the brewers – and because party political divisions between Conservatives and Liberals came to assume much greater salience.

Henry Mayhew's Investigations

Other currents contributed to the development of social investigation at the same period. In the 1840s Chadwick had sought to awaken the public's awareness to the social consequences of urbanism for public health. In the middle years of the century public awareness of poverty – to the extent that awareness existed – came from the writings of novelists such as Dickens, Disraeli, Charles Kingsley and Mrs Gaskell. Around 1850 a journalist called Henry Mayhew published a number of accounts of working-class life in London and the larger cities which were important pioneering social investigations. Earlier social investigations had used a variety of techniques – official statistics, questioning those in positions of administrative authority, calling witnesses before a commission or parliamentary committee – but they did not include going out and talking to members of the working classes in their own environments. Moreover, to the extent that members of the statistical societies investigated the condition of the working classes, they were concerned with 'social discipline' via such topics as overcrowding, domestic management, religious affiliation, church-going, literacy and school attendance. The broader social and economic environment was not thought to have much relevance to individual behaviour.

Henry Mayhew, acting as metropolitan reporter for the *Morning Chronicle*, set out to explore the condition of the working class and produced a series of well-observed descriptions of the lives of a variety of working-class occupations which first appeared as newspaper articles between 1849 and 1851 and were then republished in 1861 as *London Labour and the London Poor*.

Mayhew, the son of a London solicitor, was born in 1812 and spent his life in journalism and various literary and dramatic efforts. He seems to have embarked on his survey of London in 1849 in response to the devastating cholera epidemic of that year, which struck with as much force as the earlier epidemic of 1832. His work had many facets, among them being the fact that it was the first empirical survey of poverty as such.

> Under the term 'poor' I shall include all those persons whose incomings are insufficient for the satisfaction of their wants – a want being, according to my idea, contra-distinguished from a mere desire by a positive physical pain, instead of mental uneasiness accompanying it. The large and comparatively unknown body of people included in this definition I shall contemplate in two distinct classes, viz, the *honest* and the *dishonest*. (Mayhew, quoted in Yeo, 1973, p. 60)

He broke the former down into the 'striving' and the 'disabled', thus distinguishing three groups, those that *will* work, those that *cannot* work, and those that *won't* work.

Mayhew looked particularly at the connection between poverty, employment and the wages and working conditions of particular occupations. He posited an association between poverty and low wages and proceeded to make case-studies of occupations such as Spitalfields weavers, casual dock labourers and many kinds of needle-women. Though writing as a journalist, Mayhew declared: 'My vocation is to collect facts and register opinions.' He gathered a large amount of statistical data and made very laborious wage calculations. His accounts of different occupations were based upon interviews with a cross-section of workers in a trade about their employment and life-style, producing some of the most vivid nineteenth-century evidence about the condition of the metropolitan working classes. His use of qualitative evidence and awareness of subcultures among the poor was far superior to the later, quantitatively more precise, work of Charles Booth and Seebohm Rowntree. It is also noteworthy that Mayhew's inquiries were carried out by a small team which he directed (Yeo, 1973, pp. 66–72).

Mayhew's well-documented revelations shocked mid-Victorian Britain and made clear the extent of deprivation and want in the heart of the metropolis. As with Chadwick in 1842, there was a sense of revealing a part of England unknown to the better-off sections of the population. Mayhew himself saw those he described as 'a large body of persons of whom the public had less knowledge than of the most distant tribes of the earth'. A reviewer commented that he had produced a book 'full of facts entirely new; throws light where utter darkness has hitherto existed'. He was also important because his work was free from the moralism and sentiment so common among Victorian writers. He did have the journalist's touch, the search for the individual story and quotation, the eye for the colourful 'character' who would catch the reader's imagination. But he also had the objective stance of the social investigator and the ability to cross the wide social gulf between himself and those he described.

Moreover his aim was quite directly to influence social action:

> My earnest hope is that the book may serve to give the rich a more intimate knowledge of the sufferings of the poor and cause those who are in 'high places' and those of whom much is expected, to bestir themselves to improve the condition of a class of people whose misery, ignorance, and vice amidst all the immense wealth and great knowledge of 'the finest city in the world', is, to say the very least, a national disgrace to us. (Mayhew, 1861, Vol. 2, p. iv)

The Influence of Charles Booth

It was not until about 1880, however, that the first significant steps towards modern scientific social investigation by social survey were taken. The nineteenth-century inquiries described so far all made use of evidence gathered for the purposes of inquiry and strived to use evidence (not always successfully) which was objective and reliable. But almost without exception such evidence was impressionistic rather than precise, and failed to provide a complete or a representative picture of the condition either of the whole population or of the working-class part of it. This was certainly true of Mayhew, who produced brilliant sketches and vignettes of particular occupations, without being able to say how typical such occupations were or how their economic condition compared with the rest of the population. Though focused upon policy-relevant subjects, many investigations were less than truly scientific in their methods of research.

It would be a mistake to place too great an emphasis upon the changes brought about by Charles Booth (1840–1916), yet it is in no small measure due to him that applied social research in Britain took a more scientific direction (and became particularly associated with the study of poverty).

Charles Booth was not a professional social scientist. He was a Liverpool ship-owner and businessman who had spare-time interests in philanthropy and scientific inquiry. Like many at the time, he was influenced by works published in the 1880s such as Mearn's *The Bitter Cry of Outcast London* of 1883 and Henry George's *Progress and Poverty*, published in 1881 (see Keating, 1976). He was concerned about the individual cases of hardship which were given publicity but wondered how typical they were. Specifically he doubted the evidence of the early socialist H. M. Hyndman that one-quarter of the population of London were living in poverty, based on a primitive study which the Social Democratic Foundation had carried out in working-class districts in London. Late in 1885 he called on Hyndman to tell him so.

Mr Booth was quite frank . . . he told me plainly that in his opinion we had grossly overstated the case . . . [and] that he himself intended to make, at his own expense, an elaborate inquiry into the condition of the workers of London: the wages they received and the amount of subsistence they could obtain for the money remuneration they were paid, he being quite certain he would prove us to be in the wrong. (Hyndman, quoted in Pfautz, 1967, p. 22)

His business experience and positivist outlook inclined him to a systematic study of social conditions. Rational and scientific inquiry seemed to offer a way of resolving the conflicting claims about the condition of the working classes which became particularly salient in the 1880s. Disinterested and methodical investigation could throw light on questions of burning public interest.

There is some dispute as to whether Hyndman's account of the origin of Booth's research is correct (Hennock, 1976, pp. 70–3) but the general aim was clear. The condition of the working class in one of the world's greatest cities was in need of systematic investigation. The method which Booth and his collaborators employed gave a firm statistical basis to the impressionistic accounts of poverty and deprivation widespread at the time. Their work made the estimates of poverty more precise, and provided estimates which gave an approximately correct picture for London as a whole. As he said later:

> The lives of the poor lay hidden from view behind a curtain on which were painted terrible pictures: starving children, suffering women, overworked men; houses of drunkenness and vice, monsters and demons of inhumanity; giants of disease and despair. Did these pictures truly represent what lay behind, or did they bear to the facts a relation similar to that which the pictures outside a booth at some country fair bear to the performance of the show within?

Booth wanted to give some definite quantitative meaning to the term 'starving millions'. As he told the Statistical Society in 1887, the 'helplessness' of all levels of society to influence the world in which they lived was manifest. Among other things it led to

> socialistic theories, passionate suggestions of ignorance, setting at naught the nature of man, and neglecting all the fundamental facts of human existence. To relieve this sense of helplessness, the problems of human life must be better stated. The *a priori* reasoning of political economy, orthodox and unorthodox alike, fails from want of reality. At its base are a series of assumptions very imperfectly connected with the observed facts of life. We need to begin with a true picture of the modern industrial organism, the interchange of service, the exercise of faculty, the demands and satisfaction of desire. (Booth, quoted in B. Webb, 1938, p. 270)

Two subjects in particular, poverty and work, became the focus for his research over nearly two decades. His aim was to obtain data for the working-class population of London on 'the relative destitution, poverty or comfort of the home' and, secondly, 'the character of the work from which the various bread-winners in the family derived their livelihood'. Some information he could get from the censuses of 1881 and 1891, but this was limited. On the other hand selective studies did not produce a comprehensive picture of the life of the people of London and led to the sorts of biases which he was trying to overcome. So he determined to make a complete investigation of his own, using a team of helpers and beginning in the East End, in Tower Hamlets. One of those who assisted him was the young Beatrice Potter (later Beatrice Webb), who described in her autobiography his method of working.

For most of his information he relied on what she later called 'wholesale interviewing' – interviews with school attendance officers, the people who possessed the most detailed knowledge of parents of school children and their living conditions. This method of collecting such a vast amount of information was his first innovation. He attempted systematically to survey the whole population of families with children of school age by using the school attendance officers as his informants.

Beatrice Webb described him working as follows.

> Charles Booth, or one or other of his secretaries, would extract from the school-attendance officer, bit by bit, the extensive and intimate information with regard to each family, the memory of those willing witnesses amplifying and illustrating the precisely recorded facts in their notebooks . . . [T]his method . . . blocked the working of personal bias . . . [S]hort of deliberate and malicious falsification, it was impracticable for anyone taking part in extracting and swiftly recording specific facts about every individual in every street throughout the Metropolis, to produce a result which seriously, and a total which materially, falsified the aggregate of particulars. (B. Webb, 1938, p. 278)

The main features of Booth's lengthy studies, carried on in his spare time between his business activities, are well known (Simey and Simey, 1960; Pfautz, 1967; Fried and Elman, 1971). The first results of this investigation were published in 1889, the whole findings of his survey appeared gradually in the seventeen volumes of the *Life and Labour of the People of London* between 1889 and 1903. The central findings of his work on poverty depended on dividing the population into eight classes, A to H.

Class A   The lowest class comprising occasional labourers, loafers and semi-criminals.

Class B   The very poor comprising casual labour with hand-to-mouth existence and chronic want.

Class C and D   The poor including those whose earnings are small because of inequality of employment and those whose work, though regular, is ill-paid.

Class E and F   The regularly paid and fairly paid working-class of all grades.

Class G and H   Lower and upper middle-class and all above this level.
                             (Booth, 1889–1903, *Poverty Series II*, p. 20)

Booth classified the population of London, excluding the inmates of institutions, into one of these eight classes according to their income.

Thereby he began to make systematic distinctions between different classes of the poor. One of Booth's major innovations was to introduce the concept of the poverty line, an income level below which a family would be said to be living in poverty. This he set at £1 a week.

His initial work was focused on East London, later extended to the whole of the city. The final results of his inquiries into poverty showed that 30·7 per cent of the population of London was below the poverty line, 'at all times more or less in want'. (See Table 1.1.)

Table 1.1 *Booth's Statistics of Poverty*

Classes					
A	(lowest)	37,610	or	0·9%	in poverty,
B	(very poor)	316,834	or	7·5%	30·7%
C and D	(poor)	938,293	or	22·3%	
E and F	(working-class, comfortable)	2,166,503	or	51·5%	in comfort,
G and H	(middle-class and above)	749,930	or	17·8%	69·3%
		4,209,170		100%	
Inmates of institutions		99,830			
		4,390,000			

Source: Booth, 1889–1903, *Poverty Series II*, p. 21.

These findings reverberated through the worlds of politics and philanthropy. Far from disproving Hyndman, Booth showed that the proportion of London's population living in poverty was even higher than Hyndman had claimed. The fact that he produced this finding also shows the objectivity with which he pursued the study, which was for him a major scientific enterprise. That about one million Londoners – one-third of the population – lived below the poverty line (as he defined it) was a major revelation, all the more authoritative because of the scientific backing given to it by his methods. The research suggested that poverty was less the result of personal inadequacy or failure, but was linked to underlying social and economic factors. For example, Booth's studies of employment and earnings showed that a large proportion of the poor were poor because in their regular work they were paid at less than the poverty line. He also showed that about one-third of the population lived in housing conditions of overcrowding and squalor, with two to three persons per room, and death rates which varied considerably, and almost exactly in line with the incidence of poverty. He also highlighted the problems of poverty in old age. The old were not poor through personal failings, but because there was no income provision for working-class wage-earners once they had become too old to work.

Booth thus provided the first real statistics of the incidence of poverty, which were necessary if policy solutions to the social consequences of industrial progress were to be found. As he once wrote, 'In intensity of feeling and not in statistics lies the power to move the world. But by statistics must this power be guided if it would move the world right.' The seventeen volumes of Booth's massive survey contain much more – important studies, for example, of casual employment and underemployment and their connections with poverty – but it is for his work showing the extent of poverty that Booth is chiefly remembered.

Charles Booth's monumental study was important methodologically both for the precision of its measurement of poverty and for the representative coverage of the population of London, which no previous inquiry had achieved. What conclusions were to be drawn from the findings were less clear. Beatrice Potter parted company from Booth's inquiry because she was more interested in collective action than in pursuing the investigation. Booth himself tended to conservatism and did not see that his findings pointed directly to the need for radical changes in social policy. Others might draw the conclusion that private charity was ineffective but he himself did not become a staunch advocate of state intervention.

Booth had started his inquiries in two areas, Tower Hamlets and Hackney, then broadened his study to cover the whole of the East End of London and finally extended it to cover the whole of London. When his results for the whole of London were published the Charity Organisation Society, among others, questioned whether the results could be generalised to the country as a whole; was London representative of England or of Great Britain? An answer to this question was provided by the work of Seebohm Rowntree.

Seebohm Rowntree's Study of York

Seebohm Rowntree, like Booth, was from the family of an industrialist. His father was the Quaker cocoa manufacturer, philanthropist and pioneer of industrial welfare, Joseph Rowntree. Living in York where the family business was located, Seebohm Rowntree was much impressed by Booth's studies of London and determined to see how far conditions in a country town compared with London. He therefore undertook in 1899 a survey of York, which was published in 1901 as *Poverty: A Study of Town Life*. This work stands alongside Booth's *Life and Labour* as one of the two most important early scientific investigations in British empirical social research. It was important in part because it confirmed Booth's results. Rowntree found, to his surprise, that 28 per cent of the population of York lived below the poverty standard as he defined it. This lent strong support to the view that approximately one-third of the urban population of Great Britain was living in poverty. Booth's findings could not be dismissed as peculiar to London.

Rowntree's work was equally important in other ways, in how he designed the study and measured and analysed poverty. First, he differed from Booth in that he did not rely on intermediaries (school attendance officers) to provide him with information. Instead he set out to find out information about the income, occupation and housing of every wage-earner in York, and he did so at first hand by using interviewers to go to talk to the families themselves in their homes. This was a most important innovation at the time, though it is nowadays a feature of social survey research which is entirely taken for granted.

Secondly, Rowntree tried to put the measurement of poverty on a firmer scientific basis. Booth had more or less arbitrarily, though not unreasonably, selected £1 per week as his poverty line. But was this the correct figure? If one moved the line up (say, to 25s), the numbers in poverty would increase. If one moved the line down, the numbers of the poor would decrease. It was therefore important to ensure that the level one was measuring was the right level. Rowntree tackled the problem from a biological foundation. He asked what was the minimum food intake required for a family of two adults and three children, where the husband worked in heavy manual work. Using the estimates of an American nutritionist, Atwater, he calculated how many calories per day each member of the family would need and converted these calorie intakes into food, chosen to be as cheap and nutritious as possible. He thus calculated that such a family would require a certain sum of money per week for food. On to this had to be added money for rent, light and fuels calculated according to restrictive assumptions, plus the cost of clothing 'necessary for health' and of the 'plainest and most economical description'. A small addition was made for other items such as the fares of the bread-winner going to work. This produced an estimate of the 'minimum weekly expenditure upon which physical efficiency can be maintained in York' of 21s 8d in 1899, made up as follows for a family of two adults and three children.

	s	d
Food	12	9
Rent (say)	4	0
Clothing, light, fuel, etc.	4	11
	21	8

For larger or smaller families the figures would be adjusted accordingly. Rowntree emphasised that the standards he had adopted were 'stringent to severity and bare of all creature comforts' and that no allowance was made for expenditure beyond the maintenance of mere physical efficiency. Nevertheless, using standards calculated in this way for each size of family, he found that 28 per cent of the total population of York were living in poverty.

Rowntree's third innovation was to distinguish between ideal and actual patterns of expenditure and the effect of this difference upon the incidence of poverty. For a family might have an income at or above Rowntree's minimum but not spend it in such a way as to meet the bare necessities. He therefore distinguished between primary and secondary poverty. Primary poverty was found in families whose total earnings were insufficient to obtain the minimum necessary for the maintenance of merely physical efficiency, assuming that they budgeted according to Rowntree's strict scheme. In other words, no matter how they budgeted they could not meet the minimum requirements. Secondary poverty was found in families whose total earnings *would have* been sufficient for the maintenance of mainly physical efficiency *were it not* that some portion of it was absorbed by other expenditure, either useful (for example, additional clothes, furniture, or a newspaper) or wasteful (for example, alcohol, or tobacco, or gambling). In other words, poverty was a consequence of not following his stringent budget, rather than an absolutely inadequate income. In this 1899 study 10 per cent of the population were identified as living in primary poverty and 18 per cent in secondary poverty.

Though this distinction is an important one, it contained a subjective element which lays it open to criticism. For determining what is a necessity, or 'useful', and what is a luxury, or 'wasteful', involves judgement and often moral judgement. Rowntree relied partly on the observations of his interviewers of families who were in obvious want and squalor despite an apparently adequate income, and his views about justifiable forms of expenditure (for example, on leisure activities) were tinged by his religious beliefs. His approach to the measurement of poverty in terms of a scientifically determined absolute standard of poverty in money terms was an important one, and one which has continued to be used. But he did not resolve the problem of what is a minimum necessity. In Britain, for example, it is unlikely that the cost of a car would be included in a contemporary poverty line budget, yet in the United States it would.

Rowntree's final innovation was the concept of the *poverty cycle*, the idea that poverty is not a constant for a particular family throughout its existence but fluctuates according to the family's stage in the life-cycle. Similarly, not all families are in poverty at all times. They are especially likely to suffer poverty at particular times. The two particular points of vulnerability which Rowntree identified were in the years when a couple had young children, who were an additional strain on an income which might have been adequate for two adults alone; and when two adults (whose children had grown up and left home) reached old age, and their income fell dramatically when the wage-earner ceased earning. These were the days before old age pensions, of course, and the most a wage-earner could expect might be a very small benefit from a friendly society, if he had belonged to one and contributed to it regularly over most of his working life.

Booth's work in London had a greater immediate impact upon politics and social policy than did Rowntree's, though the study of York provided important confirmation of the London findings. As a scientific investigation, however, Rowntree's work was a more rigorous and definitive study of the subject and was to have more influence in the future. It has been discussed in some detail in order to demonstrate the contribution of scientific investigation to the delineation of social conditions and social problems.

Rowntree's political sympathies were Liberal, and whereas 'Booth seems to have become increasingly uncertain as to what measures of reform were appropriate in the light of his research, Rowntree became increasingly certain' (P. Abrams, 1968, p. 139). His demonstration of the poverty cycle and the connections between family, life-cycle and economic condition made him an early advocate of the minimum wage and of the establishment of a state social security system. After 1901 Rowntree became much involved in a programme of research on the relationship between patterns of landholding and social welfare, undertaken in close collaboration with the Liberal Party (Briggs, 1961). This was lost with the First World War. It provides a reminder, however, that not all socially useful research necessarily has a positive outcome.

Sidney and Beatrice Webb

If Booth and Rowntree are remembered for their empirical researches, the important impact of Sidney and Beatrice Webb in developing applied social science was somewhat different. In the long run, like Booth and Rowntree, they had a formidable influence upon twentieth-century British social policy. The influence of Booth and Rowntree, however, rested on the technical mastery and political impact of their inquiries, not upon their own political views or involvements, which have left little lasting trace. In the Webbs' case, their contribution to methodology was relatively slight, but they had far more impact as politically engaged social scientists, institutional innovators, members of committees and (in Sidney's case in later life) as politician and minister. A good deal of this influence may be attributed to their conception of social science as an instrument of policy analysis.

Beatrice Webb (1858–1943), who came from a comfortable, upper-middle-class background, had cut her teeth as a social investigator by working with Booth for several years. Her social awareness had been slowly awakened but, once aroused, her interest developed and she became a formidable force in English social administration. Sidney Webb (1859–1947) was the son of a radical London accountant, educated in Switzerland and Germany and later at London University, who met Beatrice through a common interest in the co-operative movement. They became engaged in 1891 and were married in 1892, living thereafter on Beatrice's private income which gave them economic independence. Early social research owed a good deal to the surplus wealth of some members of the English upper-middle class.

The Webbs' personal life revolved around their work; their honeymoon, for instance, was spent studying social conditions in Ireland and Scotland. Within two years of their marriage they produced in 1894 *The History of Trade Unionism*, a classic of English social history. They then published in 1897 *Industrial Democracy*, and a second edition of Beatrice's *The Co-Operative Movement in Great Britain*, followed by a mammoth programme of work including histories of English local government and of the Poor Law, more on trade unions, combined with active political work in the London School Board and the newly formed London County Council.

Unlike Booth, the Webbs did not aim to produce a comprehensive 'instantaneous photograph', a picture of society as it was at one point in time. Their aim was rather to develop the analytical history of the way in which particular forms of social organisation had developed, starting with trade unionism as a social institution. Their approach to research was thus more historical than statistical and tended to rest on very comprehensive researches in historical archives. The Webbs approached social study without preconceptions, not trying to test ideas but to accumulate facts inductively and produce generalisations on the basis of these facts (Warner, 1979).

The aim of the Webbs in doing all their research was severely practical.

> The very continuance of social science or sociology as a separate category of study will depend on the world's experience of the practical utility of such a parcelling out of knowledge at the particular stage of the world's history that we may have attained.

The Webbs believed that it was possible to combine scientific research into social institutions with active participation in their operation. Indeed the influence of each on the other was reciprocal and beneficial. They themselves combined a life spent in prodigious amounts of research and writing with active political interests through the Fabian Society and the Labour Party. Sidney was for some years a Labour MP and later a peer (Lord Passfield), holding ministerial office in the Labour governments of 1924 and 1929–31. As one historian of the period has written,

> both in research and action, as writers, intellectuals, politicians and administrators, the Webbs were ubiquitous; they were the link – often the only link – between the worlds of Bloomsbury and Poplar, between the 'high politics' of Cabinet and Empire and the low politics of the poor rate and municipal reform.

The Webbs' methods of work and influences can be illustrated from the history of the Royal Commission on the Poor Laws, 1905–9, the first major review of the Poor Law since the 1832–4 Commission and the 1834 Act. The 1905–9 Commission, unlike its predecessor, was composed of experts in the field of social administration. Its chairman, Lord George Hamilton, was a retired politician and its other seventeen members included four senior officials of the Poor Law administration, representatives from the Local Government Board, two economists, two Labour leaders (one of them George Lansbury), four members (including C. S. Loch, Helen Bosanquet and Octavia Hill of housing fame) who were attached to the Charity Organisation Society, and two social investigators, Charles Booth (who had to retire through ill-health in 1908) and Beatrice Webb.

The commission, as an independent body reporting to the King, was instructed to inquire into the workings of the Poor Law and also into the means adopted outside the Poor Law 'for meeting distress arising from want of employment, particularly during periods of severe industrial depression'. Much of the work of the commission was spent on hearing oral evidence, of which that of J. S. Davy, head of the Poor Law division of the local government board was the most weighty. Davy was still in favour of the principles of less eligibility, and thought that other services such as education and unemployment relief could be provided within the Poor Law. But much of the evidence – forty-seven volumes in all were published – both given orally before the commission and collected at its request, tended to point away from a strict application of the principles of 1834. Beatrice Webb played an important part in this, both in suggesting inquiries which should be carried out for the commission and in influencing the line of questioning at sessions for the taking of evidence. As she noted at one point, the evidence all pointed 'away from bad administration as the cause of pauperism and towards bad conditions among large classes of the population as the overwhelmingly important fact'. In the end the commission produced two reports. The Majority Report, signed by the chairman and fourteen members, recommended that the role of guardians should be replaced by local authorities. Considerable reshaping of the Poor Law, to be renamed 'public assistance', was required and even modification in principle. But the Poor Law would remain as an all-embracing social institution. *All* social services, it was envisaged, would come under the remit of the public assistance committees. The signatories of the Majority Report still saw poverty as largely a personal failing on the part of individuals. 'The causes of distress are not only economic and industrial; in their origin and character they are largely moral.'

The Minority Report, mainly written by the Webbs (though Sidney was not a member of the commission), was signed by Beatrice, George Lansbury, Francis Chandler (a trade unionist) and the Reverend Wakefield (later Bishop of Birmingham). Its argument was simple, and novel. Destitution, not pauperism, was the problem. The phenomenon of poverty was a social condition resulting from the condition and organisation of the economy. For many in poverty, their conditions of life were such that they could not escape unaided. What was needed was not moral improvement but social reorganisation. What was needed was mobilisation of the community's resources to *prevent* destitution before it occurred. To this end, the Minority Report (although it agreed with the majority about transferring responsibility to local authorities) recommended dismantling the Poor Law. It favoured administrative specialisation. Separate government departments would deal with education, health, pensions, and so on. A Ministry of Labour should be set up to organise the labour market for the able-bodied (B. Webb, 1948, ch. 7).

The analysis of poverty contained in the Minority Report illustrates the influence both of Booth and Rowntree, and the Webbs. The scientific findings of the former bolstered the analysis of poverty as a social condition. But it was the influence of the Webbs through Beatrice's membership of the commission that communicated these findings and incorporated them in policy recommendations. Social research had, indirectly, a major influence upon the content of a most important Royal Commission report. Its importance was not immediate, since neither Majority nor Minority Reports were acted upon immediately. Too many interested parties, such as the local government board, were fiercely opposed to change. Yet if the Royal Commission had little immediate effect, the Minority Report and its outlook were prescient. It anticipated much of the modern welfare state and though its short-term influence on policy (though not on ideas) was slight, in the long term much of the Webbs' vision has been implemented.

In passing, a further indirect contribution of the Webbs to applied social science may be mentioned. They were both founders of the

Fabian Society, and in 1894 a wealthy Fabian, Henry Hutchinson of Derby, died, leaving a legacy and appointing Sidney Webb as his executor. Webb conceived the idea of establishing a school of economics – an idea supposedly thought up at breakfast with Beatrice, Graham Wallas and George Bernard Shaw – using the legacy to do so. Although the legacy provided for the furthering of the aims of the Fabian Society, Webb persuaded his fellow Fabians that it should be used to found the London School of Economics and Political Science, opened in 1895, which would be devoted to research and not to propaganda. Both he and Beatrice believed that socialists would only be effective if they could understand the society which they were trying to reform much more fully than they did in the 1890s. As Webb wrote to Mrs Shaw in 1899, 'only in this path of scientific study lies any hope of remedying social evils, or relieving individual misery' (Caine, 1963, p. 95). The LSE became, from the beginning, the most important centre of academic social research in Britain, a position it retained until at least the 1960s.

The three most important aspects of the Webbs' contribution to applied social research were that, first, they developed historical and institutional analysis in the social policy field. Secondly, they demonstrated the influence which a social scientist could have through the work of a Royal Commission or official committee, an influence which other social scientists since have exercised on a number of important committees. And, thirdly, they blended social science and political action, especially through their work in the Fabian Society, and this has given British social administration a particular character. The Webbs were not detached scientists in an ivory tower, though they believed in the value of objective knowledge and chose for LSE the Latin motto *Rerum Cognoscere Causas*, 'To know the causes of things'.

Institutionalisation Begins

Nineteenth-century British social research, outside government, thus provides a picture of various organised attempts, in the statistical and philosophical societies and the NAPSS, by wealthy middle-class amateur social investigators to throw light on current social conditions. By modern standards the procedures they used were fairly primitive. This was partly due to lack of scientific support from the universities. At this time social science was not taught in English universities, there was no recognised status of empirical social researcher – for most nineteenth-century figures it was a spare-time activity – and no institutional setting of a permanent kind in which social science could develop. Until at least the First World War progress in social investigation depended on wealthy private individuals of ability who were interested in investigating social conditions. Mayhew made his living as a journalist and his investigations were a part of this work. Booth, Rowntree and the Webbs had private incomes which enabled them to support financially their own social investigations – in the case of the Webbs to devote their whole time to it.

Outside government, social research was not successfully institutionalised.

> The history of British sociology before 1914 – indeed before 1945 – is in no sense a success story . . . [T]his failure was not at all an effect of inadequate intellectual resources. Many men of great capacity were deeply concerned with problems of social order and disorder at every level of generality. The critical difficulty was more immediately structural. It was a problem of institutionalisation. (P. Abrams, 1968, p. 4)

Looking exclusively at empirical research (without any aspirations to develop a general science of society) the same is true. There was a great deal of empirical research of one sort or another done in Britain in the nineteenth century, yet it was marked by lack of continuity, an absence of cumulation. Those who did social research typically worked in a non-academic setting, often doing research in their spare time and with their own money. There was no recognised status of 'social researcher' or 'social scientist'. Only in one part of government was inquiry a legitimate primary task. Statisticians in the General Register Office, however, had a narrow conception of 'research' and confined their work to medical and demographic fields. Most of those who contributed to the Statistical Society of London relied on statistics generated by the institution in which they worked, whether a hospital, business or government department. They did not carry out original inquiries of their own. So few men carried on empirical social research that it was difficult to recruit successors to those who did. Sociology was not taught in the universities. Nobody thought of himself as a sociologist, social research was not institutionalised (Cole, 1972, p. 108ff.).

Around the turn of the twentieth century the picture began to change. With the establishment of the London School of Economics in 1895 a modest British university base for social science was established which in time was to grow to considerable proportions. Government involvement in social policy through the growth of social insurance led to some early statistical investigations which went beyond the demographic head-counting of the General Register Office. The development of philanthropic foundations in the early years of the twentieth century provided alternative sources of support to the wealth of private individuals. Twentieth-century changes in the organisation of social science research are discussed in Chapter 6 so will not receive detailed attention here. The point can, however, be made that slowly in Britain, somewhat more rapidly in the United States, the conditions fostering applied social research changed. Nineteenth-century social research was in some ways very different from its late twentieth-century counterpart.

The Influence of A. L. Bowley

The change is illustrated by the part played by A. L. Bowley, Professor of Statistics at the London School of Economics. From this academic base Bowley undertook empirical investigations of poverty in the manner of Rowntree, though using a slightly different measure of the poverty line, based on actual spending patterns, and taking into account the varying food needs of children of different ages. In 1912 he made a study of primary poverty in five towns – Reading, Northampton, Stanley, Warrington and Bolton – published as *Livelihood and Poverty* in 1915. A follow-up study, with Margaret Hogg, *Has Poverty Diminished?*, appeared in 1925.

Bowley's main innovation, one of lasting and great importance, was the introduction of *random sampling* into social survey research. The significance of this idea can hardly be overestimated. Before Bowley, if an investigator wanted to provide a representative picture of the condition of a population he had to try to collect data on the whole population, or a part of it selected in terms of a particular criterion, usually geographical. Thus Booth started his work in two relatively small areas and gradually expanded the geographical coverage. Rowntree confined his study to one relatively small town. Booth relied on school attendance officers for his evidence, since by using them he could hope to achieve a more complete coverage of the population than by any other method. Rowntree, within York, wanted to get a representative picture so he arranged for every wage-earning family in the town to be interviewed. Both aimed at complete coverage of the population in relatively restricted geographical areas. Neither Booth nor Rowntree was able to provide an estimate of the proportion of the total population of Great Britain which lived in poverty; this was too great an undertaking.

Bowley's introduction of random sampling was based upon advances in the statistical theory of probability. The important practical consequence of this theory was the discovery that a population as a whole could be satisfactorily studied by studying only a sample of the population, *provided that the sample was selected randomly*. Thus a town of 10,000 families could be studied by interviewing one in ten of the families (1,000) and the results could be generalised from the sample to the population if the families were selected in a random manner. (In practice, one way of doing this might be to list all the families in the town in street order, and within streets by number of house. Take an arbitrary starting point between one and ten, say six, and then take every *n*th – sixth – family on the list, working your way right through it.) If the sample were selected randomly, then quite a small fraction of the whole population could be interviewed to provide an estimate for the whole population. Bowley used this method in the study of the five towns.

Bowley's ideas in the early 1900s were only adopted gradually, and only fully after 1945. But the idea of sampling in social survey research is one of the single most important developments in social research this century, because it provides such a powerful means of getting data about the whole population. This greatly strengthened the practical usefulness of social survey research, an advantage which came to be more and more appreciated as time went on. Moreover it introduced a more 'scientific' element into social research, in the sense that random sampling derived from statistical theory. Henceforth survey research in Britain had increasingly close links with the discipline of statistics.

Social Surveys between the Wars

Several important surveys of social conditions were carried out in the interwar period in addition to Bowley and Hogg's re-study. A number of studies were carried out in particular cities – by P. Ford in Southampton (1934), Henry Mess on Tyneside (1928) and by D. Caradog Jones on Merseyside (1934). This last survey, largely funded by the Rockefeller Foundation, proceeded inductively to provide an exhaustive statistical picture of the area.

> The survey claims to be scientific in the sense that observation and inference are made in an impartial spirit: the sole object has been to arrive at and present the true facts . . . It is left to others to decide how bad conditions can be changed, although recommendations are on occasion proffered. (D. C. Jones, 1934, p. x)

Also carried out at this period was the massive *New Survey of Life and Labour in London*, directed by Sir Hubert Llewellyn Smith, the retired permanent secretary of the Ministry of Labour who had worked with Booth on the original survey and whom Beveridge brought to LSE to direct the enterprise. The results of the research, partly funded by the Rockefeller Foundation, were published in nine volumes between 1930 and 1935 (Smith, 1930–5). The first volume, providing an overview of changes in the previous forty years, consists of a series of descriptive chapters on the cost of living, earnings, rents, travel, health, education, recreation, employment and unemployment, poor relief and crime. The tone is one of pure description: there is no explanation of what the problem being tackled is, simply an enumeration of the empirical evidence about different aspects of London life. The 'problem', such as it is, is said to be the question: 'What has been the change [since Booth] in the numerical relation of poverty to well-being?' (op. cit., Vol. 1, p. 55). Again the empiricist emphasis is explicitly acknowledged:

> the present volume . . . is only concerned to a minor degree with analysing the causes and influences by which that development [over forty years] has been stimulated, hindered or deflected. It is of course impossible to present a coherent picture of development without touching on causation . . . but these references are only incidental and illustrative. (op. cit., Vol. 1, p. 57)

Later volumes present studies of London's industries, life and leisure and reports of surveys carried out by the investigation. These were of two types, the first a street survey, following closely the methods of Booth and relying on reports from school attendance officers, supplemented by other sources such as employment exchanges, boards of guardians and the police. The second type of survey was a house sample, drawn by A. L. Bowley using probability methods, which contacted 12,000 working-class households in the eastern area of London (op. cit., Vol. 3, p. 3). Both surveys agreed closely in the main empirical finding of the *New Survey* that the proportion of the population living in poverty was, at about 10 per cent, one-third of the level which Booth had found. Despite the meticulous empirical methods used, and the precision with which key terms such as 'poverty' were defined, the main results of the survey are presented in a purely empiricist form. Moreover, despite all the massive effort involved, the painstaking replication of Booth's procedure represented no great advance upon the earlier study, apart from the fact that sampling methods were used and a survey of householders was carried out.

In 1935 Rowntree undertook a second study of poverty in York, published in 1941 as *Poverty and Progress*. He redefined the poverty line for this inquiry (Townsend, 1954, 1962), but the study is of methodological interest for his attempts to measure the accuracy of sampling. Although the study was based on a complete enumeration, Rowntree then drew samples of 1 in 10, 1 in 20, 1 in 30, 1 in 40 and 1 in 50 from his data and compared the sample results with the population results, in general confirming the precision and accuracy of sampling as against complete enumeration.

A number of other detailed investigations of the interwar period – into unemployment, housing, health and nutrition – also made a marked impact. The studies of unemployment by Bakke (1933) and the Pilgrim Trust (1938), of housing by Hutt (1933) and Simon and Inman (1935), of nutrition and health by Boyd Orr (1936) and Titmuss (1938), all documented the deprivation and distress wrought by economic depression on top of poor working-class living standards even in times of full employment.

> [T]he result was a considerable step forward in the investigation of the social condition of Britain. Using the new techniques of scientific social inquiry, most of the contemporary social problems were studied with an intensity which was almost unprecedented. Impressionistic surveys of social conditions were increasingly being replaced by the products of scientific investigation, building upon the foundations of the earlier pioneers . . . Rarely in so short a space of time have so many aspects of British social life been so exhaustively examined. (Stevenson, 1977, p. 53)

Another development in this period was the community 'self-survey', the study of a local area carried out by people resident within it. A guide to such surveys published in the mid-1930s throws light on the expectations which were held about the value of social research. A survey is defined as 'a fact-finding study, dealing chiefly with working-class poverty and with the nature and problems of the community' (Wells, 1935, p. 13). Booth's research was seen as a landmark which set the pattern for all subsequent studies. His influence had been felt in the Liberal social legislations of 1906–14, in the LCC and in demonstrating the inefficacy of haphazard measures of social relief. Similar hopes were held out for the main interwar surveys. At the local level, surveys such as Mess's study of Tyneside (1928) had the effect of stirring the waters, showing the need for reforms and increasing interest in undertaking them. In some cases the local authorities in the area were pushed into action; in other cases, additional voluntary efforts (such as the creation of the Tyneside Council of Social Service) resulted. More generally, local social surveys had a general educational value for the members of the local community who undertook them, focusing their attention on the history, geography and social processes of the locality studied. The aim of the local social survey was 'the description of the conditions under which the workers live, and often also an attempt to arouse interest and action directed by the inhabitants of the locality studied towards their own social problems' (Wells, 1935, p. 80).

There are obvious affinities with the earlier social survey movement in the United States (see Gordon, 1973), which never caught on to the same extent in Britain. The conception of the local social survey, however, is very similar to that of the larger, more professionally conducted British inquiries. Indeed in the period up to 1945, despite changes in the sponsorship and organisation of survey research, a common conception of the task and character of applied social research held sway, one reflected in Caradog Jones's postwar definition: 'the primary aim of the social survey is to make an accurate and impartial collection and presentation of facts, the results of careful observation, not of hearsay' (1948, p. 11).

The Historical Continuity

This common conception is important because it still exercises a predominant influence upon the character of applied social research in Britain today. There is strong historical continuity between the classic surveys of Booth, Rowntree and Bowley and modern research. If one looks at studies of poverty, for example, there are marked parallels between the earlier studies and those of Brian Abel-Smith and Peter Townsend (1965), which reintroduced poverty into national political debate in the 1960s (Banting, 1979, ch. 3) and the more recent work of Richard Layard *et al.* (1978). Townsend's approach (1979) has been more theoretical but emphasises the very close association between social inquiry and social intervention characteristic of the older inquiries.

What are the main elements in this common conception? Social surveys – the characteristic kind of social research – are seen as factual inquiries in the Baconian manner. Discovery of the facts may permit subsequent generalisation, but the gathering of data is not carried out in terms of a theoretical or conceptual scheme. It is inductive. Moreover the factual character of the data so obtained is essentially unproblematical. Secondly, there is a strong *implicit* normative element. Although on the face of it purely empirical, value elements are built into the approach and analysis of data. A prime example is Rowntree's distinction between 'primary' and 'secondary' poverty. These elements are, however, largely unrecognised by their authors. Thirdly, there is taken to be a relatively automatic connection between surveys and action, between knowledge and policy. Some people, such as Booth, did harbour doubts about the conclusions to which their research pointed. But the general motivation for undertaking social investigation was the desire to achieve social improvement and social reform, from Chadwick onwards. Even nineteenth-century government statisticians like William Farr were also supporters of social action in a quiet way. Rowntree was actively involved in Liberal Party politics. The interwar surveys were designed to draw attention to the adverse conditions in which the working classes lived. Fourthly, little of the research discussed was influenced to a significant extent by academic social science, apart from the introduction of random sam-

pling from statistics by Bowley. This was largely due to the underde-
veloped state of the social sciences until the early twentieth century,
but it is noteworthy that even the *New Survey of Life and Labour in
London*, carried out from LSE, did not in its conception bear much
imprint of disciplines such as economics, sociology or anthropology,
then taught there.

How is one to account for these distinctive features of applied social
science in Britain? One reason lies in the enduring strengths of
empiricism and positivism in English intellectual life. An empirical,
piecemeal approach to social issues was characteristic, coupled with a
belief that the scientific, rational study of society could contribute
directly to the conduct of public affairs. 'Positivism' is a much over-
used term, but most of those discussed in this chapter shared a belief
that social questions could be treated in a manner assumed to be that of
the natural scientist. The limitations of such a view of social science will
be discussed in the next chapter. There is no doubt, however, that it
has marked empirical social research, keeping it closely to the direct
observation and recording of facts, as these were conceived.

A second important influence, already discussed, was the failure to
institutionalise academic social science until a late date. In this respect
a comparison with the United States is instructive. Although the
American social survey movement was not based in universities, the
teaching of subjects like sociology in American universities from an
earlier date brought empirical research more quickly into contact with
general ideas. At the University of Chicago, for example, in the 1920s,
much empirical research was carried out which fitted into a more
general theory of urban structure despite being very matter-of-fact in
its character (Faris, 1970; Bulmer, 1981a). Such an intellectually
nurturing context was absent in Britain.

A marked characteristic of British social inquiry has been its reformist and moralistic tinge.

> The passion of the English for discussing everything in terms of
> morality has often been noted by foreigners . . . The passion in this
> country for laying down how men ought to behave and how society
> ought to be reorganised in order that they may behave better has led
> us to neglect . . . how far reorganisations of society are capable of
> changing their behaviour. The desire to reform is excellent, the
> fervour to improve the condition of our fellow human beings is
> admirable, but they are – on the theoretical level – worthless unless
> they take into account new knowledge. (Annan, 1959, p. 18)

It may seem paradoxical to stress this aspect when discussing empirical
research. Yet it was strongly present in the work of nineteenth-century
investigators like Chadwick and twentieth-century ones like Seebohm

Rowntree. His later work such as the study of *English Life and Leisure* (1951) is heavily tinged with moralism; in his earlier studies it was more carefully veiled.

A further explanation for the particular character of English social research is to be found in the nature of the British intellectual and political elite. A reformist orientation flourished because those who did social research were often assured that their findings would be listened to by politicians and other policy-makers. The 'intellectual aristocracy' identified by Annan (1955) (into which Booth married), was complemented by the Fabian connections which developed around the Webbs and Bernard Shaw. There was no separate intelligentsia (Anderson, 1968) but an intellectual elite closely integrated with the ruling circles of late Victorian and Edwardian society. Indeed the links were so close as to draw people away from social investigation towards administration, party politics, or various kinds of administration. Applied social research was encouraged by a social structure in which simple political responses to social problems were easily available and plausible, and there was a failure to realise that social problems were more *fundamentally* problematical than they appeared (P. Abrams, 1968, pp. 148–9, 152–3).

For all these reasons, applied social research in Britain up to 1945 had a distinct character which continues to mark it. The organisation of social research today is vastly different – with very large government spending, much stronger social science departments and research units in the universities and a flourishing commercial market research sector – but many of the same general characteristics are present which existed historically.

2

Models of the Relationship between Knowledge and Policy

Empirical social research of the type discussed in the opening chapter has several characteristics: it is meticulous in its procedures, precise in its measurements, careful in the extent to which generalisations are made from the cases studied to a larger population – and frequently boring and even trivial in its content. The great contributions of Booth and Rowntree, for example, stand out while the painstaking labours of many investigators of their time and earlier are forgotten (Cole, 1972). This is no doubt true of much social and political theory as well. The undistinguished practitioners of the past are not remembered any more than those who carried out unremarkable pieces of social research.

Yet the intellectual taint of triviality and boredom sticks more to empirical research than it does to more bookish and abstract pursuits, however remote and arid their concerns (see Thompson, 1978). Nothing is easier to dismiss than 'mere' empirical research. In the intellectual pecking order of disciplines such as sociology and political science, generalisation and theoretical flair confers more prestige than adeptness in empirical research. Despite lip-service paid to the bringing together of theory and research in particular inquiries, the more abstract and the more concrete remain particularly far apart in contemporary British social sciences such as sociology (see Payne *et al.*, 1981). This in turn has important effects on the potential usability of social science. If '[t]here are no sociological theories about society in general on which a structure of indicators can at present be based' (Moser, 1978, p. 208), then government statistical work, for example, is likely to be uninformed by the insights of social science and to remain at the purely empirical level.

This chapter is concerned to examine the contribution of the social *sciences* – disciplines such as sociology, psychology and political science – to the study of policy, by considering models of the relationship between social knowledge and social policy. What influence can research exercise upon policy? What are the different ways in which these effects are felt? What different expectations do policy-makers have of social research and social science? In this respect the discussion is more abstract than that in Chapter 1, for it is concerned with the general relationship between knowledge and policy. Nevertheless, the last chapter provides a starting point. If there remains a large gap between social science as a body of knowledge and social research as a socially useful activity, may it be that some of the practitioners of empirical inquiry actually believe that it is possible to conduct research free from significant contact with a body of general ideas which might inform their work? Though far less true in the United States, it is certainly the case in Britain that the strain of empiricism runs deep in influencing the form taken by 'useful' research.

Empiricism

What is meant by 'empiricism'? The term must be distinguished from 'empirical', which denotes that the propositions of social science must be tested against observational data to survive as tenable generalisations. Rather 'empiricism' refers to a conception of social research involving the production of accurate data – meticulous, precise, generalisable – in which the data themselves constitute an end of the research. It is summed up in the catchphrase 'the facts speak for themselves'. The terms 'empiricist' and 'empirical' are not used consistently by social scientists. Some sociologists, for example, use 'empiricist' as a pejorative term referring to any kind of empirical inquiry. This is not the sense in which it is used here. In this book 'empiricist' denotes a view of empirical social inquiry which holds that such inquiry is primarily factual in nature and that the task of social research is to produce 'facts', either for the use of policy-makers, or in order to influence the policy-making process.

The empiricist model of the relationship between research and policy implicitly or explicitly used is the following. Society is a highly complex entity about which governments, firms and other organisations need adequate information on which to base policies which they pursue and implement. The task of social research is to provide as precise, reliable and generalisable factual information as possible about the state of society or parts of society at a particular time. This information, when fed into the policy-making process, will enable policy-makers, or 'political administrators', to use Heclo and Wildavsky's term (1974, pp. 2–3), to reach the best decisions on the basis of the information available.

This view of social research as a superior kind of fact-gathering is

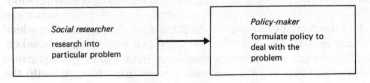

Social researcher
research into
particular problem

Policy-maker
formulate policy to
deal with the
problem

embodied in the role of the Government Statistical Service and the Social Survey Division of OPCS. (Both are post-Second World War developments in British central government.) It is also characteristic of the work of a very large proportion of local government social researchers, whose task is to provide 'the unbiased facts to which future policy should be adapted. Their job is to tell the truth; it is management's job to deal with the policy implications' (Benjamin, 1973, p. 26).

That characteristic British institution the Royal Commission or departmental committee of inquiry also provides many instances of such empiricism in making use of social research. Many Royal Commissions have undertaken substantial research, discussed further in Chapter 5. Andrew Shonfield has described the typical procedure:

> just plunge into your subject; collect as many facts as you can; think about them hard as you go along; and at the end use your common sense as you *feel* for the practicable to select a few good proposals . . . This method derives from a view of public affairs which puts the functions of an investigator on essentially the same footing as those of a common-law judge. Such a person is supposed to know all about the underlying theoretical assumptions of those whose affairs he is examining. All he needs is facts. (Shonfield, 1980, p. 59)

The Royal Commission on the Distribution of Income and Wealth (RCDIW, 1974–80), undertook a very large programme of research and synthesis of statistical material which was formed by a similar approach. The commission's role was primarily a factual one. The chairman, Lord Diamond, explained that:

> we strive to be impartial and objective. Each of us [the commissioners] has his or her own opinions about whether income and wealth should or should not be more equally distributed but we are not asked to report on these opinions. We are all united in wishing to present the facts in ways which are helpful to people whatever opinions they hold. (Bulmer, 1980a, p. 159)

This emphasis fitted in with a particular view of the likely influence of the Royal Commission on government. The RCDIW did not make recommendations for government action, but confined itself to exposition of the (very complicated) facts about income and wealth.

> Recommendations often get filed and left there, because the government and the civil service are very good at making decisions – ministers and their advisers combined – if they have got the facts . . .
> It is facts that are wanted, and it is no great restriction that you

cannot go on from facts to make recommendations. (Lord Diamond, quoted in Bulmer, 1980a, p. 163)

Such an emphasis on factual inquiry in research inquiries supported directly or indirectly by government meshes too with the British tradition of quantitative social inquiry discussed in Chapter 1. Social survey research in Britain is the province of the statistician to a far greater extent than in North America, where sociologists and political scientists have played a notable part in methodological developments. The statistician's view of a social survey, reflected in a standard textbook like *Survey Methods in Social Investigation* (1971), is that it is a factual inquiry.

[M]any, perhaps most, of the social research surveys mentioned in this book are fact-collecting enquiries, just as are the bulk of Government Social Survey or market research enquiries. Nor is the preoccupation of social scientists with descriptive, fact-finding enquiry anything to be ashamed of. (Moser and Kalton, 1971, p. 486)

A particular conception of the role of the social research has also been fostered by academic writers. David Glass, the influential LSE sociologist and demographer, stated in his inaugural lecture in 1949 that social research was integrally bound up with social intervention. Social and economic planning in the postwar world was 'here to stay', and social research was required both in the formulation of policy and in testing and advancing the implementation of policy. Yet the task was not easy, for the social researcher working in government 'would still have to fight against the irrational elements in policy-making and against the self-satisfaction of ignorance' (Glass, 1950, p. 18). Discussing examples from town planning, public health and housing, Glass showed how social research could, potentially, throw light on problems facing policy-makers, even though in practice the findings of research tended to be ignored. In housing, for example, 'a housing policy based on research requires much new research' (1950, pp. 27–8). The predominant tone was to stress the practical usefulness of research, its essentially commonsensical and empiricist character, and to strike a note of optimism that research would be a means of overcoming the 'ignorance' and 'prejudice' of politicians and administrators.

This blend of social interventionism and empiricism is also found in the work of one of the leading early practitioners of social survey research in Britain, Mark Abrams. Writing in 1951, he trenchantly stated the role which social surveys could play in social amelioration and improvement. He defined a survey as 'a process by which quantitative facts are collected about the social aspects of a community's composition and activities'. Its findings could be expressed in numerical form and they were usually utilitarian, 'carried out as an indispensable first step in measuring the dimensions of a social problem, ascertaining its causes, and then deciding upon remedial action' (M. Abrams, 1951, p. 2). Social surveys provided a method by which society could obtain precise information about itself and thus achieve social change 'in a peaceful and coherent manner' (p. 124). In the postwar period, surveys of housing, poverty and social conditions were supplemented by town planning and transport surveys. 'We now all realise that the modern community needs social engineering . . . and that in such engineering the social survey is a necessary and valuable preliminary to planning' (p. 125). Abrams saw particular value in the social survey, too, in enhancing communication between rulers and governed, drawing on early findings from American mass communications research. Systematic research was needed to enlighten the administrator about the primary group ties of the working class, the kind of 'goods' from which people derive psychic rewards, the goals to which they orient their lives, and how to put across the 'facts' resulting from research to a working-class audience.

> Half a century ago the social survey in the hands of Booth, Rowntree and Bowley provided the state with an analysis of poverty which possibly saved Britain from violence and revolution and set her on the road to economic democracy. Today, the same research tool must be applied to the analysis of effective communication if political democracy is to be added to economic democracy. (M. Abrams, 1951, p. 143)

Abrams's stands squarely in the classic survey tradition discussed in Chapter 1.

David Glass's lasting influence, however, has lain in the field of population studies and Mark Abrams's in the fields of market research and opinion polling. A slightly different group of academics has been the torch-bearer, in the third quarter of the twentieth century, of the tradition of Booth and Rowntree. The academic base of applied research in Britain has tended to lie in departments of social administration, a subject developed from 1950 onwards under the influence of Richard Titmuss. This subject has several distinct characteristics: a concern with social welfare and social justice; a blending of the different social sciences, such as economics, sociology and psychology, with history and philosophy; a focus upon social policy-making, both descriptively and normatively; and an empirical slant more marked than that of recent British sociology. The tradition of Booth and Rowntree lives on more strongly in social administration departments than elsewhere. A good deal of applied research is also carried out by specialists in industrial relations, race relations and criminology, but with these exceptions social policy and administration is the most important academic base for applied research. It is therefore highly significant that it has tended to adhere to empiricist methods, inquiry of a simple fact-finding kind. Carry out a survey to determine the facts of the situation, and the main features of the phenomenon will be made clear. A study of LSE students, for example (Blackstone *et al.*, 1970), turned these methods upon the institution which had been the main base of social administration since its inception in an attempt to understand the student protests there of 1967, the equivalent in Britain of the Berkeley movement of 1964. As Arthur Stinchcombe observed (1970), the study entirely lacked any theory and any hypotheses about the relationship between power structures, career structures, the world-views of students and campus political action. It was representative of the 'Marxified Fabianism' characteristic of British sociology and social administration of the period.

The explanation of the empiricist leanings of such a style of work lies in the quasi-political character of much social policy research. The study of social administration, at least in the 1950s and 1960s, had marked social democratic leanings, indicated by the involvement of leading practitioners such as Richard Titmuss, David Donnison, Peter Townsend and Brian Abel-Smith as active members of the Fabian Society and at periods as advisers to the Labour Party.

> Titmuss was not only a careful investigator of social life; his work was also a moral statement, and he became a philosophical leader not only of an academic generation but also of parts of the Labour Party. This group of intellectuals was convinced that myths about the generosity of the welfare state were blinding Britons to the persistence of hardship and inequalities in their midst. They therefore set out in the 1950s to map the contours of British society, and to generate the ideas and evidence that would legitimate social reform. Their research was explicitly political; its aim was to reshape policy-makers' interpretation of their environment. (Banting, 1979, p. 7)

This in itself need not necessarily affect scholarly work, as the capacity of economists to combine academic economic analysis of an objective kind with political advice and commitment shows. It is perfectly possible to maintain scientific detachment while playing another role as political advocate. The powerful blend of economic theory and economic indicators insulates economists, to some extent at least, from criticism as being *parti pris* in their academic work.

Much social administration research is also impeccably scholarly and objective in its form. Donnison's work on housing in the late 1950s (Donnison *et al.*, 1961) and Abel-Smith and Townsend's earlier work on poverty (1965) are meticulous factual studies whose impact was all the greater through the quiet force of their careful research. If the form was scientific, however, the objective of doing the research was at least partially political, to provide evidence in favour of reform of housing policy or social security policy. Description leads more or less directly to prescription, research to policy initiatives. The prescriptive element is stronger and more overt than in Lord Diamond's picture of the research role of his Royal Commission, but the task of social research is essentially the same – to make clear the facts of the case on the basis of which sound policy can be formulated.

This endorsement of a simple model of the research role is possible because of closeness to policy-making. If one believes that it is possible to influence government directly through politicians, this encourages a view of research as 'fact-finding' to serve as evidence to buttress the case for policy change. There are many examples of this – *The Poor and the Poorest* was clearly intended to (and did) have major political impact; the notable PEP (Political and Economic Planning) study of racial discrimination (Daniel, 1968) was published to (and did) influence the passage of the 1968 Race Relations Act through the House of Commons.

These tendencies have been enhanced by the interdisciplinary character of social policy and administration as a subject and the lack of a common core of ideas which can be related to the theories of a single discipline.

> Do we have a subject of our own, or are we merely a bunch of ex-economists, political scientists and historians, would-be psychologists, philosophers and sociologists, that could be better employed in the purer atmosphere of these major disciplines? (Donnison, 1973, p. 35)

The attempt to apply the social sciences, including philosophy, to the analysis and solution of a changing range of social problems throws up challenging intellectual tasks of disciplinary integration.

Several different solutions have been found, none of them entirely satisfactory. One is to carry out research within the perspective and intellectual framework of a single discipline, as an applied branch of that subject. Thus studies are carried out on the economics of health, or the sociology of race relations, or the psychology of child-rearing, which are essentially applied economics, or applied sociology, or applied psychology. From a policy point of view such research may be criticised as painting a partial picture, from within a single intellectual framework. Could housing policy, for example, be formulated simply in terms of the insights provided by the sociology of housing, ignoring the historical and economic dimensions of the British system of housing?

A second course is sometimes then followed, which involves carrying out an interdisciplinary study in which a single discipline dominates. Different sorts of factors are taken into account within an explanatory framework provided by a single discipline. Cost-benefit analysis in economics is an excellent example (cf. Layard, 1972). The framework and unit of measurement is economic, but non-economic factors are included by giving them a monetary value. Thus in the study of airport location, monetary values can be given to factors such as airport noise, environmental damage, time taken in travel to different locations, and so on. In criminology, on the other hand, the focus has mainly been upon social and/or psychological factors, while economic influences have tended to be subsumed under social variables (economic incentives to commit crime treated as an aspect of class or status position).

Frequently, however, a third approach to interdisciplinary study is preferred which involves seeking the lowest common denominator of the disciplines concerned. This is usually found in their methodologies, in the preferred variables and measuring tools of the participating disciplines, with de-emphasis of the explanatory framework. As Glennerster and Hoyle have shown in relation to educational research, the conflict between a policy and disciplinary orientation is difficult to resolve. Some types of research – sociological studies of school organisation, for example – have been cast at too high a level of abstraction to be useful in studying substantive problems. On the other hand there is too ready a tendency to seek the lowest common denominator of the *form* of science without substantial intellectual content.

> [E]ducation has suffered from what might be called the non-disciplinary approach. Many examples of educational research use the tools of the social sciences – tests, surveys, etc. – but have little theoretical basis. These studies are often useful at the level of description, but lack explanatory power. The administrator or politician is likely to welcome description, for this leaves him with a considerable degree of freedom to formulate his own policies. (Glennerster and Hoyle, 1972, p. 196)

The empiricist tendencies of social administration are built into the intellectual structure of the subject and can only be countered by more explicit attention to problems of conceptualisation, theory and explanation. The situation has been succinctly summed up as follows.

> [In British] social policy and administration we begin with fact-finding and end in moral rhetoric, still lacking those explanatory

theories which might show the process as a whole and reveal the relations of the separate problems to one another. (Pinker, 1971, p. 12)

The Limitations of Empiricism

The empiricist character of much British social policy research is a serious weakness which reduces the impact that the social sciences might have upon society through trivialising their intellectual contribution. Good social science research requires a significant problem. Social science is a special kind of problem-solving by which disciplined and logical social investigation attempts to answer questions about the social world and human existence. The social scientist is a man with a problem or he is nothing.

> The naive empiricist thinks that we begin by collecting and analysing our experiences, and so ascend the ladder of science . . . But if I am ordered to record what you are now experiencing, I shall hardly know how to obey that ambiguous order. Am I to report what I am writing; that I hear a bell ringing; a newsboy shouting; a loudspeaker droning; or am I to report, perhaps, that these noises irritate me? A science needs points of view, and theoretical problems. (K. R. Popper, 1961, p. 106)

The inadequacy of a 'factual' approach to social investigation is that data have to be collected in terms of categories. These categories or concepts are a means of organising the observations made into some sort of order. The 'bucket theory of the mind' (see K. R. Popper, 1972, pp. 341–61) treats this as unproblematic: one simply dips in one's bucket and pulls out an array of facts, which one then has to make sense of inductively.

The interdependence of theory and observation is a commonplace of the philosophy of science which hardly needs extended discussion. Generalisation and observation are interdependent. Concepts and theories are not imposed as *a priori* categories but are used in the context of a particular problem and a particular set of observations. There is a constant interplay between the observation of realities and the formation of concepts, between research and theorising, between perception and explanation. The genesis of any theory is the result of an interplay between observational sophistication and theoretical specification (Bulmer, 1979, p. 659). Social *science*, as distinct from social research of an empiricist kind, involves bringing general ideas into play in empirical inquiry.

So far as the making of policy is concerned, this suggests that a more mature understanding of science is necessary for progress to be made. As Michael Rutter has observed:

> research is not primarily concerned with the collection of facts nor even with the derivation and testing of laws. Rather it provides a means (or, more accurately, many different means) of posing and answering questions. Science is not a body of knowledge. Instead it involves a process of inquiry – a means of finding out about something. (1977, p. 107)

The model of the relationship between research and policy which emerges is therefore rather different from the simple empiricist one.

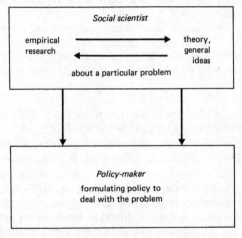

Different social sciences display different degrees of integration between empirical research and theory. Of policy-relevant social sciences, the fit is certainly tightest in economics. The influence and persuasiveness of economists in the counsels of government owes much to this degree of scientific maturity which few other social sciences can match. (Experimental psychology is perhaps an exception, but many of its propositions are so stunningly trivial, banal, or irrelevant to policy as to place it on the margins. Other fields of psychology produce much more relevant scientific findings, but there is much more contention over them.)

Sociology, the other social science which might be thought to have most to contribute to the study of social policy, displays in Britain conflicting tendencies but in general a lack of engagement with policy issues. In part the explanation for this is historical, in the relation between the academic subjects of sociology and social administration. The British tradition of empirical social inquiry, from Rowntree and the Webbs onwards, has been based on very close links between social scientists and social democratic politicians. A social structure in which simple political responses to social problems were easily available and plausible fostered intimacy between social researchers and policy-makers. Sociology as a distinct subject only began to develop strongly when it became clear that social problems were more fundamentally problematical than they had been in the British experience (P. Abrams, 1968, p. 153), but the result in the long run was the marked divergence of the theoretical and empirical streams. In the period 1945–60 the two subjects were in close academic conjunction, but have since drawn quite far apart. In sociology this has been due in part to scepticism about the intellectual merits of empiricism and positivism (see Rex, 1961) and in social administration to scepticism about the usefulness of certain types of general theory.

Sociologists have not helped their case by their emphasis on the distinctiveness of sociological theory. Although it is a caricature, Alasdair McIntyre's picture of the general theorist is not too far from the more empirically minded social scientist's view of contemporary sociology.

There was once a man who aspired to be the author of the general theory of holes. When asked 'What kind of hole – holes dug by children in the sand for amusement, holes dug by gardeners to plant lettuce seedlings, tank traps, holes made by roadmakers?' he would reply indignantly that he wished for a *general* theory that would explain all of these. He rejected *ab initio* the – as he saw it – pathetically common-sense view that of the digging of different kinds of holes there are quite different kinds of explanations to be given: why then he would ask do we have the concept of a hole? Lacking the explanations to which he originally aspired, he then fell to discovering statistically significant correlations; he found for example that there is a correlation between the aggregate hole-digging achievement of a society as measured, or at least one day to be measured, by econometric techniques, and its degree of tech-nological development. The United States surpasses both Paraguay and Upper Volta in hole-digging. He also discovered that war accelerates hole-digging; there are more holes in Vietnam than there were. These observations, he would always insist, were neut-ral and value-free. This man's achievement has passed totally unnoticed except by me. Had he, however, turned his talents to political science, had he concerned himself not with holes, but with modernisation, urbanisation or violence, I find it difficult to believe that he might not have achieved high office in the American Political Science Association. (1972, p. 8)

There is evidence, too, that the impulses to empirical inquiry in contemporary British sociology have become somewhat weakened (*Sociology*, 1981; for a more extended account see Payne *et al.*, 1981). Coupled with a degree of radicalisation of the subject, leading to distrust of the state and its works, the net outcome has been that today sociology does not play a pre-eminent role in the study of social policy. The theme of the limitations of empiricism has been played upon so strongly that not only is it exhausted, but the counter-view that 'theory speaks for itself' has come to be taken far more seriously than policy research. (For one example of its consequences see Hindess, 1977.)

The above is a very general characterisation, to which there are exceptions. It may be helpful to look briefly at one or two areas in which research brings together theory and evidence to illuminate problems within a sociological framework which are also of interest to policy-makers. Research on education is one field in which sociological approaches have had a considerable impact on policy, though perhaps more in the 1950s and early 1960s than in the 1970s. The findings of studies by Jean Floud, A. H. Halsey and F. M. Martin (1956), J. W. B. Douglas (1964) and the Plowden Committee (1967) into the social determinants of educational success all exercised a powerful influence upon policy in both primary and secondary education, supporting the case for comprehensivisation and for positive discrimination.

Sociological studies of the workings of labour markets have provided findings relevant to the deliberations of policy-makers. Subjects studied include the contraction of vulnerable industries and redundancy (Kahn, 1964; Martin and Fryer, 1973; Bulmer, 1977); the effects of industrial relocation (Mann, 1973); and the workings of the labour market at the local level (Blackburn and Mann, 1979). To the extent that such studies develop theories of the middle range (advocated by Robert Merton and T. H. Marshall), they demonstrate the value of a perspective upon social policy informed by social science and not just consisting of an assemblage of empirical data.

Studies in the sociology of poverty also demonstrate the potential fruitfulness of a more inclusive theoretical treatment of a problem. The debate over the 'culture of poverty' stimulated originally by Oscar Lewis, has provoked lively theoretical discussion about the nature of poverty as a phenomenon and the social mechanisms which sustain it (see Valentine, 1967; Leacock, 1971). Recent British research on transmitted deprivation derives from this debate – specifically the idea that social disadvantage is passed on from one generation to the next – and has led to a number of interesting empirical studies (for example, Coffield *et al.*, 1981). If the outcome of work in these fields is predominantly negative – to suggest that the 'culture of poverty' hypothesis is wrong and that the intergenerational transmission of deprivation is unproven – it has been concerned with ideas and generalisations. Indeed the falsification of theoretical propositions in this way might be regarded as a good example of Popperian methodology. It is only by setting up theories and testing these against evidence that progress can be made. Social policy is a particularly good field for the competition and confrontation of different alternative perspectives and explanations. By generating competing models, empirical testing is forced and some judgements permitted about the merits of alternative theories (cf. Blume, 1979).

This process is well demonstrated in a field on the boundary between sociology and psychology, that of parent–child relations. Empirical studies of maternal deprivation, for example, have suggested the harm which can be caused in early life by disruption of the mother–child bond (Bowlby, 1951). The testing of this theory has been careful and prolonged and in the course of it considerable doubt has been cast upon the original formulation (Rutter, 1972). More attention is now devoted to the quality of parent–child interaction and to the question of whether there are critical periods in a child's development. Others have argued that a focus on the early years is exaggerated (Clarke and Clarke, 1976). The point is that specific theoretical hypotheses about child development, with direct policy implications, have provoked a lively scientific exchange. In the medium to long term this is likely to be much more fruitful for policy than merely assembling the facts, however reliably or comprehensively.

The Engineering Model

A model of social scientist interacting with policy-maker to bring to bear the insights of social science – rather than merely the factual products of social research – does not take the discussion very far. What sort of interaction occurs? What form does the influence exercised by the social scientist take? What use is made of social science, and how? One influential account of this relationship is to draw an analogy with the engineer, a notion perhaps given unintended impetus by Karl Popper's belief in 'piecemeal social engineering'. Social science provides the evidence and conclusions to help solve a policy problem. The social scientist is a technician who commands the knowledge to make the necessary investigation and interpret the results.

The model is a linear one. A problem exists; information or understanding is lacking either to generate a solution to the problem or to select among alternative solutions; research provides the missing knowledge; and a solution is reached. Typically a single study will be involved. This – with its data, analysis and conclusions – will affect the choices that decision-makers face. Implicit in such an approach is agreement upon ends. It is assumed that policy-makers and researchers agree upon what the desired end-state should be. The role of research is to help in the identification and selection of appropriate means to reach that goal (Weiss, 1977a, pp. 11–12). Such a view of the influence of research upon policy can be represented thus:

The engineer (or the doctor) provides the role model for this kind of applied research. It involves the making of a sharp distinction between basic and applied research. The task of basic researchers is to develop and test a logico-deductive system of hypotheses and propositions. Theoretical knowledge is very general. Theoretical contributions are intended to systematise knowledge and stimulate empirical research. Applied social researchers, on the other hand, are concerned with the research applications of existing theoretical knowledge. Their task is to collect empirical data to solve specific problems. They are skilled in empirical research, and have the interpersonal skills to communicate their findings directly to policy-makers. 'They are, so to speak, social engineers' (Janowitz, 1972, p. 3).

An early statement of this conception of the applied researcher is to be found in Hans Zetterberg's *Social Theory and Social Practice* (1962), where the author uses physiology and medicine as the basis for an analogy, arguing that the applied social researcher (like the doctor) should be able to offer prescriptive recommendations on the basis of the special knowledge which he possesses. Unfortunately the examples adduced, such as advising public librarians, are not particularly impressive. The model of the social scientist as social engineer is nevertheless clear (see also Dror, 1971; MacRae, 1976).

In Britain the engineering model has received a powerful impetus from the influential Rothschild Report of 1971, which distinguished sharply between basic and applied research. Applied research for government, Rothschild argued, should be done on a customer/contractor basis. A customer (perhaps a government department) would commission research from a separate contractor (perhaps a research institute or university department). The customer, although he could be advised by the contractor, would set the objectives and the limits within which the contractor would work. The customer pays the contractor for his services (Rothschild, 1971). The model for such a role for research was taken from technology. Though Rothschild did not refer specifically to social research in his recommendations, he has nevertheless been read as endorsing the appropriateness of the engineering model for social science.

The most powerful advocacy of such an approach has perhaps come from James S. Coleman, the American sociologist, who has distinguished sharply between 'policy research' and 'discipline research', arguing strongly that only the former can contribute effectively to social policy-making (1972). Policy research, as he defines it, has a number of characteristics. It is time-bound, designed to meet deadlines set by the policy-maker. Partial information at the time action is taken is more effective than complete information after the deadline has passed. In policy research the correctness of the predictions or results is more important than the parsimony or elegance of the theory. Models used should be relatively simple and robust. In policy research, too, the choice of variables is different from that in discipline research, where there are ordinarily 'independent' and 'dependent' variables. There are results of outcomes of policy; there are policy variables, which have been or are amenable to policy control; and there are situational variables, which play a part in the processes being studied but are not amenable to policy manipulation. The focus of research should be upon policy variables and outcomes which the policy-maker can influence.

Further distinguishing characteristics of policy research are that it is only the first stage of a social learning process. The ultimate product is not a contribution to knowledge in the discipline but a social policy modified by the research results. Moreover policy research starts with a problem defined outside the discipline. This requires careful translation into research terms without loss of meaning. While values implied by the canons of scientific method govern the *execution* of policy research, values from the world of action govern the formulation of policy research problems. There are a number of other distinguishing characteristics which Coleman (1972) identifies, drawing on his own research for the Department of Health, Education and Welfare, *Equality of Educational Opportunity* (Coleman *et al.*, 1966).

The thrust of Coleman's analysis is to suggest a number of characteristics which distinguish policy research sharply from discipline-based research. A strictly scientific model of research is employed, but it differs in marked respects from scientific research within a discipline. Most notably it serves different ends from those of discipline-based research and this has many consequences for the design and execution of research which lead to Coleman implicitly adopting the engineering analogy. Indeed he explicitly criticises much existing applied research as being not very relevant to policy problems, a curious misapplication of the paraphernalia of discipline research outside the discipline. It is of very little use in short- and medium-term policy formation and tends to address problems intrinsic to the discipline rather than problems in the real world (Coleman, 1972, p. 22).

Coleman writes authoritatively on the basis of first-hand experience to present one of the most forceful recent statements of the engineering model. He has also pointed out that in recent years much policy research has been carried out in the United States outside universities in independent research institutes and firms, such as Rand Corporation, Abt Associates, Mathematica, and a number of others, which have been set up specifically to meet the requirements of government-funded policy research. Like market research formerly, policy research has tended to move outside the university because the university is too irregular, irresponsible and unpredictable a setting for the efficient execution of policy research once it is regularised. It may be that the development of policy research involves distancing from academic discipline research *and* from academic organisations.

The model of the social scientist employing his empirical and analytical skills to answer problems and questions posed by policy-makers is an attractive one. It suggests that the social scientist can be socially useful, making an important contribution to national issues. The scientific status of social science is recognised both in its methods and explanatory theories. The professional status of research is much enhanced, while the social scientist is accorded a position of power as a technical expert comparable to that of the engineer or doctor. So what is wrong with it?

One powerful line of criticism suggests that the engineering model misstates and misunderstands the nature of the policy-making process.

> Information and analysis provide only one route among several to social problem-solving – because . . . a great deal of the world's problem-solving is and ought to be accomplished through various forms of social interaction that substitute action for thought, understanding or analysis . . . In addition . . . other forms of information and analysis – ordinary knowledge and causal analysis foremost amongst them – are often sufficient or better for social problem-solving. (Lindblom and Cohen, 1979, p. 10)

Policy research in the engineering model, it is argued, misunderstands the policy-making process, fails to take account of the complex processes by which decisions are reached, exaggerates the role of the 'decision-maker' for whom research is carried out and gives unwarranted authority to the research input which the policy researcher provides. The results of policy research lack the degree of conclusiveness which their practitioners claim, either as scientific knowledge or as confirmation of ordinary knowledge.

Two strands in this criticism are particularly important. One concerns the nature of the policy-making process. If the policy-making process is confused, messy, inconclusive, invoking mutual bargaining, the unintended consequences of actions, disjointed incrementalism and uncertain outcomes, the neat rationality of either David Glass's postwar optimism or modern 'policy science' is really beside the point. If the world does not work in a wholly rational way, the impact of a social science designed specifically to serve policy will be correspondingly reduced.

The second strand concerns the scientific status of the results of policy research in the engineering model. Perhaps Rothschild exempted social science from the customer/contractor principle because he recognised that many social sciences are unable to satisfy the customer by providing hard and fast answers to discrete 'technical' questions. Subjects like psychology and sociology are not well placed to provide definitive answers to questions like: how can (certain types of) vandalism be reduced? How can employee absenteeism be reduced? How can educational performance (of certain pupils) be improved? How can the health (of certain groups) be made better? Certainly some of the factors involved may be identified, and a distinction made between situation variables and policy variables, the latter being amenable to manipulation by the policy-maker. The findings of such research, however, are not only rarely absolutely conclusive, they frequently only explain a small proportion of the variance observed in the dependent variable. The scientific claims made for policy research in the engineering model are frequently much too strong.

What alternatives, then, are available?

The Enlightenment Model

The engineering model employs a fundamental distinction between basic and applied research. Applied social science involves using the insights of basic social science theory, together with rigorous methods common to both basic and applied research, to tackle problems defined for the researcher by the customer or client. As the influential Dainton Report (1971, p. 5) pointed out in the same year as Rothschild, such a distinction is unsatisfactory. The objectives 'pure' and 'applied' imply a division where none should exist and their use can be harmful. Supposedly theoretical research may have important practical consequences; supposedly applied research may have theoretical pay-off. The same point has been made by Peter Rossi *et al.*, who point out that the distinction between pure and applied research is blurred. Though differing in objective,

> one can scarcely begin to solve societal problems until one understands them; conversely, one only understands a societal problem when potentially effective solutions to it can be imagined . . . basic

and applied social research share the science and craftlore of the social science disciplines, but differ in their artful aspects: the theories, methods and procedures of basic and applied research are quite similar but the style of work encountered in each camp is not. (Rossi *et al.*, 1978, p. 173)

This view of the nature of applied research has had many adherents in the history of the social sciences, particularly sociology. Florian Znaniecki (1940) in *The Social Role of the Man of Knowledge* discussed the fusion of the roles of sage and technological leader, insisting that technical specialists alone can not effectively apply social science knowledge. William F. Ogburn, himself something of a technical specialist in statistical studies of social change, insisted that basic and practical research tended to merge. Basic research sometimes produced results of great benefit to mankind; research on practical social problems (such as race relations) not infrequently yielded knowledge that is fundamental (Ogburn, 1964, p. 332).

Its most persuasive recent adherent is perhaps Morris Janowitz. Janowitz argues that the sociologist is part of the process which he or she is studying, not outside it. For example, in studying the 'causes' of social problems as well as the technical means for analysing the issues, the sociologist has to make explicit criteria and standards of performance that are being applied. Minimum income levels and the procedures for welfare administration need to be considered, with a view not only to what is but to what is possible (Janowitz, 1972).

It is not the sociologist's task to *recommend* alternative policies and to insist that some administrative options are 'better' than others. But if he is not a proper catalyst of social change, neither ought a sociologist to serve as a justifier of received patterns, legitimating them with *post factum* omniscience as a product of 'inevitability'. If the sociologist may not expatiate upon what 'ought to be', he is still privileged to deal with another realm, 'the realm of what can be'. (Gouldner, 1954, p. 28)

The sociologist has to recognise that he is interacting with subject and audience, whom the findings may influence directly or indirectly. The findings and ideas which are put forward come in time to be part of the general culture, and specific social science theories and findings may become part of the defensive ideology of particular groups, as in the influence of social research upon the self-perceptions of criminals and delinquents. (For one example see McVicar, 1979.)

The enlightenment model assumes the overriding importance of the social context, and focuses on developing various types of knowledge that can be utilised by policy-makers and professions. While it seeks specific answers its emphasis is on creating the intellectual conditions for problem solving . . . rational inquiry and intellectual debate require social and political conditions of academic freedom. The consequence of effective sociological inquiry is to contribute to political freedom and social voluntarism by weakening myths, refuting distortions, and preventing an imbalanced view of social reality from dominating collective decisions. (Janowitz, 1972, pp. 5–6)

Empirical evidence in support of such a view of the role of applied social science is found in recent studies of policy- and decision-makers in government by Caplan (1976), Knorr (1977) and Weiss (1980a). The neat model of the social engineer does not seem to accord with how government officials actually make use of social research. They seem to employ it more to orient themselves to problems than to find solutions to discrete policy problems. Research provides the intellectual background of concepts, orientations and empirical generalisations that inform policy. It is used to orient decision-makers to problems, to think about and specify the problematic elements in a situation, to get new ideas. Policy-makers use research to *formulate* problems and to set the agenda for future policy actions. Much of this use is not direct, but a result of long-term infiltration of social science concepts, theories and findings with the general intellectual culture of a society.

Carol Weiss draws the conclusion from these findings that the narrow focus of the applied researcher as social engineer is not a necessary condition for good applied social research. There need not be complete acceptance of the fundamental goals, priorities and political constraints of the decision-maker. Decision-makers (at least in the United States) believe it is a good thing to have controversial research, challenging research, research that makes them rethink comfortable assumptions. Value consensus is not a prerequisite for useful policy research. There is a role for research as social criticism. There is a place for research based on variant theoretical premises. As new concepts and data emerge, their gradual cumulative effect can be to change the conventions policy-makers abide by and to reorder the goals and priorities of policy-makers (Weiss, 1977a).

Such a picture also accords with a critical assessment of the intellectual achievements of the social sciences as scientific disciplines. Sociology, for example, has not made advances comparable to those in subjects like medicine, physics or agriculture. It cannot point to technological innovations such as nuclear weapons, or nuclear electricity, new forms of therapy, or new improvements in food production. Nor are its cognitive accomplishments on a par with many other sciences, as the present plurality of approaches within sociology demonstrates. Moreover applied research in sociology is not comparable to applied research in the natural sciences and medicine in that it does not involve the application of scientifically tested general principles to the explanation and management of specific social problems; such general principles do not exist as yet.

One influential statement of the task of sociology has been made by Edward Shils in pointing out the limitations of a technicist conception of social science in aid of the policy-maker.

> The proper calling today of sociology is the illumination of opinion. Having its point of departure in the opinion of the human beings who make up the society, it is its task to return to opinion, clarified and deepened by dispassionate study and systematic reflection . . . Like the *philosophes* [of the Enlightenment], sociologists will be the commentators and illuminators of the current scene . . . they have a theory that [has] assimilated the best in the ideas of the Enlightenment and strengthened it by progress in a great variety of disciplines cultivated since the eighteenth century. Some sociologists might feel that this definition of the calling of sociology is one that undoes the progress of the subject. On the contrary, it shows the right direction for a subject that is at once a science, a moral discipline and a body of opinion. (Shils, 1961, p. 1441)

Conclusion

The relative merits of the engineering and enlightenment models will be further discussed in the final chapter. It is now time, however, to descend a little from the rather abstract level at which the preceding discussion has been conducted. Though a considerable number of empirical studies have been referred to there has not been much detailed reference to the procedures of empirical research. In the next three chapters the utilisation of social research in policy-making will be discussed in much more detail by means of examples. In Chapters 3 and 4 different stages of the research process will be highlighted, using illustrations from the study of deprivation, physical handicap and health. In Chapter 5 the different case of the use of research by governmental commissions is considered in depth. In all three chapters the underlying concern is with issues raised in this chapter: the poverty of empiricism; the doubtful usefulness of an engineering model of application; and the different ways in which applied social research may provide enlightenment about the problems being considered.

3

Conceptualising Problems and Designing Research: 'Deprivation' and 'Disadvantage'

The limitations of the 'bucket' theory of the generation of social knowledge may be demonstrated by looking in some detail at several stages of the process of research. Methodology textbooks conventionally emphasise the steps through which research passes, including:

- problem-finding;
- concept definition and specification;
- formulation of hypotheses;
- selection of sample;
- collection of data, after design and testing of the research instruments;
- editing, coding and processing of data;
- analysis of data;
- report-writing, policy conclusions.

How research is conducted has important consequences for the uses which can be made of the results in the policy process. For example, if care is not taken in the selection of the sample, the generalisability of the results may be in doubt and their usefulness as a basis for drawing inferences about government action limited. Meeting the requirement of representativeness is very important in policy research.

Many of the basic principles of social research methodology are familiar or, if not, can be acquired from standard texts. The aim of the discussion in this and the next chapter is not to go over such familiar ground but rather to focus upon different stages of the research process and show how the way in which research is approached and conducted has implications for its utilisation. In this chapter particular attention is paid to problem-finding, to concept definition and to the formulation of hypotheses, using the example of the study of 'deprivation' or 'disadvantage'. In the next chapter particular attention is paid to problems of measurement and explanation, using the examples of physical disability and health and illness.

Problem-Finding in Policy Research

An essential question to ask of any piece of policy research is: whose 'problem' is being investigated? A 'problem' in social science can mean one of various things. It may refer to a policy problem, or to a problem of a more philosophical kind thrown up by the philosophy of history, or to problems generated by, and intrinsic to, academic disciplines (Greer, 1969, pp. 8–18). One argument of this book is that the line between these different types of problem cannot be drawn too sharply. Although principally concerned with policy problems, those of direct practical social concern, other kinds of problem cannot be excluded. Moreover the search for solutions to problems is likely to require the social scientist to draw on the theories and explanations offered by different social science disciplines.

Problem definition exposes the researcher to several kinds of pitfall. The simplest is that facing someone working on behalf of a pressure group, investigating the problems of a particular category of people (for example, the elderly). If the problem definition of the pressure group is accepted at face value it is likely to bias the conduct of the research and gloss over important issues which need to be taken account of in policy formulation, such as the relationship between different types of disadvantage, or how the scarce resources available for social policy fields are to be allocated. Surveys may show, for example, that falling income and poor pension provision upon retirement make it desirable to raise the legal retirement age in order to enable those between 65 and 70 to remain at work if they wish and thus maintain their incomes. To implement such a policy, however (as has in fact been done in the United States), merely creates other problems for other sections of society – for example, those entering the labour market at a time of contraction of job vacancies, who are faced with a situation where vacancies are not being created by retirement.

This reference to the interests involved is also a reminder that what is a problem for government is not necessarily a problem in everyone's eyes, and vice versa. The state may perceive as problems issues which others deny to be significant problems while itself ignoring issues which members of the society consider to be problems. Examples of the former would include the use of marihuana in Western countries and excessive state concern with the political affiliations of state employees and others. Topics tending to be ignored by governments might include the effects of nuclear energy programmes or the consequences of widespread excess alcohol consumption. It is now a commonplace of the sociology of social problems that what counts as a 'problem' is socially defined.

A question to be asked about a problem then, is: for whom is this issue a problem? The posing of such a question may lead to a question being seen in a new light. The study of British race relations, for example, has tended to focus upon the black population, their situation and behaviour. It can be very plausibly argued, however, that the focus should be as much upon the white population and how they define 'race' as a problem. In the case of welfare fraud, great attention is focused on what is alleged to be a major 'problem', 'scrounging', while less attention is given to other forms of abuse (for example, tax evasion) or crime (for example, commercial fraud). The fact that many people entitled to welfare benefits may not be receiving them is regarded as less important than that a small minority may be receiving them illegally. Values enter into problem selection and formulation sometimes to a greater extent than at other times.

There is a tendency, however, particularly among those favouring the engineering model, to see applied social science as a means of providing technocratic solutions to problems.

> The typical American word for an unsatisfactory social state is 'problem', something, that is, which can be solved and thereby disposed of; and the typical word for ameliorative social action is 'program', something, that is, which has a pre-ordained beginning, middle and end . . . There is a distinct tendency to see public social provision as emergency breakdown and repair rather than a service and maintenance contract. (Hope, 1978, p. 250)

The use of the terminology of social problems to treat current issues as matters of social sickness rather than social cleavage and conflict has been widely commented on (see Rule, 1978, ch. 1). A problem – whether race, pollution, poverty, or the city – can be safely agreed to be a bad thing by all, and the social scientist is then brought in to treat the problem in the manner that the doctor diagnoses illness. The participation of the expert social scientist in the diagnosis of problems is a limited one and, as was argued in the previous chapter, a limiting one. It may be more discomfiting if the social scientist draws attention to the existence of conflicting interests, lack of consensus, social cleavage and political conflict over the right course of action to be followed. The enlightenment model can, however, accommodate the part played by social science within such a political system whereas the engineering model cannot.

Concept Formulation: 'Deprivation'

The social scientist's choice of problem is given exact form when he or she comes to define and specify the concepts to be used in a particular study. Yet if the terms involved are at all complex, the implications of such definitions are far from the simplicities of the tradition of British survey research. At this point it is most useful to turn to the discussion of a specific example.

An interesting case of the complexity of research is provided by the concept of 'deprivation'. This has a central place in the study of social policy, where it has developed out of the study of more specific social problems such as poverty, malnutrition, ill-health, bad housing conditions, and so on. Defining some of these specific concepts can be problematical; the concept of the poverty line, for example, is not simple and straightforward. But 'deprivation' is at a higher level of generality and relates to a broad range of concerns within social policy and social work studies.

Deprivation may be defined as a state of mind in which an individual or set of individuals is without something which one believes they should not be without. What is it, however, that they are without? Is it material resources, or access to services, or affection and psychological support, or what? Different disciplines give different answers to the question. The study of maternal deprivation (see Bowlby, 1951; Ainsworth, 1962) is concerned with the consequences of lack of maternal love. Adequate mothering implies a loving relationship between mother and baby, which leads to an attachment which is unbroken, which provides adequate stimulation, in which the mothering is provided by one person, and which occurs in the child's own family. The absence of one or more of these characteristics is said to constitute maternal deprivation, with harmful consequences for the child. For example, a child's ability to form deep interpersonal relationships in adulthood may be based in part on having formed satisfactory bonds with other people in the first three years of life. Other psychologists, however, have preferred to use deprivation to refer to lack of sensory stimulation alone, as being more specific and measurable (Casler, 1961). Runciman's (1966) sociological approach, on the other hand, treats deprivation as a lack of financial and material resources, without any reference to lack of psychological stimulus. Yet other approaches treat deprivation as synonymous with psycho-social disadvantage (Eckland and Kent, 1968).

It is hardly news that different disciplines define the concept in different ways. Yet this cannot be ignored in the study of social policy, for the researcher must define his terms and justify the definition selected. How is a choice made between the different competing definitions? Perhaps more difficult still is the fact that the concept is not even used consistently within a single framework, reflecting the woolliness and lack of precision of many social science concepts. Maternal deprivation, for example, has been used to cover 'every undesirable interaction between mother and child – rejection, hostility, cruelty, over-indulgence, repressive control, lack of affection and the like'

(Ainsworth, 1962). A review by Michael Rutter of research in the field concludes that:

> The concept of maternal deprivation has undoubtedly been useful in focusing attention on the sometimes grave consequences of deficient or disturbed care in early life. However, it is now evident that the experiences included under the term 'maternal deprivation' are too heterogeneous and the effects too varied for it to continue to have any usefulness. It has served its purpose and should now be abandoned. That 'bad' care of children in early life can have 'bad' effects, both short-term and long-term, can be accepted as proven. What is now needed is a more precise delineation of the different aspects of 'badness', together with an analysis of their separate effects and of the reasons why children differ in their responses. (1972, p. 128)

For example, if deprivation is taken to refer to 'dispossession' or 'loss', then its appropriateness to mother–child interaction is not clear, for research suggests that it is lack or distortion of maternal care, rather than actual 'loss', which leads to short- and long-term psychological damage.

The very vagueness of the term 'deprivation' can be an advantage. A major research programme has been based on the idea of deprivation transmitted from one generation to another. Yet a review of the social science literature carried out for this programme concluded that the term 'deprivation' should be abandoned. There was no doubt that people continued to suffer various forms of personal and social disadvantage – in terms of income, poor housing, racial discrimination, and so on. The term 'deprivation', however, generated semantic confusion and lack of clarity.

> The word almost functions as a projective test in which each person reads into the concept his own biases and prejudices, regardless of how the word has been used in the article or book in question. The result has been an inordinate amount of fruitless friction and heat concerning words and their usage. (Rutter and Madge, 1976, p. 2).

Such differences in problem definition and usage do not reflect only differences in disciplinary perspective. They are also grounded in more basic philosophical differences in approach which can be reflected in empirical research. A common element in approaches to deprivation is the idea that those who are deprived of some social or psychological state are unable in some sense to lead 'a full life'. Spelling out the criteria by which one would decide what is a full life, however, is much more problematical.

In empirical research one can, of course, set out criteria of deprivation clearly and then investigate their incidence. For example, one can define a measure of housing stress and then look empirically to see to what extent families of particular types suffer from such stress. All reasonable people, it can be argued, may agree on the facts. But is this so? If different types of deprivation are compared – for example, housing with health with income – empirical investigators in different fields tend to find that they have been using different criteria to define the concept. In studies using census indicators one is confined to the variables actually available from the census, yet very often such studies proceed in the data-dredging manner regardless of problems of comparability. Moreover, some results (for example, Holtermann, 1975) tend to show that there is not a very high degree of overlap between different kinds of deprivation.

If one tries to specify more clearly what may be called 'a full life', however, one has to draw on a conception of what human beings and their societies are capable of, in order to have an ideal. This is partly a philosophical matter, taking a view of 'a society in which men may have perfected themselves and their relations with each other or, in which they have not because it is believed that they cannot, these relations are the ones best suited to their enduring frailties' (Hawthorn and Carter, 1977, pp. 4–5).

The concept of deprivation, Hawthorn and Carter argue, is an essentially contested concept. The application of the concept of 'deprivation' depends upon one's prior conception of what it is to be deprived. Four distinct models of deprivation can be identified in use in Britain since 1942. These are set out ideal-typically as the patriarchal, *laissez-faire*, liberal and egalitarian models. The patriarchal approach views men as weak and greedy, in need of protection from themselves as well as each other. Protection is best assured in a hierarchical community in which the strong protect the weak and the weak serve the strong, a society modelled on the idealised family or small-scale settlement. *Laissez-faire* proponents, on the other hand, suppose that men are intrinsically different, particularly in their abilities and aptitudes. Given free rein, this results in a vigorous, creative and therefore successful society. Liberals also presuppose dissimilarity, but emphasise its value for individuals themselves. A society must be judged in terms of the extent to which it enables the individual to fulfil his own potential. Egalitarianism, like patriarchalism, assumes the similarity of individuals, but sees this as a strength and a virtue. What appear as individual failings are not so at all, but social ones brought about by inequalities (Hawthorn and Carter, 1977, pp. 5–6).

As a result of these differing social ideals, there are differing views as to what constitutes the most important social problems; what constitutes their causes; and what social action is required to deal with the disjunction between actuality and the ideal state of affairs. These differences are summarised in Table 3.1.

From this analysis the conclusion is drawn that discussions of social problems and social policy cannot be only discussions of the facts.

> They must also and necessarily be moral and so in practice political. Accordingly, a definition of what is to count as a social problem, and so a definition of something one might wish to call 'deprivation', cannot be neutral. It has to be committed. And as such, in a morally heterogeneous society, it has to be contested. (Hawthorn and Carter, 1977, p. 7)

Not only is the concept of 'deprivation' itself contestable, but the possible components of deprivation when it is studied empirically are open to dispute. There is little disagreement, perhaps, about how to characterise people's age and sex, and determining their housing conditions poses few problems. As one goes on to consider income, education, psychological characteristics, the neighbourhoods in which people live or their participation in the market, agreement on what constitutes deprivation is progressively less likely. The moral and political element does not wholly determine how the definition is framed, but it does intrude into empirical inquiry.

The argument being put forward should not be misunderstood. It is not one of relativism, of the dependence of empirical research findings upon the prior moral and political perspective of the observer. What is being argued is that the definition of 'deprivation' is more fundamentally problematical than many empirical researchers would admit. The study of social problems therefore requires prior and explicit attention to definitional problems and to the intellectual framework within which a particular study is being carried out. One cannot just plunge into the facts, in the worst tradition of the 'bucket' theory of the mind, and draw out conclusions which can then be applied or made useful to the policy-maker. One requires an intellectual framework within which to set the observations and out of which to develop adequate definitions of the phenomena under investigation.

In the case of deprivation, some investigators have drawn back from using the term. Rutter and Madge advocate substituting the term 'disadvantage', which has broader connotations of unfavourable conditions or circumstances, detriment, loss, injury or prejudice, and avoids the vacuity of meaning which they discern in 'deprivation'. Others have sought a solution in broadening and building moral components directly into the definition. The Southwark community development project, for example, defines deprivation as:

Table 3.1 *Four Ideal-Typical Models of the Nature of Social Problems*

	Paternalist	*Laissez-faire*	*Liberal*	*Egalitarian*
The ideal society	Moral community; mutual care and service, necessarily hierarchical	Perfect competition:	Individual fulfilment	Equality of deserts: economic power, economic rewards, or status
Central social problems (including 'deprivations')	Absence of community; absence of mutual care and service; deviance	Inhibited competition: individual and institutional (including political) interference	Lack of freedom for fulfilment	Inequality of deserts
Causes of central social problems	Rapid structural change; insufficient moral socialisation or education	Individual deficiencies; institutional impediments to competition	External impediments to individual freedom	External impediments to full equality
Intervention required to further ideal	Controlled or arrested structural change; moral education	Eugenics, etc.; removal of impediments	Removal of impediments; education	Structural change to facilitate equality

Source: Hawthorn and Carter, 1977, p. 6a.

an unjustifiable gap between those who can and those who cannot secure for themselves the living conditions and standards generally regarded as necessary in a particular society at any point in time . . . deprivation is about relative access to and control over resources within the structure of opportunity that comprises our society. (A. Davis *et al.*, 1977)

Such a definition comes close to defining deprivation in terms of inequality, rather than in terms of lacking or being without certain characteristics.

The stage of conceptual definition and specification thus involves taking basic decisions about an empirical inquiry which will influence its course and outcome. Where concepts are at all complex theoretically, attention must be paid to their meaning in case an ill-thought-out or careless definition glosses over major dimensions of importance. The theoretical implications of most social science concepts are inescapable, and it is this among other things which renders empiricism such an inadequate philosophy of social inquiry.

Designing Research: the Level of Analysis

When concepts have been defined, the next stage to be considered is the design of the research, including the formulation of hypotheses and selection of the sample. This is partly a matter of good technical practice, but decisions taken at this stage also embody broader assumptions which frame or set the stage for the data collection and analysis which is to follow. The importance of considering such assumptions will now be shown by discussing the level of analysis used in the study of deprivation.

Deprivation, however it is defined, is not spread randomly across the population. It is concentrated among particular social groups and it tends to be concentrated in particular areas. Within cities, in particular, there are areas which are poorly endowed with a number of basic resources including services for housing, education, employment and health, and where poverty is most widespread. Such deprived areas do not contain all the poor and disadvantaged of one city, but on aggregate they are likely to be worse off and to be the areas where the occurrence of multiple deprivation is most likely. Urban deprivation has in recent years in Britain been studied by academics from a number of different disciplines. It has become the focus of several policy initiatives by government (see Lawless, 1979).

This raises an interesting methodological question. To what extent, in studying deprivation or disadvantage, is it more useful to direct attention to the characteristics of *individuals* or to the characteristics of *areas*? The problem is a familiar one. The psychologist tends to focus on the individual, the sociologist on the collectivity and its attribute. Both may study samples of the population, but the focus in doing so is different. The former tends to produce explanations in terms of the behaviour of a single person, the latter in terms of the common characteristics of groups and their interaction. For example, studies of unemployment make it clear that those unemployed are likely to be older than those in work, are more likely to lack work skills, to have a history of unskilled work, to be of lower social class, to be chronically sick and to be suffering from marked personality disorders. Some of these factors are social, the last one is psychological. But all are couched at the individual level. If, on the other hand, one looks at variations in the unemployment *rate* one observes changes which are unrelated to states of the individual. If the national rate is 4 per cent in one year and 8 per cent three years later, it is implausible that such changes are due to changes in the characteristics of individuals. They are more likely to be due to changes in the macro-economic system which have consequent effects upon the level of unemployment. The type of explanation of changes in the level of unemployment is therefore different from the explanation of why some people are unemployed and others are not.

The concept of a system, and explanations couched in terms of a system, is a familiar one in the social sciences. Many social problems cannot be studied adequately at the individual level. Though psychological explanation still strongly imbues the teaching of social work, in the study of social policy it is more common to look for structural factors which may explain why psycho-social problems vary in frequency over time. By extension, interest has developed in the geographical distribution of social problems and in explaining the spatial distribution of such characteristics.

It is well established descriptively that there are important geographical variations in a whole range of social characteristics between countries, between regions in the same country, between areas (such as towns) in the same region and between areas within a single town or city. Indeed the study of such variation is a growing part of social geography (see E. Jones and Eyles, 1977; Coates *et al.*, 1977). Within social policy, the extent and importance of local geographical variation has been documented for personal social services (B. Davies, 1968), for education (Byrne *et al.*, 1975), for income (Berthoud, 1976, ch. 6) and for health (RAWP, 1976), among others. Indeed Davies has formulated the concept of 'territorial justice' to indicate the lack of fit between unequal geographical spread of services and resources and their optimal distribution in relation to population. It is now well documented that the level of public provision of a range of services, as well as the distribution of income, wealth, health and a range of other objective social conditions, are not equally distributed, nor is their unequal distribution explained away in terms of the age, sex or social class structure of the area.

The immediate methodological question is what is the status of such observed geographical variations. Are they merely descriptive data? Or can one thereby *explain* a certain proportion of variance; does geography to some extent determine the distribution of social characteristics? Or do spatial factors constrain the social framework without determining it? Or are spatial differences merely a symptom of more important social divisions? Geographers, of course, tend to assume that space is by definition of central interest, but one does not need to adopt that assumption in social policy studies. Space may certainly play some part in social administration (see Massam, 1975). For example, the size of an area and a local authority may make a difference to the efficiency and quality of its services. To argue that, however, is rather different from arguing that space is in the same sense a determinant of life chances, comparable in importance to social class, income, education, housing, and so on.

The methodological problem is important practically because of the extent to which governments in Britain have in recent years sought to develop policies for tackling urban deprivation at the areal level. There are a number of reasons why area-based policies should have seemed attractive. The limited geographical area covered by the units of English local government permits central government to discriminate between authorities in resource allocation and the meeting of needs of different areas (Foster *et al.*, 1980). Some problems, moreover, are intrinsically problems of an area, notably environmental and planning problems. These can best be tackled at the level of the area as a whole. Moreover, run-down and deprived inner city areas are fairly visible to the naked eye, with their old and decrepit housing, poor public amenities, low standard of maintenance, and so on. It seems fairly obvious that social problems exist in the area, so why not formulate policies to deal with these problems? Finally, if socially deprived individuals and households are indeed heavily concentrated in particular areas, then tackling the major social problems of such areas will help most of the deprived people.

Since the late 1960s a variety of programmes have been directed to small geographical areas, following the logic of this analysis. The earliest influential statement of such a policy was the preference of the Plowden Committee (1967) on primary education for what they termed 'positive discrimination', intervention in particular, seriously deprived, areas to try to bring them closer to the level of provision elsewhere by giving them additional resources. The educational priority area (EPA) programme followed directly from Plowden and was an action research project designed to raise educational standards and monitor the effects of the action programme in selected deprived inner city areas. Specifically, it sought to improve the children's educational performance, raise the morale of teachers, increase parental involvement and enhance the sense of responsibility for their communities of the people living in them (Town, 1978, p. 169). Plowden introduced the idea that certain areas have prior claims over others. The EPA experiment sought to improve the life chances of deprived children by directing extra resources to deprived areas, making the schools in those areas 'as good as the best in the country' (Halsey, 1972).

The Home Office community development project (CDP), launched in 1969, was similarly an action research programme in twelve local areas, designed to tackle social deprivation through the better operation and co-ordination of existing social services and to increase community response by encouraging self-help and people's participation in the decision-making process of the organisations and services which affect them. The CDP's objectives were primarily 'to improve the quality of individual, family and community life in areas of multiple deprivation, through programmes of social action related to local needs, aspirations and resources' (Town, 1978, p. 176). Subsidiary aims were to record and describe the methods used in such programmes and to evaluate their effectiveness by means of research. The twelve areas selected were mostly twilight districts of inner cities, characterised by poor housing stock, high unemployment and poor economic outlook, a concentration of social problems and heavy demands on local social service departments.

A number of other programmes were also developed at different times, including urban aid, the comprehensive community programmes, the inner area studies, and planning strategies such as general improvement areas and housing action areas. (They are conveniently summarised in Lawless, 1979). All, however, rested on the same assumption, that by identifying areas in which deprived persons were concentrated and by directing resources to those areas, one was thereby most effectively tackling the problem of urban deprivation.

The analyses produced by a number of these projects have concentrated on the routes and processes by which people living in those areas came to be there, the factors keeping them there and their likelihood of moving away. Low pay, poor economic prospects and poverty are clearly identified as one group of important factors. Like Booth (1889–1903) in London and Caradog Jones (1934) in Liverpool, much of the spatial concentration of poverty may be explained by the adverse employment situation in inner city areas, with precarious job security, low wage rates and high unemployment. Housing conditions too are important. In the public sector these centre on 'problem' (council) estates, whose low status has been acquired through the mechanisms of local authorities' procedures for allocating 'difficult' tenants. In the private housing sector deprived inner city areas tend to have run-down private accommodation judged in terms of size, quality and amenity standards. Multi-occupation and high rents compound the difficulties in the private sector. As far as education is concerned, inner city schools are less successful in attracting staff, occupy old buildings and have a higher concentration of children suffering from particular social disadvantages (Gittus, 1976).

> Urban deprivation is the structural inability to compete effectively in those markets which most affect people's life chances – the employment, education and housing markets . . . The three markets are closely interlinked such that disadvantage in one will often determine disadvantage in the others. If a child's parents are poor and live in an inner city area of decay, the chances are that he will go to a poor school; his education will be deficient and the opportunities for advancement through examination success will be low or absent. He will . . . likely emerge at the earliest opportunity to take up a job which offers low pay, low security and no future. His social position and lack of money will effectively disqualify him from competing effectively in the housing market, and in areas of acute housing shortage he may well end up once more in an inner city area – if he ever left. (Edwards, 1978, p. 226)

There has been considerable methodological controversy about the appropriateness of particular indicators in studies of deprivation (Little and Mabey, 1972; Bebbington and Davies, 1980; Carley, 1981, pp. 143–50). The use of crime and delinquency rates, truancy rates, suicide data and other indices of social pathology and personal handicap has been criticised as focusing upon the individual rather than upon the social structure. A more serious criticism, however, is whether it is appropriate to focus so heavily upon the areal level in devising programmes to counter urban deprivation.

This critique of area-based policies starts from the fact that area-based policies rest on correlations between aggregate statistics and the characteristics of an area. For example, in studies of housing stress, indicators of stress may be the proportion of households *in an area* living at a density of more than 1.5 persons per room; or without access to a fixed bath; or without exclusive use of an inside toilet. The inference is drawn from this that a high proportion of the population of such an area is living under conditions of housing stress. This is true. But two other propositions are *not* true:

(a) that all people living in areas of high housing stress themselves live under conditions of housing stress;

(b) that all people living under conditions of housing stress live in areas where housing stress is concentrated.

This result is replicated when one looks at the distribution of other types of social disadvantage. In the London EPA project, for example, J. Barnes showed that identifying EPA schools did not enable one to direct resources exclusively to the deprived children. For every two disadvantaged children located in EPA schools, there were five disadvantaged children in schools outside the EPA schools; in other words, disadvantaged children were widely scattered. Moreover, even within EPA schools the disadvantaged were only a minority and were outnumbered by those who were not disadvantaged. Directing resources to EPA schools only reached a proportion of deprived children (Barnes, 1975).

R. Berthoud has made a similar point in discussing income distribution within London. It is possible to identify areas of low income within the city, measured in terms of median income. When, however, one then focuses upon these areas of low median income, variation among households *within* those wards is about as great as variation in income levels *between* wards across the capital (though the median is different). There are scattered across London pockets of rich people; even quite small geographical areas are not socially homogeneous. As Berthoud points out, a crude indicator of the wealth of an area could be the number of Rolls Royces in that area. But if one observed a high concentration of Rolls Royces in Chelsea and Belgravia, it does not follow that living in that area is what makes people rich. Conversely, there may be a danger in overemphasising the extent to which living in poor or deprived areas *alone* makes people poor (Berthoud, 1976).

Holtermann's statistical analysis of urban deprivation using census indicators points to a similar conclusion. She examined the extent to which districts with a high rate of deprivation on one indicator had a high rate of deprivation on other indicators, and found the spatial coincidence to be far from complete. Enumeration districts in the 'worst' 15 per cent on male unemployment, overcrowding and poor household amenities only accounted for one-fifth of the 'worst' enumeration districts. A more general point also emerges from her work, that 'the degree of spatial concentration of individual aspects of deprivation is really quite low' (Holtermann, 1975, p. 39). On unemployment, 15 per cent of enumeration districts contained only 36 per cent of the unemployed. The other 85 per cent of enumeration districts contained 64 per cent of the unemployed.

The Ecological Fallacy

The results of these studies may be generalised as follows. Areas identified in terms of having a high proportion of deprived persons or households (however defined) living within them are indeed areas in which deprivation is concentrated *to some extent*. The extent to which this is the case may, however, easily and unintentionally be exaggerated. This is because:

(a) Not all persons living in areas identified as being deprived are themselves deprived. Indeed it is perfectly possible that the deprived constitute only a minority of the population of deprived areas.

(b) Not all deprived persons live in deprived areas. Many live outside them. Indeed, only a minority of the deprived may live in such deprived areas. It is perfectly possible that a majority of the deprived live elsewhere.

(c) Where the focus is upon more than one type of deprivation, there is no assurance that different kinds of deprivation will all be concentrated in particular deprived areas, even if such deprivations are linked at the individual level. For even if there is overlap in the case of individuals, there may not be overlap within particular areas. The main exception in Britain to this generalisation appears to be Glasgow, where such an overlap does appear to occur.

The statistical basis for these conclusions about the geographical distribution of deprivation is the existence of what is known as the ecological fallacy. Correlations between aggregate data about areas do not permit one to make inferences about the association between the characteristics of individuals (Robinson, 1950).

Consider in Table 3.2 hypothetical data sets showing the relationship between income and education for 1,000 people. In set (a) there is no association between education and income. No higher proportion of those with more education have higher incomes compared to those with lower incomes. In set (b) there is a perfect association between education and income. Those with more education have only high incomes; those with less education only low incomes. In both sets, however, *the marginal totals are the same*. Ecological correlations are calculated using the marginal totals (or their equivalent). A perfect ecological correlation can be consistent with a perfect individual correlation. Equally, it may be consistent with the presence of no association at all at the individual level.

Robinson demonstrated this classically for the relationship between colour and illiteracy in the United States. If one listed the percentage

Table 3.2   *A comparison of Hypothetical Data Sets Showing the Relationship between Income and Education*

(a)	Education beyond age 18	Education up to age 18	Total
High income	40	160	200
Low income	160	640	800
Total	200	800	1,000
(b)			
High income	200	0	200
Low income	0	800	800
Total	200	800	1,000

illiterate and the percentage black in each state of the union, the ecological correlation between colour and illiteracy was $r = +0.773$. If, however, one took the percentage illiterate and the percentage black as properties of individuals – that is, one distinguished between whites who were illiterate, blacks who were illiterate, whites who were literate and blacks who were literate – and then calculated the individual correlation, the result was $r = +0.203$. In this case the ecological correlation was three and a half times the individual correlation. Robinson also provided a mathematical proof of his result. He argues that it is more likely that the ecological and individual correlation will differ than that they will be the same.

The importance of the ecological fallacy is that it cautions against too ready an extrapolation from characteristics of areas to characteristics of individuals. For example, if a particular area had a high proportion of the population living in conditions of housing stress *and* a high proportion of the population suffering from psychological problems such as depression, it does not follow that *at the individual level* there is any association between the two. It would be quite possible that there was a much lower association than appeared from the area level data; or even no association at all. Working with data for the area (aggregate) alone, one's inferences about individuals within that area are necessarily uncertain.

Just as the scientific conclusions drawn from aggregate data may be invalid, so too the policy measures taken may be ineffective, because they are based on a false diagnosis. There is undoubtedly some intuitive appeal in the idea that social problems cluster together in particular areas. Townsend (1976) suggests that the exaggeration arises from notions of association and contamination, congregation, inheritance and environmental influence. Destitute, poor, mentally ill and criminal people are believed to seek refuge in certain areas because they feel easy in each other's company and more secure. Poverty, criminality and a range of other social problems are believed to be strongly rooted in certain geographical areas. There is a further belief that these characteristics are self-generating. Whether the theoretical explanation is in terms of the 'culture of poverty' (Lewis, 1966; Banfield, 1970) or the 'cycle of deprivation' (Coffield *et al.*, 1981, pp. 1–3, 157–70), there is a tendency to place the blame both on the area *and* on the victim, rather than on features of the economic and social structure. Both the 'culture of poverty' and 'cycle of deprivation' theories have come under critical scrutiny (Valentine, 1967; Leacock, 1971; Coffield, 1981). Each has been criticised for providing too facile an explanation for the persistence of deprivation and disadvantage. To the extent that they provide tacit support for an area-based policy, they are doubly unsatisfactory. The ecological fallacy can become a policy fallacy. Area-based policies for resource allocation, as Townsend points out, have severe weaknesses. First, however socially or economically deprived areas are defined, unless half the areas in the country are included there will be more disadvantaged people living outside such areas than inside them. Yet, clearly, to include as many as half the areas in the country does not facilitate direction of resources to a few areas. The EPA and CDP schemes were small demonstration projects; a national policy for resource allocation at the local level would require clearer guidance than this. Secondly, within all or nearly all areas defined as deprived there will be more persons who are *not* deprived than are deprived. Thus a policy of directing resources to deprived areas would not necessarily reach deprived people. For example, putting extra resources into EPA schools could, theoretically, not benefit any of the children for whom they were intended but provide benefits exclusively for children not from deprived backgrounds. This would be unlikely in practice, but the point is that area-based resource allocation does not necessarily ensure that resources reach those for whom they are intended.

Conclusion

This rather extended discussion of urban deprivation is intended to show how the way in which a problem is conceptualised and how hypotheses are framed can have a profound impact upon the subsequent analysis. Such features of the research process cannot be ignored, or in cases where they are, assumptions are smuggled into the analysis which distort the results without the investigator being aware of them. A theory-free approach to social policy research is more likely to plunge the investigator into error and oversimplification than it is to lead directly to usable data for policy-making.

4

Measurement and Explanation: Physical Handicap and Health and Illness

When the initial stages of problem formulation, concept definition and research design have been passed, the investigator then has to design and test research instruments by which to gather data, collect the data and analyse it. This is the most labour-intensive and time-consuming part of the research process, for which, again, good technical practice is indispensable and detailed guidance is available in textbooks on research methods. Nevertheless at these later stages of research, also, awkward problems of a more general kind rear their heads and further undermine an empiricist approach to the procedures of social research. This chapter will consider two aspects of the process of data collection and analysis: what is involved in the measurement of phenomena; and how explanations of phenomena are constructed. In discussing measurement, the example used will be physical disability. In discussing explanation, the example drawn on will be geographical and social inequalities in the incidence of health and illness.

The Measurement of Physical Disability

Social science critics of empirical research are fond of maintaining that much research is an elaborate way of proving the obvious, or that the results of such work are so stunningly trivial as to be not worth the effort expended upon them. The real meat lies in difficult theoretical concepts like alienation, anomie, or mental 'health', not easily susceptible to empirical investigation. On the other hand, practically minded empiricists sometimes proceed as if all one needs is clear definitions and well-chosen indicators, and then everything will be straightforward and the results of research directly applicable in policy. A good case with which to examine these views is the study of physical disability. Here, apparently, one has a phenomenon which is fairly straightforward and easy to define. Physical handicap is surely much more unambiguous than the fraught conceptual area of mental handicap and mental illness. Is it not possible to measure the incidence and effects of physical disability in the community in order to determine the right policies to adopt for dealing with it?

In fact physical disability turns out to be less straightforward and more inherently problematical from a research point of view than one would expect. Both conceptually and in terms of measurement it is a more complex phenomenon than at first sight appears, yet because of its obvious importance within social policy some solution to the difficulties encountered must be sought.

Physical disability is an obvious social problem. The physically disabled are incapacitated from doing certain things and they have certain needs which they cannot meet themselves. These include problems of mobility and personal self-sufficiency; of work and occupation; and of household and family relationships. Yet immediately one says this complex policy issues are raised. Personal physical needs are clearest, but work and wider social relationships raise a number of policy choices. What policies should there be for providing sheltered employment? Do employers discriminate in filling a quota of disabled workers? Should they do so? What are the effects of disability upon social relationships within the family and beyond?

Underlying these immediate policy problems are theoretical problems. What is the place of the disabled person in society? Should he/she be integrated into society or disengaged from it? Theories of disengagement show the disabled person moving from the centre to the periphery of society, disengaging from society rather in the way that ageing can lead to social and psychological withdrawal. The disabled come to play more limited and marginal roles; they seek to hide their disabilities from people in everyday life and carry on activities outside the mainstream. Theories of segregation postulate that the disabled have different needs and interests from other members of society and therefore develop patterns of social activity which emphasise their separateness. They tend to confine their relationships to a few close members of their families, and possibly to fellow disabled whom they meet in special associations of the disabled. Such theories are significant because they have immediate effects on how services develop. For example, do spastics prefer to live with other spastics, with other kinds of disabled persons, or in ordinary households? What policies are pursued seem likely to be influenced by the kinds of theories that underlie service provision.

Official categorisations of disability tend to be framed in terms of clinical type and degree of impairment of motor activities. The standard of comparison is how the condition of the disabled person compares with that of a normal healthy person of the same sex/age. Yet, as Sally Sainsbury has pointed out, it is also necessary to look at the social situation and social relationships of the disabled. In doing this, reference group theory is likely to prove useful. What are the points of reference to which someone looks in assessing his or her own social situation? The *membership* reference group refers to groups to which the person belongs: the family; or those suffering a particular disability, such as the blind, the deaf or paraplegics; or those with particular interests. The *comparative* reference group is a group with which the person compares himself or herself on a wider basis, such as someone of that person's age and sex in outside employment. Studying disability involves setting the analysis in a theoretical framework such as reference group theory (Sainsbury, 1970, ch. 1). This is a good example of the conceptualisation function of applied research, discussed in Chapter 2.

The study of disability also entails taking account of the different standpoints from which disability may be viewed. Reference group theory focuses upon how the disabled see themselves and how they conceptualise their social situation. One must also look, however, at how they are seen and defined by various kinds of officialdom and the consequences which these definitions have for their treatment. To those two different perspectives the social scientist's own interpretive framework must be added, which will not necessarily coincide with either of the two alternatives mentioned. This is clearly shown in the studies by Sainsbury (1970, 1973) and Blaxter (1976a). The differences between the three standpoints in approaching the problem of disability have major consequences for the way in which the problem is tackled in policy terms. Knowledge about the particular social problem is set in the context of a particular body of theoretical knowledge. As Keynes observed in another context, practical men who believe themselves to be entirely free from any intellectual influences are usually the slaves of a body of influential (and possibly out-of-date) ideas.

The difficulties in specifying disability carry over when one turns to its measurement. By comparison with the definition and empirical identification of mental states such as those labelled 'schizophrenia', it might be thought that the measurement of physical disability would pose few problems. Can one not determine fairly unambiguously the extent to which someone's physical faculties are impaired? Official definitions of disability, reflecting how it is conceptualised in practice, appear in their origins to be essentially commonsensical. In awarding war pensions and industrial injuries benefits, DHSS make a comparison between the condition of a disabled person and that of a normal healthy person of the same age. Assessment on this basis measures the general handicap imposed by loss of faculty. Loss of faculty may be defined as the loss of physical or mental capacity to lead a normally occupied life and does not depend on the way in which the disablement affects the particular circumstances of the individual. A normally occupied life includes work as well as household and social activities and leisure pursuits.

To be included on the Department of Employment Register of Disabled Persons, a person must be substantially handicapped on account of injury or disease arising from imperfect development of any organ or congenital deformity, in obtaining or keeping work suited to his or her age, qualification and experience, the disablement being likely to last twelve months or more. DHSS advice in 1968 to local authorities on whom to include on their register of the disabled merely stated that the person should be considered to be 'substantially and permanently handicapped' (Sainsbury, 1970, pp. 24–5). Such classifications set up criteria in terms of 'substantial' handicap, or handicap based on 'loss of faculty'.

A different approach is in terms of criteria of physical or economic independence. In the administration of social security benefits, for example, the amount of benefit payable to a disabled person is determined by four principles – a means-tested assessment of need, the assessment of earnings in normal employment, the assessment of unemployability and the principle of payment to meet certain special needs. Thus, in addition to standard rules, economic independence and position in the labour market are likely to be prime determinants of a disabled person's supplementary benefit. The wage stop, for example, is relaxed for some types of disabled person.

Physical independence is used as a criterion in the provision of some services. Local authorities provide residential accommodation for persons who, by reason of age, infirmity or any other circumstances, are in need of care and attention not otherwise available to them (Sainsbury, 1973, p. 24). In practice, however, no consistent criterion of self-care seems to be applied in determining who is institutionalised – a person's capacity for physical independence may not be the only factor leading to his being placed in a situation of total dependence.

Yet another official approach to disability is in terms of compensation for the occurrence of disability, depending on how the disability originated. This includes persons disabled in employment as a result of industrial accidents; persons disabled as a result of war service in the armed forces; those who can prove at common law that negligence led to their disablement; and those eligible for compensation for criminal injury. In each of these cases there are wide disparities in the criteria used for making official judgements (Sainsbury, 1973, pp. 26–32).

Empirically, the use of such differing concepts of disability does not produce uniform results. The same benefit or service may be subject to a number of tests, each based on a different principle. The same principle may be used to determine eligibility for more than one benefit.

As might be expected, the populations defined by each of the concepts and principles are not coterminous, though there may be considerable overlap between them. Indeed, each principle is used to define a number of different populations, though these may overlap in varying degrees. Finally, there are some disabled persons who remain unidentified, not because they are not sufficiently disabled, but because their needs are not recognised by current provisions. (Sainsbury, 1973, p. 31)

There is thus considerable variability in the proportion of the population eligible for different benefits and services who are identified as disabled, both between different types of service provision and between different geographical areas.

These variations in the conceptualisation of disability in practice are reflected in the operational definition of the phenomenon, both in administrative activity and in research. How is disability measured when data are gathered upon particular individuals? What measures have been used in the past and which is the optimum measure which might be recommended for future research? How can one devise measures which go beyond the familiar generic classification in terms of condition, for example, those suffering from blindness as distinct from multiple sclerosis?

Several distinct measures of functional capacity have been developed. The most strongly developed are assessments of the motor capacity of a disabled person. These are based on the assumption that it is possible to identify and isolate components of everyday action which can be measured. Capacity to perform these movements can then be used as an indicator of a person's capacity to meet the requirements of daily life. Typically standard tests are used, involving prescribed operations such as asking people to step on and off a platform of a certain height, to bend down and touch the floor, or to lift articles of a certain weight, and so on. Results from such tests achieve very high rates of reliability – if different judges rate the same person at one point in time. Results are less satisfactory as a standardised measure. A test on the same person on different days may give different scores. Objectivity in such tests seems to be particularly difficult to achieve in the middle ranges of impairment (between the most and the least severe disabilities), where factors other than motor impairment determine the extent to which people can be independent in their daily living.

This directs attention to one general weakness of such measures. They tend to focus attention upon the most severely disabled, who have difficulty with basic actions such as eating, drinking, going to the toilet, washing, dressing, sitting, standing and walking a short distance. Their use in assessing industrial injury benefit reflects the fact that it is the most severe disabilities which confer a right to it. Such a measure, however, does not identify other disabilities (such as chronic bronchitis or deafness) which might have a major impact upon a person's capacity to lead a normal working and home life, but does not prevent him or her performing basic motor tasks.

A further general weakness of such a measure is that it fails to identify disabilities such as mental handicap or mental illness whose symptoms are not primarily impairment of motor capacity. For example, a mentally handicapped person might carry out the set motor tasks but still experience difficulty in accomplishing basic activities of everyday life. Thirdly, motor capacity is not the only component of physical disability narrowly defined. The effects of exhaustion, and problems of mental co-ordination, are not adequately measured by such tests, yet these may have a major impact upon a person's capacity to perform certain basic tasks in looking after himself.

An alternative to measures of motor capacity is a direct measure of self-care and household care. Assessments are based on the assumption that extent of disability may be measured by assessing a person's ability to perform a variety of tasks necessary to everyday life – such as going to the lavatory, making a cup of tea, washing, and so on. Short lists of activities can be used to make assessments, using a crude scoring system. The problem with this type of measure is that individual circumstances vary, people's environments are different, and this makes standardised measurement very difficult. Such studies also need further data on impairment of physical and mental faculties, such as speech and sight defects, hearing, breathlessness, incontinence, difficulties of mental co-ordination, and so on. The relationship between difficulties such as these and self-care is imperfectly understood.

Table 4.1   *Extract from the Interview Schedule of a National Survey of Handicap and Impairment*

The following panel is used to find degree of handicap. Note that the main question should be repeated every three or four items. Then, for any item found difficult (needing help/supervision), ask question (*a*) at head of columns (2) and (3), below, to sort out those who can do it, even with difficulty, from those who cannot.

Note there are two variations in the main question.
A   For young children (in most cases the under-12s): does (name) need more help or supervision than other children of his/her age? . . . then ask each item (i)–(ix) separately, coding 'O' in column (1) if 'no difficulty of supervision'.
B   *Where a proxy is taken because informant is mentally impaired*: as for A, omitting reference to age.

Introduce Can we talk about looking after yourself (if proxy, name person)? Some people have difficulty in doing things for themselves. Some of them may not apply to you, but could we run through them one by one?

	(1) No difficulty or supervision	(2) If difficulty or supervision ask (*a*) But can you do it yourself, even with difficulty?		(3) Notes for the interviewer
15 Do you generally have difficulty in (or alternative versions A or B above):		Yes can do	No cannot do	
(i) getting in and out of bed on your own?	0	2	3	If uses *hoist* – code 3 in column (3).
(ii) getting to or using the WC?	0	4	6	If never uses WC because bedfast – code 6 in column (3) If incontinent – code 6 in column (3).
(iii) having an all-over wash (or bathing yourself if bath used)?	0	2	3	If subject cannot use bath, but can wash his body and limbs with difficulty – code 2 in column (2).
Repeat question				
(iv) washing your hands and face?	0	2	3	
(v) putting on shoes and socks or stockings yourself?	0	2	3	If doesn't dress, wear shoes, etc., because bedfast or never goes out, code as appropriate in column (3).
(vi) doing up buttons and zips yourself?	0	4	6	If special clothing for handicapped bought, e.g. cannot do up buttons so wears 'pull-on' clothes – code in column (3).
Repeat question				If, however, wears, say, casual shoes because he prefers them – code in column (1) if no difficulty, or (2) if some difficulty.
(vii) dressing, other than buttons and shoes?	0	2	3	
(viii) feeding yourself?	0	4	6	If food has to be cut up, code in column (3).

(ix)	*WOMEN AND CHILDREN ONLY* combing and brushing your hair?	0	2	3	
(x)	*MEN ONLY* shaving yourself?	0	2	3	GRAND TOTAL CATEGORY
	TOTAL COLUMN SCORE	0			

Source: Harris and Head, 1971, p. 42.

Measures of dependence seek to determine the extent to which basic activities, such as dressing, eating, going to the toilet, and domestic tasks can be carried out without assistance or, if assistance is required, what degree of assistance is required. Table 4.1, an extract from the interview schedule in a manual of guidance for surveys of handicap and impairment (Harris and Head, 1971) shows one type of research approach in this way. The sorts of areas covered by such research instruments include mobility, self-care, domestic duties and work.

A fourth type of measure is one related to work. In Britain, for example, under the Disabled Persons Employment Act of 1944 this type of assessment is used to judge a person's fitness for work according to what is considered appropriate in an able-bodied person of the same age. In a US study quoted by Sainsbury an effort is made to distinguish the severely disabled from the occupationally disabled from those suffering from secondary work limitations. Measures based on work suffer from being less applicable to women at home than to men; does housework count as 'work', and if so by what standards should it be assessed?

Sainsbury's own approach to the study of disability provides yet another alternative (Sainsbury, 1973, pp. 48ff.). Her solution to the problem of measurement involves rejection of a measure of minimum physical independence as the sole indicator of incapacity, in favour of a focus on the *consequences* of disability. Disability is defined as the incapacity for commanding the range of choices generally available to persons within a society. To assess the consequences of disability therefore requires a measure of the degree to which disability forces people to depart from the mainstream of life. The problem is conceptualised not as a dichotomy between disablement and non-disablement, but as a continuum. Disability is seen in terms of its impact upon the whole way of life of an individual. On the basis of interviews with 150 disabled people, Sainsbury constructed a nine-item index which measured the extent to which people were limited in their social capacity. The items included were doing heavy housework; doing heavy shopping; preparing and cooking a hot meal; going up and down stairs; running to catch a bus; cutting toenails; washing down or bathing; hanging out washing; and tying a good knot in string. The index is constructed with reference to respondents' subjective assessments of their ability to perform tasks. This raises some difficulties, but a comparison between such replies and a performance test for a small sample showed a very high level of agreement. Its limitations in terms of the mentally ill, those with conditions like epilepsy and those who fail to recognise restrictions on their activities are admitted. This social concept of disability also permits comparison between the physically and mentally handicapped and those who suffer from other kinds of social disadvantage.

A comparison of these five different measures of disability shows that the study of the phenomenon is by no means unambiguous or without theoretical implications. Indeed there is a bewildering variety of procedures for identifying and assessing disabled persons,

> from the apparently objective and standard tests of motor capacity, to those measuring capacity for work, which may be determined by a host of other factors besides degree and type of disability – motivation, the type of work available, the general supply of work, the availability of rehabilitation and training schemes, education, level of skill, and so on. (Sainsbury, 1973, p. 46)

The most recent major social survey of disability in Britain, carried out by OPCS and published in 1971 (Harris *et al.*, 1971), was done for the DHSS. The definition of persons to be identified as disabled which was used combined a number of different characteristics:

- those who had a limb or part of a limb missing owing to a defect at birth or subsequent accident;
- those who are bedfast or housebound;
- those who need a lot of help in using the WC, personal toilet, dressing, etc.;
- those who have difficulty walking without help, kneeling, bending, or going up and down stairs;
- those who have difficulty in washing, dressing, or performing their toilet, feeding themselves, or gripping or holding things;
- those who suffer from some permanent disability (including blindness) which stops or limits their working or getting about or taking care of themselves.

One aim of the OPCS study was to estimate the number of people who might qualify for an attendance allowance. It was therefore essential to identify among the most severely handicapped those who needed someone else to look after most of their wants. The measures of handicap used in the study therefore put most emphasis on dependence and independence in self-care. How far could impaired people look after themselves as far as their basic needs were concerned?

The complexities of such a measure can be shown from the criteria used to determine whether a respondent needed special care. The most severely handicapped were identified at the first stage if *one* of the following four conditions applied:

(a) the person was not able to understand the questions or give rational answers – for example, the mentally impaired or senile;
(b) the person was permanently bedfast;
(c) the person was not bedfast but confined to a chair and unable to get in and out of the chair without the aid of some other person;
(d) the person needed someone to supply most of his or her personal needs.

The most severely handicapped were then grouped in three groups, 1, 2, 3, of decreasing severity of handicap, according to their ability to perform various functions. Briefly summarised (from Harris, 1971, pp. 254–6), these were:

Group 1   Person needs help using bedpan or pot every night, *plus* unable to perform at least four of following: feed self; drink without help; go to WC even with help; dress self; move self in bed (list A); *plus* at least eight of a long list of criteria relating to washing and toilet functions (list B).

Group 2   Person does not need help with bedpan, but at least three items from list A and eight from list B are checked, *OR* does need help with bedpan, but neither A nor B apply.

Group 3   Person included for special care at the first stage but not included in groups 1 or 2.

An even more elaborate classification was required for those not identified at the first stage in terms of one of the four criteria, but still suffering from severe or appreciable handicaps. The classification was based on a question very similar to that given in Table 4.1. Major items were getting to or using the WC, doing up buttons and zips and feeding; the other items were rated as less important. Each item was given a weight and the respondent was scored according to the pattern of responses for each item. Those with higher scores were classified as more severely handicapped (Harris *et al.*, 1971, pp. 256–62). Thus all those who were impaired could be classified on a scale from 1 (most severe) to 8 (least severe). The results of the survey were then presented (Harris *et al.*, 1971, p. 17) in the form of national estimates obtained by multiplying the results of the national survey by the sampling fraction. The following summary of the results shows the numbers estimated to be in different disability groups.

Degree of handicap	Total number of persons	
Very severe, needing special care		
1 + 2	24,000	
3	133,000	157,000
Severe, needing considerable support		
4	102,000	
5	254,000	356,000
Appreciable, needing some support		
6	616,000	
Minor/no, needing little or no support for everyday living activities		
7	680,000	
8a non-motor	737,000	1,942,000
8b motor	525,000	

The authors of the study anticipate problems in the interpretation of their results.

> There is no clear line between the categories, and when one reads or talks about 'the disabled' or 'the handicapped', it is difficult to know what condition is being described. Some champions of the cause of the handicapped will doubtless use the total of 3 million as the number of handicapped, and give 'typical' examples of the almost helpless to illustrate their plight. It may be that others will try to minimise the number of handicapped, by considering only those who need constant attendance. (Harris *et al.*, 1971, p. 17)

There is, however, a further and less obvious point which the present discussion has been concerned to emphasise. The administrator or politician using the results will appreciate that they can be read in different ways depending on the standpoint of the reader. What is less obvious is that the results obtained depend crucially upon the concepts and definitions used, how individuals are assigned into categories and the measurement process used to perform such a classification.

In addition to carrying out the national survey, Harris and Head (1971) prepared guidelines on the conduct of sample surveys of the handicapped and disabled, from which Table 4.1 is taken. This was in response to the Chronically Sick and Disabled Persons Act of 1970 which placed a duty upon all local authorities and hospitals to identify and compile registers of the chronically sick and disabled living in their areas or institutions. As a result, local authorities throughout England and Wales were required to carry out investigations, either of a sample survey type or a complete enumeration. A study of this inquiry process – to be discussed more fully in Chapter 6 – was carried out by M. Brown and R. Bowl (1976) of the University of Birmingham.

One of the most important findings of Brown and Bowl's study was the importance of clear definitions. Even though Harris and Head's national guidelines were available, not all local authorities used them. In fact, when carrying out an investigation, almost half of local authorities in the study did not define chronic sickness and impairment for the purposes of the research. The other half did define handicap and, of these, four-fifths used the nationally recommended definition from the OPCS survey. Failure to define terms had deleterious effects on the research results and was associated with identifying fewer handicapped and disabled people in an area. So care (or lack of it) in definition and measurement has quite direct practical consequences.

The Study of Health

The varieties of approach in applied social science are well illustrated when one looks at the field of health and illness. Here is an area of social policy of both direct practical and broader theoretical interest. How, where and how well health care is delivered to the population is a matter of central concern in social administration, while 'life chances' (see Dahrendorf, 1980) are reducible in the last analysis literally to matters of life and death. The study of the distribution of health care between different geographical areas and different social groups provides a good case-study of the way in which social research can be used.

The unequal geographical distribution of health care in Britain raises philosophical issues about service provision. Should the same quality of care not be available to everyone equitably regardless of where they happen to live? Should not random variation in the level of service between different areas be reduced so far as is possible in order to equalise the right to adequate treatment? This conception has been summed up in the term 'territorial justice' (B. Davies, 1968). Similar issues are raised by social class differences in the incidence of ill-health and in the use of services. How does one account for marked variations between the classes which persist over time even when overall improvements in health occur? What sort of interventions would be needed to try to reduce social class inequalities in health?

Both geographical and social class inequalities in health have been of direct policy concern in the British health service in recent years. In 1975 the Resource Allocation Working Party (RAWP) was set up by the government to review arrangements for distributing capital and revenue from central government to region, area and district health authorities 'with a view to establishing a method of securing, as soon as practicable, a pattern of distribution responsive objectively, equitably and efficiently to relative need' (RAWP, 1976, p. 5). In 1977 the Secretary of State for Social Services set up a working group on inequalities in health to review information about differences in health status between social classes, to consider possible causes and implications for policy and to suggest further research. Their reports, published in 1976 and 1980 respectively, both had a major impact upon opinion, and the RAWP report led to important shifts in the allocation of resources within the NHS. Both were solidly grounded in social science research, yet illustrate clearly that 'the facts' do not speak for themselves.

Geographical Inequalities

The main problem tackled in the RAWP exercise was how to measure relative need for health care, in order to establish the share of available revenue to which each health region would be entitled on a basis of need. When this was attempted there was found to be a mismatch between the concept of need and available data. On the incidence of ill-health in the community, one of the best indicators available was regional hospital inpatient and outpatient caseloads. However, this was rejected as a measure of the need for health care because it reflected the supply of health care rather than the demand for it. Caseloads in health (as in other services such as personal social services) reflect the resources available for a particular service in different parts of an organisation at one point in time. They do not necessarily reflect different degrees of need nor do they take account of unmet need. So it became very important to pick a measure of the state of health of populations in different regions quite independent of supply.

The final RAWP recommendations were worked out using a complicated formula (RAWP, 1976, pp. 26, 101). Its object was to establish for each region a revenue target, taking into account measures of variation in the relevant social characteristics between different regions. The calculation began with the mid-year population estimates for each region. These figures were then weighted by factors which reflected differences in need for services between regions. The most obvious weighting factors were age and sex; the proportion of elderly persons and children, of men and women in a population will directly influence the need for health care. Then the RAWP group had to find a satisfactory measure of morbidity, since there were known to be significant regional differences in the distribution of ill-health which had to be measured.

Three alternative measures of morbidity were considered. One was the DHSS records of recipients of sickness benefit. Although this would indicate absence from work through sickness, it was rejected as a measure because it did not cover children, the elderly, and many married women; it was a measure related to the industrial structure, and the ability to continue work with a morbid condition would be influenced by the nature of employment; and it reflected primarily need for GP, not hospital, care which was the focus of the RAWP exercise. A second alternative source was self-reported sickness data from the General Household Survey (GHS). There was clear evidence of marked regional variation both in this and in GP consultation rates, but this source was also rejected, partly because of inadequate coverage down to the level of health regions, partly because there are differences in perception and reporting of self-reported sickness. (Rainwater, 1968, for example, has argued that there may be a 'culture of sickness' and low body esteem among the poor, with higher levels of tolerance for ill-health which would in turn affect self-reports of sickness.)

The third source of data, the one chosen, was in fact *mortality* statistics. These, the most comprehensive and reliable of the three sources considered, were correlated with regional variations in *morbidity* as shown in the DHSS sickness and GHS data. Apart from certain medical conditions such as pregnancy and skin complaints, mortality data was judged the best available indicator of geographical variations in morbidity. There are still statistical problems about whether the dead can be considered a representative sample of the living – they are older, their formative health experiences may have occurred many years earlier, and so on – but these were overridden by the comprehensiveness and quality of the mortality data available for health regions.

So the regional population figures were weighted to reflect the differences in mortality experience, as measured by standardised mortality ratios (SMRs), and, after further adjustments for administrative factors, they were used to produce weighted populations combined proportionately to revenue expenditure on each service. These figures were then used in the report to recommend orders of magnitude for the changes needed in the allocation of resources between health regions, in particular away from the more favoured metropolitan health regions to those in other parts of the country. When the government proceeded to implement these changes on a modest scale in 1976 there was much resistance and a considerable public outcry. The Secretary of State, Barbara Castle, made it clear the object was to increase the level of resources to those regions which were relatively deprived, on the basis of objective assessments made by RAWP of the relative need of each region for revenue resources.

This major example of an attempt to achieve greater territorial justice in the distribution of health resources shows both the complexity of social measurement and indicator construction (see Carley, 1981) and the necessity for clear conceptual definitions in attempts to measure factors such as the need for health care or relative deprivation in terms of health resources in different regions. In particular, measures based on outputs from the existing service were rejected as an adequate measure of the need for health care. An empiricist approach to this problem would be manifestly inadequate since before measuring the phenomenon decisions must be taken about what it is that is being measured and how it is to be measured.

Social Class Inequalities

Social class differences in health and illness demonstrate even more clearly than regional differences the need for conceptual clarity and analytic sophistication in approaching empirical evidence. Indeed as a problem area it is a very good example of Michael Rutter's point about the meaning of 'research' for policy-makers and its use in policy-making, quoted already in Chapter 2. It bears repeating.

> [R]esearch is not primarily concerned with the collection of facts nor even with the derivation and testing of laws. Rather it provides a means (or, more accurately, many different means) of posing and answering questions. Science is not a body of knowledge. Instead it involves a process of enquiry – a means of finding out about something (1977, p. 107).

Rutter quotes with approval Medawar's view of science as the construction of a story about a Possible World which is invented and criticised and modified as one goes along.

Social class differences in health cannot be treated within an entirely empiricist framework because from the outset decisions have to be taken as to what is meant by 'social class'. For these purposes the Registrar-General's social class classification is the one most commonly used in Britain, indeed it was originally developed to analyse social class differences in mortality in Britain (Leete and Fox, 1977). Paradoxically, however, interest in social class and health has remained high because of the striking empirical regularities which have been observed, for example, in mortality data by social class, over time (see Table 4.2). Despite falling mortality and other improvements in health, class differences have persisted. Indeed, 'there is so much evidence demonstrating differences in mortality and morbidity between the social classes that it is difficult to select from the evidence' (Brotherston, 1976, p. 73).

Table 4.2 *Male Standardised Mortality Ratios, by Social Class, for England and Wales*

Social class	1921–3 (age 20–64)	1930–2 (age 20–64)	1949–53 (age 20–64)	1959–63 (age 15–64)	1970–2 (age 15–64)
I	82	90	98	76	77
II	94	94	86	81	81
III	95	97	101	100	104
IV	101	102	94	103	114
V	125	111	118	143	137
All social classes	100	100	100	100	100

Source: Registrar-General, 1977, p. 174.

Useful surveys by Brotherston (1976), Blaxter (1976b), Kosa and Zola (1976), Illsley (1980) and Blaxter (1981) present selected evidence. The most comprehensive review is that of the DHSS working group (DHSS, 1980). The analysis of morbidity and mortality using such data may be illustrated by one example from work based on the General Household Survey. How well founded was the RAWP assumption that mortality differentials could be treated as a proxy for morbidity differentials? The General Household Survey, since 1971, has collected evidence upon self-reported illness, classified as acute (was there any illness or injury which restricted activity during a two-week reference period?), chronic ('does illness limit your activities compared with most people of your own age?') and handicapping. In the GHS respondents are classified into the Registrar-General's six socio-economic groups (I to VI) rather than six social classes (I to V with III divided into IIIM and IIIN), but the two classifications are broadly comparable and the socio-economic groups may be regarded as equivalent to the corresponding social class (that is, socio-economic group I = social class I; socio-economic group VI = social class V, and so on) (Reid, 1977, pp. 34–42).

Figure 4.1 shows the comparison between socio-economic groups for these three types of illness. The gradient is less steep for acute illness, more steep for chronic illness alone and for chronic and handicapping illness together. If one regards the latter as the most objective condition, the rate in socio-economic group VI is well over two times the rate in socio-economic group I.

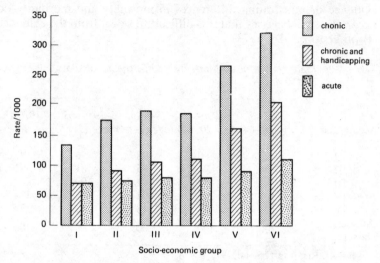

Figure 4.1   *Rates of self-reported illness by socio-economic group, per 1,000 people, men and women, all ages, in Great Britain.*
Source: Blaxter, 1976b, p. 116, based on the General Household Survey, 1972.

Mobility varies by age and sex. These variables may now be introduced, and morbidity differentials compared to mortality differentials. This is shown in Figure 4.2 which compares the morbidity experience of men in socio-economic groups I and VI with mortality in the same classes, expressed as percentage deviations from the average experience of people in a particular sex/age group. Although Rein (1969) has argued that class mortality is not an index of class morbidity, this is not supported by the GHS evidence. Figure 4.2 suggests that the two are associated, though morbidity differences appear to be greater, particularly for younger men in socio-economic group VI. This latter finding also undermines the argument that mortality rates in the lowest social class are as high as they are simply as a result of downward lifetime mobility, as the less fit and healthy gravitate to the lowest social class. This hypothesis is disproved by the observation that rates of chronic and handicapping illness are higher in the age group 15–44 years for socio-economic group VI than for the age group 45–64 years.

The experience of women is shown in Figure 4.3. This comparison of socio-economic groups I and VI also does not support Rein's contention that mortality and morbidity are not necessarily connected. Social class differences remain pronounced, though not as marked as in the case of men. The interpretation of these data is complicated by the fact that married women are classified by their husband's social class. How this affects the result is uncertain.

Figure 4.2   *Rates of illness compared with mortality for men in socio-economic groups I and VI.*
Source: Blaxter, 1976b, pp. 117–18.

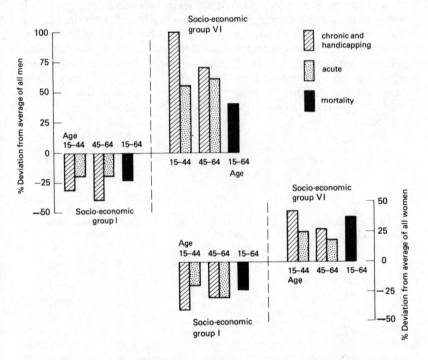

Figure 4.3   *Rates of illness compared with mortality for women in socio-economic groups I and VI.*
Source: Blaxter, 1976b, pp. 117–18.

Note: Figures 4.2 and 4.3 compare morbidity data for socio-economic group VI with mortality data for social class V. Since the two groups are not identical, the similarities and differences shown are indicative rather than precise comparisons.

This brief extract of GHS data shows that morbidity is greater among lower social classes and that therefore they would appear to need more medical help than those in higher social classes. Do they receive it? An attempt to answer this question can be made using data from the General Household Survey. Table 4.3 shows consultation indices for GP and hospital care. These are worked out by dividing the rate of consultation per 1,000 people in a two-week period (from GHS data) by the prevalence per 1,000 people of chronic handicapping illness (also from GHS data), separately for GP and hospital visits. This shows that even though in terms of numerical frequency those from lower social classes may use GPs more, in relation to the amount of illness they perceive themselves as suffering from there is a marked class gradient. For every visit that a man in socio-economic group VI with a chronic handicapping illness pays to his doctor, a similar man in socio-economic group I pays two visits. For women, the differential is even greater; one visit compared to three visits. A very similar class gradient is observed for specialist hospital care. These findings support what has been formulated by Tudor Hart (1975), with only slight exaggeration, as the 'inverse care' law: 'the availability of good medical care tends to vary inversely with the need of the population served.'

Table 4.3   *Consultation Indices Comparing the Prevalence of Chronic Handicapping Illness with General Practitioner and Hospital Outpatient Consultation Rates*

Socio-economic group	General practitioner index [a]		Hospital outpatient index [b]	
	M	F	M	F
I	1·20	2·03	1·29	1·56
II	1·04	1·34	0·99	1·08
III	0·91	1·29	1·02	1·05
IV	0·84	1·20	0·93	0·84
V	0·75	0·76	0·66	0·58
VI	0·59	0·69	0·63	0·49

[a] Rate per 1,000 people of general practitioner consultations in a two-week period/ prevalence rates per 1,000 people of chronic handicapping illness.
[b] Rate per 1,000 people of hospital outpatient consultation in a three-month period/ prevalence rate per 1,000 people of chronic handicapping illness.
  Source: Blaxter, 1976b, p. 120, analysing data from the General Household Survey, 1972.

The Explanation of Health Inequalities

Here, then, is a small sample of compelling evidence of major social influences on health and the provision of health care, which are of direct policy relevance, and of concern, when considering the extent and incidence of social deprivation. Moreover, simply to set out the evidence is the beginning of the process of inquiry. As many medical sociologists have observed, rates of illness analysed in relation to categories such as age, sex, social class, region, marital status, or even occupation, though providing essential evidence, offer little by way of explanation. Gross demographic population categories are essentially meaningless when treated as 'causal' variables indicative of social processes.

> These may be convenient, easily-studied labels for subdividing populations, but they are not dynamic social ideas and cannot, except in a very limited superficial sense, represent the kind of social phenomena that may cause disease or anything else. (Suchman, 1967, pp. 109–10)

The complexity of behaviour lying behind demographic statistics has been pointed out also by Raymond Illsley in a wide-ranging review of current medical sociology.

> The so-called 'hard data' of vital statistics are invaluable but their interpretation is uncertain without more detailed knowledge and direct observations which allow us to explore the subjective meanings of behaviour and thus to substitute evidence for inference in our search for explanation. (1980, pp. 35–6)

Two brief examples of the kinds of analysis which may be carried out to probe further the meaning of broad demographic regularities will be cited. Social class differences in fertility, premarital conception, illegitimacy and perinatal mortality are well documented and show consistent trends over time (for a review see Illsley, 1980, pp. 11–44). Taking one of these variables, fertility, one may ask why it is that families of unskilled manual workers tend on average to be larger than families of skilled manual workers. An illuminating small-scale study of this question in Aberdeen by Askham (1975) shows how such a problem may be investigated. Her strategy was two-fold. At the theoretical level she set out to make explicit the kinds of model on the basis of which hypotheses could be formulated to explain the fertility of the lower working class. Four distinct models were identified. A model of personal inadequacy, which receives wide support among the public though little among social scientists, emphasises that among members of the lowest social class are found those with low IQs, personality problems, physical deficiencies, and so on. These individual deficiencies militate against a planned approach to family formation and birth control. A second, more sociological, model is that of the culture of poverty, formulated by Oscar Lewis. There is, it is argued, a separate subculture of poverty, transmitted from one generation to another, with its own values, beliefs and norms and its own system of socialisation. A norm of larger family size in the subculture of the poor is thus a culturally reinforced pattern of behaviour.

The situational model posits that lower-class groups are distinguished basically by a lack of resources or by social deprivation. The lack of generalised command over goods and services, in the long term as well as in the short term, affects not only economic opportunities but also educational and occupational opportunities, lack of political power, housing class – in short, the 'life chances' of a whole social stratum. Fertility behaviour is then a response to this disadvantaged situation.

The fourth model, the adaptational, suggests that the fertility behaviour of the unskilled working class is an adaptation to a particular situation of deprivation, reinforced by a series of values, norms and beliefs. The situation and the behaviour interact. Behaviour is guided by a continual process of adaptation to mutually reinforcing, causally connected, social disadvantages. Although deprivations exist statistically in aggregate form for the class as a whole, they are not just acquired at birth or during childhood, but are experienced in a temporal sequence through the individual's life. Not all are experienced by each person to the same extent. This adaptational pattern is reflected in fertility behaviour.

Askham set out to test the hypothesis that the greater the impact of situational factors such as economic and social deprivation, insecurity and powerlessness, the greater the need for adaptation in terms of norms and behaviour patterns involving no planning ahead and being unable to control one's own environment. The greater the need for this type of adaptation the more likely it is that a couple will have a large family, since such adaptation hinders both the motivation for small families and the ability to control and restrict the family size achieved.

This outline illustrates the complexity of explaining social class differences in fertility behaviour. The research design of Askham's study provided another means of insight into the problem. Carried out in Aberdeen, instead of simply comparing large families in social class V with small families in social class III, Askham thought it would be useful to look at the 'deviant cases', those with large families in social class III and with small families in social class V (see Table 4.4). This permitted comparisons of fertility behaviour between families of similar size in different social classes ($a \longleftrightarrow d$ and $c \longleftrightarrow b$), between families of different sizes in the same social class ($a \longleftrightarrow c$ and $d \longleftrightarrow b$), as well as between small class III and large class V families ($a \longleftrightarrow b$). This deliberate search for negative evidence, together with the explicit formulation of prior hypotheses, illustrates the merits of a Popperian approach to scientific investigation. Many of the problems faced in the

Table 4.4   *The Research Design of J. Askham:* Fertility and Deprivation

	SOCIAL CLASS	
	IIIM	V
Small families (2 children)	*a*	*d*
Large families (4 children or more)	*c*	*b*

Source: derived from Askham, 1975, pp. 20–4.

study of social influences in medical care – of which this is one example – open up complex and intractable problems of explanation, the surface of which is not even scratched by empiricist data collection. Prior thought and careful theoretical specification are indispensable if some scientific understanding of the social causation of medical phenomena is to be gained.

George Brown's work (Brown *et al.*, 1975, Brown and Harris, 1978) upon the social causes of depression in working-class women is another case of an influential piece of medical research which probes a gross statistical correlation to try to explain the social processes by which structural variables are associated with depression. The aim of the research is to specify the causal links between structure (belonging to the working class) and psychiatric disorder (evidence of depressive illness). This is then investigated by looking at whether there is a causal link between stressful life events and the onset of depressive illness. Were there events in the life of the depressed person or immediate relatives involving some element of danger – such as significant changes in health, social status or way of life? The research is then concerned to determine what factors affect vulnerability to onset of disturbance once stressful life events have occurred.

The detailed analytic procedures used in Brown's study have been analysed in another book in this series (Marsh, 1982, ch. 5). The point to emphasise here – demonstrated in Figure 4.4 – is the complex theoretical structure of the connection between a social class differential and the outcome for a particular individual in a particular social class. The causal model hypothesises that the onset of a severe event or major difficulty may lead to a depressive episode; but that the likelihood of this occurring is also influenced by amplifying factors: whether the woman has a job; the number of children at home; relative intimacy between the woman and her partner; and whether or not she lost her mother at an early age. Psychological factors, particularly low self-esteem, may also play a precipitating role.

The procedure followed by Brown and his collaborators is in fact merely a much more elaborate and sophisticated version of the

procedure followed earlier in this discussion when examining the
relationship between social class and ill-health, using GHS data. The
analysis began with a simple comparison between illness in different
social classes, looking at different types of illness. The relationship was
then *elaborated* by looking at differences between highest and lowest
social classes in terms of age and sex, and a comparison was also made
between morbidity and mortality. Such *analytic* use of social surveys
permits one to try to make inferences about causes.

To explain these relations and establish causes, a definite question
must be posed. To do this specific variables or combinations of
variables must first be conceived and then isolated, and the effects of
their presence or absence predicted. The prediction constitutes a

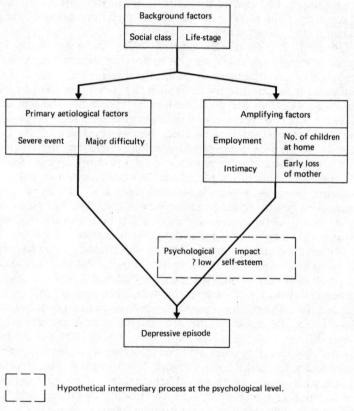

Figure 4.4   *A simplified causal model of the relationship between social class
and depression.*
Source: Brown et al., 1975, p. 246.

hypothesis. In the explanatory survey we test the hypothesis by seeking out circumstances in which the effects of the presence and absence of the supposed cause can be observed and compared. We set up our survey to make the comparisons as valid as possible. (Susser, 1973, p. 8)

The procedures for the causal analysis of health data are set out by Susser (1973), following the principles established by Stouffer, Lazarsfeld, Hyman, Rosenberg and Hirshci and Selvin. Unfortunately, Brown's research is an all too rare British example of the use of such procedures, given the proclivities among social administrators and epidemiologists for unbridled empiricism. An ounce of theory is worth several pounds of data.

A number of recent attempts, arising out of the DHSS working group on inequality in health, have been made to explore theories and explanations of health inequalities (see Blaxter, 1981). Hart (1978, p. 110) represents some of the relationships involved in Figure 4.5. Her

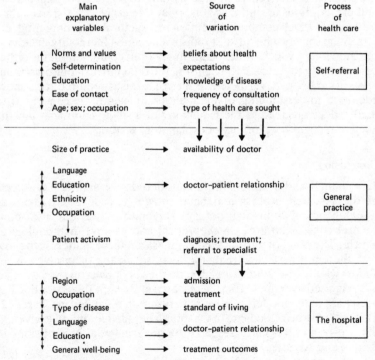

Figure 4.5   *Inequality in the national health service.*
            Source: Hart, 1978, p.110.

analysis places primary emphasis upon sociological factors in the explanation of health inequality. The report of the working group itself (DHSS, 1980, pp. 153–98) discusses explanatory factors and identifies four different types of explanation: (a) that inequalities are an artefact of the classificatory systems used in analysis; (b) that they can be accounted for by theories of natural or social selection; (c) that a materialist explanation best fits existing inequalities; or (d) that a cultural or behavioural explanation provides the best fit. Their analysis tends to favour the importance of materialist factors, while acknowledging that cultural explanations and a genetic element play some part. At the same time they recognise the complexity of explaining health inequalities, involving as it does access to, and use of, health services, specific issues in other areas of social policy and more general features of social class, material inequality and deprivation.

In a recent paper Blume (1980), the scientific secretary of the DHSS committee, has considerably extended the analysis of different theoretical approaches. He contrasts the epidemiological, social administration and sociological frameworks used in various studies, bringing out the significant differences in their assumptions, forms of explanation and prescriptions for influence on policy. He argues for the need for a framework which combines attention to structural-environmental factors in the society with 'host', predisposing, or 'vulnerability' factors in the individual, which can explain, singly or in combination, his or her susceptibility to disease. Recognising the difficulties of multidisciplinary work, Blume nevertheless argues that this is required for a more adequate understanding of inequalities in health. A concern with theory does not lead to the hegemony of a single approach, but the need to recognise a plurality of explanatory factors.

Conclusion

This chapter and Chapter 3 have considered several different aspects of the research process and have shown how decisions taken as research proceeds involve not only technical issues but also more general considerations of a theoretical and general methodological nature. The point of putting such emphasis on these matters is to show that the empiricist view that 'the facts speak for themselves' is an almost wholly discredited one, despite the very powerful sway which it has exercised over applied social research in Britain. Less attention has been paid to the models of research utilisation discussed in Chapter 2. This will now be remedied. In Chapter 5 detailed attention is given to the use of social science research by governmental commissions in Britain and America.

Similar conclusions to those reached here have emerged from the research programme on transmitted deprivation. A recent monograph from this research suggests the metaphor of a *web* of deprivation is more appropriate than a *cycle* of deprivation. A web suggests a dense network of psychological, social, historical and economic factors contributing to the existence of the condition.

> Our repeated emphasis on the complexity and on the interacting and cumulative nature of the deprivations suffered by the families is *the* central, if unoriginal, point of this study. We would claim that no single hypothesis and no group of simple hypotheses could hope to explain the intricate mesh of factors. (Coffield *et al.*, 1981, p. 163)

This reinforces the case for an approach to investigation informed by theory. The searchlight theory of knowledge provides the only hope of making sense of such manifest complexity in the real world.

5

The Use of Social Research by Governmental Commissions

Independent commissions of inquiry have played a significant part in the government both of Britain and the United States. Despite major differences between the political systems of the two countries, particularly in the relationship between executive and legislature, there are marked parallels between the role played by British Royal Commissions and American Presidential Commissions within each country. Governmental commissions therefore provide a valuable focus for a comparative case-study of the influence of social science upon public policy. To what extent, and in what ways, can social scientific knowledge be used by commissions to influence the course of their deliberations and help frame the conclusions which they reach? The aim of this chapter is to seek answers to such questions by comparing and contrasting the influence of social science upon British and American commissions. The availability of case-studies of particular commissions (Komarovsky, 1975; Bulmer, 1980b) helps in this, but the aim is to highlight general similarities and differences.

The terminology used requires initial clarification. The term 'commission' is used here to refer to special *ad hoc* bodies set up to advise on specific policy problems. There are a number of bodies in both the British and American political systems, with 'commission' in their title, which are of a rather different character. They include permanent commissions such as the Canadian-American Boundary Commission, the American Battle Monuments Commission, the Royal Commission on Historical Manuscripts and the Royal Commission on Historical Monuments. There are also permanent governmental or quasi-governmental organisations such as the Federal Communications Commission, the Interstate Commerce Commission, the Civil Service Commission, the Commission for Racial Equality, the Royal Fine Arts Commission, and so on. These are not considered here. (For uses of the word see Manfield, 1968.)

British Royal Commissions are bodies set up by the Queen in Council under the Royal Seal. There are in Britain also departmental committees, many of which in recent years have been as important as Royal Commissions, while some Royal Commissions have been established on trivial subjects. The term 'Royal Commission' is used to refer both to Royal Commissions proper and to important departmental committees, following Vernon and Mansergh (1940, p. 24), Rhodes (1975, ch. 2) and Cartwright (1975, ch. 2). Where the term 'Royal Commission' appears unqualified, it refers to Britain. American Presidential Commissions are also sometimes referred to as national governmental study commissions. They are distinguished by their importance from other bodies established by the President. Where the term 'Presidential Commission' appears unqualified in this book, it refers to the United States.

British and American Commissions Compared

Commissions have a long history on both sides of the Atlantic, going back to the origins of the Republic in America and to the early nineteenth century in Britain (Clokie and Robinson, 1937). American observers have shown a great interest in British Royal Commissions (for an excellent early survey see Gosnell, 1934), but have sometimes tended to exaggerate their differences from American Presidential Commissions. We are told, for example, that 'their symbolic, legal, constitutional, environmental, compositional and operational differences are much more important than their similarities' (F. Popper, 1970, p. 54). Another observer maintains that it is

> misleading to liken presidential commissions in this country to British royal commissions, whose detached, impartial, apolitical character they lack. Because the President, unlike the British monarch, cannot be above politics, neither can his creatures. (Derthick, 1971, pp. 633–4)

R. K. Merton suggests, without amplification, that the two types of body 'have only a cousinly resemblance, structural and functional' (1975, p. 156, n. 6). Several supposed differences are based on misunderstandings. Royal Commissions, though formally appointed by the monarch, are in fact appointed by the government of the day, and are (as the Webbs observed long ago) very much political creatures (1932, p. 156). The degree of consensus, and success in achieving implementation of their recommendations, of Royal Commissions is not markedly greater than that of Presidential Commissions. It is not true that Royal Commissions are 'more concerned with substantive, long-range, policy' or that they can make more intensive examination of their topics because they can afford a wider perspective (F. Popper, 1970, p. 55). There are of course major differences in the staffing of commissions in the two countries, and very important differences between the political systems in which they operate (Hanser, 1965, pp. 225–34). Even though executive and legislature are fused in Britain and separate in America, the similarities between commissions on both sides of the Atlantic are more striking than their differences. Both operate in broadly similar ways: being given a brief, collecting evidence, deliberating, reaching conclusions and presenting these to the head of state. In the twentieth century both have increasingly turned to social scientists for assistance, and many commissions in both countries now mount major research programmes. Commissions are one very prominent way in which social science can feed into the policy-making process, both in Britain and the United States.

Governmental commissions are established by the head of state (the monarch in Britain, the President in the USA) to advise upon a particular limited issue of public policy which is specified in the terms of reference or brief of the commission. Commissions are bodies 'to which an appeal can be made for a definitive determination of controversial facts and for a trustworthy judgement on a complex public problem' (Hanser, 1965, p. 221). The commission is a corporate group created by public act whose duty it is to collect evidence, analyse the problem, report publicly and make advisory recommendations for governmental action. The group is an *ad hoc* body, created for this specific purpose, and its life is limited to the time taken to produce a report (rarely more than four years and very often a shorter period). The members of the commission are appointed directly by the head of state, as a result of consultation within government. In Britain the decision to set up a commission and the appointment of members lies in practice with government ministers (political heads of government departments). In the USA these lie with the President and the outcome is the result of consultations within the Executive Branch.

Once established and given terms of reference, the commission is an independent body whose task it is to form an authoritative and objective judgement of the policy problem which it has been given to tackle. Its members will tend to be leading public figures from various fields, either expert in their subject, or representing particular interests, or representing the lay public, or being regarded as possessing wisdom and judgement above the ordinary. The commission is on this account both highly visible and prestigious, and its members form a group who deliberate together without having vested interests in particular programmes and policies. As a constitutional device, the commission removes contentious policy matters from the immediate political arena, whether this is the Cabinet or Parliament in Britain, or Congress or the Executive Branch in the USA. A commission is both a part, and not a part, of government. It is set up, funded and its members chosen by the state, but it is then independent and free to pursue its own course until it produces recommendations. These then are fed back into the active political arena and may or may not be acted upon. The independence of commissions confers special benefits. They can take a fresh look at problems, try to influence actors in other parts of the political system and attempt to formulate a consensus upon controversial issues which will command public acceptance. They are thus, despite their prestige and authority, a means of potential innovation and change in policy-making.

Commissions are expected to inquire and advise. Inquiry may take various forms: receiving written evidence; holding public hearings to receive evidence orally; paying visits at home and abroad to throw light on the problem being considered; drawing on bodies of existing knowledge to illuminate their subject; and commissioning new research in the time available before their work is completed. Social science can clearly play a not insignificant role at several of these stages, thereby contributing to the understanding of the problem and, potentially, to innovation in policy.

The Critical View of Commissions

The above ideal-typical characterisation of British and American commissions is what may be called the 'received' view of the work that they do. There are also a variety of 'critical' views which emphasise the unstated, implicit or unacknowledged functions of commissions and point to their value as a means of political manipulation. A common allegation is that commissions are set up merely to get politicians off the hook of a current embarrassment. Once out of the way, the issue can usually be forgotten about and the report (when it comes) shelved. What substance is there in this critical view? The manifest and the latent functions of commissions do not necessarily coincide. To what extent, for example, are they really impartial and objective bodies? Potential members of commissions are usually public figures, whose existing views are not unknown (though these are not necessarily of a partisan political kind). Governments tend to set up commissions with a view to a certain sort of outcome:

> The statesman who nominates the commission can almost always determine the course that it is going to take, since he will have a pretty good knowledge beforehand of the minds of the experts whom he puts on it while, of course, avoiding any appearance of 'packing' his team. (Dibelius, 1930, p. 254)

Potential members are likely to be screened negatively, to ensure a group which is at least open-minded, or not hostile to the broad direction of the administration's policy (Wolanin, 1975, p. 75). In general, too, members of a commission have to be considered 'sound'.

There is an assumption that those with extremist views will tend to be avoided, and this of course helps to reinforce the legitimacy and credibility of a commission in trying to produce a consensual result.

The political element may be slightly more evident in appointments to Presidential Commissions, since the President is both head of state and a politician. A particular close associate of the President, appointed to a commission, may remind or advise his fellow members of the likely Presidential reception of their proposals. British Royal Commissions, too, may have a membership selected very carefully with the likely outcome in mind. The Merrison Royal Commission on the National Health Service, 1976–1979, for example, did not include any representatives of the medical profession working in hospitals, and this fact may not have been unconnected with the attitude of the minister at that time toward that section of the medical profession. The Webbs also observed some years after the Poor Law Commission of 1906–9 that commissions 'are seldom designed for scientific research; they are primarily political organs, with political objects' (Webb and Webb, 1932, p. 156).

The latent functions of commissions become more obvious when one examines the sorts of reasons which lead to their being established in the first place. Highly cynical and self-serving motives have been attributed to governments in the setting-up of commissions. One consideration may be the need to draw attention quickly away from politicians at a particular moment. It is suggested that the Presidential Commission on the Draft in the late 1960s was set up to spare the President political embarrassment. Or commissions may be set up, in Sir Kenneth Wheare's words (1955), to 'smother, strangle, drown or tear to pieces' an issue. More commonly it is alleged that commissions are used as a device to delay or postpone action. By the time they report there may be a change of government or President, or the salience of the problem may have subsided. A. P. Herbert maintained this argument strongly for many years and wrote an abrasive appraisal of government commissions called 'Anything but action?'.

> A Royal Commission is generally appointed, not so much for digging up the truth, as for digging it in; and a government department appointing a Royal Commission is like a dog burying a bone, except that the dog does eventually return to the bone. (1961, pp. 263–4)

It has also been suggested (Drew, 1968, p. 46) that governments may set up a commission when they cannot think of anything else to do. In some circumstances the establishment of a commission may seem the most appropriate political response because it has been done before. This certainly seems to have been the case with American riot commissions, which have been set up with predictable regularity since 1919, have produced broadly similar analyses of the social conditions contributing to urban racial violence and have 'persistently failed to eliminate the miseries, persecution and exploitation of black Americans' (Platt, 1971, p. 45. See also Lipsky and Olson, 1977).

The use of riot commissions also suggests a pacification function for commissions, whereby they act as symbolic responses to political demands, damp down concern and promote stability, without involving any commitment of resources or tangible benefits to citizens. Commissions may thus be set up to deal with the politics of the situation rather than the situation itself. Since commissions invite evidence from the public and hold public hearings, these too can provide an opportunity to air grievances and reduce tension (Sulzner, 1971, pp. 445–7).

Commissions may also act as a device to enable governments to do what they want to do anyway, sometimes clothing it in the legitimacy provided by research. Lord McGregor has suggested that the Finer Committee on One-Parent Families, which reported in 1974, fulfilled this function. In such cases, 'their chief task will be to draw together and deploy existing knowledge in such a way as to present the politically influential public with the most compelling supporting arguments for their conclusions' (McGregor, 1980, p. 154). Commissions may act as a means of mobilising support for particular policies. 'Commissions can . . . help the President build support for what he has already decided to do' (Cleveland, 1964, p. 292). This task is helped by the aura of objectivity surrounding commissions, the prestige attaching to the commission because of its members and the likelihood that the recommendations of the commission will be agreed and not too radical. In some circumstances commissions can also act as a means of trying out policy proposals (and amending them if necessary), so that the commission rather than the government absorbs public reaction. It may then be easier subsequently for the government to push through its intended policies.

Another interpretation of the role of commissions is that they are a means of promoting elite participation. The British Treasury allegedly keeps a list of 'the Great and the Good' – persons deemed suitable to serve on governmental bodies and hold official appointments. In a tightly integrated, centralised society like Britain, the idea of 'the Establishment' (see Thomas, 1959) connotes an inner circle of the society's elites who are close to policy-making and have a disproportionate influence in decisions that are made. Derthick (1971) argues that American commissions are presidential in character, an extension of the President's office, and that members are drawn from the 'presidential constituency' – persons who have achieved national political or civic recognition, eminence in the media or other national organisations, who tend to be urban and cosmopolitan. The staff members they hire are usually lawyers from major metropolitan law firms, leading academics, or staff seconded from federal administrative agencies. In both societies, commissions tend to represent a particular segment of the elite and to be a means of incorporating elite members into the policy-making process.

The burden of 'critical' views of the workings of commissions is to induce cynicism and suggest that rhetoric and reality are far apart. This is misleading, because although critical views provide some insights into political and organisational realities, they exaggerate the manipulative potential of commissions. For example, the extent to which the membership of commissions is 'packed' with people who are sympathetic to the government's position (if it has one) can be grossly exaggerated (cf. Wolanin 1975, pp. 75–81). Otto Larsen's experience with the pornography commission is instructive in this respect. When invited to serve, he replied he had no experience of research concerned with obscenity and pornography. In response, he was told that the President was looking for people with knowledge of research but who had not made up their minds on the subject.

> I responded by asking if this meant that the Commission was free to move with the data and was not being formed merely to provide information to support a given policy position. The answer was an emphatic yes, and I was given some names of prominent persons who were not being put on the Commission because they had publicly committed themselves to a particular view of the issue. (Larsen, 1975, p. 19)

A common thread running through the literature on governmental commissions is the frequency with which recommendations are not acted upon by governments receiving the reports. This might be taken as evidence that commissions are really devices to avoid or postpone decisions. More plausibly, it is evidence of the relative autonomy, objectivity and lack of political partisanship of commissions, whose dispassionate study of their subject leads them to make recommendations for which politicans or the public are not prepared. Commissions, despite some limitation in the range of opinions represented among their members, do constitute a means of studying objectively policy problems at a given point in time (cf. Wolanin, 1975, pp. 73–95).

Commissions as Tools of Social Inquiry

The use of commissions to examine social policy issues was discussed in Chapter 1. Although the Royal Commission on the Poor Law organised extensive first-hand empirical inquiries, their objectivity and detachment were limited and they have been indicted for gross bias (McGregor, 1957). Nevertheless, the nineteenth-century Royal Commission was one of the mainstays of what is known as British 'blue-book sociology', the systematic collection of evidence about social conditions as part of official inquiries (Pinker, 1971, ch. 2). Marx indeed praised this method of collecting objective evidence warmly:

> The social statistics of Germany and the rest of Continental Western Europe are, by comparison with those of England, wretchedly compiled. But they raise the veil just enough to let us catch a glimpse of the Medusa head behind it. We should be appalled at the state of things at home if, as in England, our governments and parliaments appointed periodically commissions of inquiry into economic conditions; if these commissions were armed with the same plenary powers to get at the truth; if it was possible to find for this purpose men as competent, as free from partisanship and respect of persons as are the English factory-inspectors, her medical reporters on public health, her commissioners of inquiry into the exploitation of women and children, into housing and foods. (Marx, 1959, p. 9)

The social facts produced by commissions were in the public domain, where they could be used to support quite different analyses of contemporary problems – in Marx's case, a critique of the capitalist system. Commissions then and now analyse social phenomena in such a way that their results can be utilised by people of sharply different philosophical and political outlook, on the commission itself or outside (see Skolnick, 1979, p. 38; Merton, 1975, p. 159). The argument that commissions are a device for burying or smothering policy problems rather than dealing with them does not therefore hold water so far as their research function is concerned.

It is of course in the twentieth century that the part played by social science in the work of commissions has really developed. In Britain an early landmark was Beatrice Webb's contribution to the Royal Commission on the Poor Law of 1906–9, on which she wrote a Minority Report. The Webbs were, of course, indefatigable social investigators and this influence was felt in the work of the commission. In the United States commissions were first actively used as an instrument of inquiry this century by Herbert Hoover (Dean, 1969, pp. 101–16), whose background in engineering led him to believe that scientific experts would contribute much to the workings of government. Sociologists made notable contributions to the research done for two of Hoover's inquiries, the Wickersham National Commission on Law Observance and Enforcement, 1931, and the President's Committee on Recent Social Trends, 1933. Criminologists Clifford Shaw and Henry D. McKay made a major analysis of the causes of delinquency for the former (Short, 1978, pp. 23–49), while William F. Ogburn was research director and Howard Odum assistant director of the latter (Karl, 1969).

These historical examples highlight a feature of the part played by social science in early commissions. Some were officially appointed but received no official funds to pay for their work. The prime example of this was the Chicago Commission on Race Relations, 1919–22, set up by the governor of Illinois in the aftermath of the Chicago race riot of 1919. It is the classic study (1922) by a riot commission utilising social science research, which was directed by black sociologist Charles S. Johnson (Waskow, 1967; Bulmer 1981b). A good deal of the commission's time was spent trying to secure financial support. Another example was Hoover's Committee on Recent Social Trends, although in that case a half-million-dollar grant from the Rockefeller Foundation paid for its staff and expenses. Nevertheless, it was a committee appointed by and reporting to the President.

Another variant was for a commission to be appointed and funded by government, but for additional research for the commission to be funded privately. This was the case with the Webbs and the 1906–9 Poor Law Commission, where Beatrice initiated various empirical inquiries of her own and firmly told the other commissioners that she intended to pursue them (B. Webb, 1948, pp. 349, 371), paying for them herself or from other private sources. This practice of relying on outside resources still survives to some extent in Presidential Commissions, where in some cases commissioners who are state governors, congressmen, or businessmen may rely on their own staff as well as on the staff of the commission. In general, however, commissions now receive sufficient funds from government both to pay for expenses and salaries to staff and to fund research which the commission wishes to conduct. Reliance on private sources of finance is unusual. The need for a larger budget, including the costs of research, is recognised as legitimate.

Before considering in detail the workings of commissions, some relevant differences in the political culture of Britain and North America should be briefly considered. It may seem self-evident that if the task of commissions is to investigate a policy problem, then social science is likely to be relevant to that investigation. This depends, however, on the extent to which social science is perceived as offering a potential contribution to the policy-making process. L. J. Sharpe has persuasively argued that there are very significant differences in the relative political cultures of Britain and the United States in this respect.

American society is decidedly more sympathetic and receptive to the social sciences than is British society . . . The epitome of the government's response to a problem in the United States is to select the professor with the highest reputation in the field, give him a generous research budget and put him on a contract. The epitome in Britain is to set up a committee of inquiry made up largely of distinguished practitioners in the chosen policy field with a token academic who may or may not be invited by his colleagues to organise research. (1978, p. 305)

The nearest analogy to a British social scientist visiting America is an English chef visiting Paris.

The differences between the two societies arise partly from the greater emphasis in American social science upon empirical research, reliable techniques and precise data, as well as the larger scale of the organisation of research, as shown, for example, by the presence on American campuses of survey research organisations. American politics and government are much more open to bringing in academics at a high level to advise. American politicians rely to a much greater extent than British Members of Parliament upon aides and research assistance of all kinds. Turning to academics for advice is merely an extension of this practice. The American higher civil service, moreover, is more open and less tightly knit than the cadre of generalist administrators, most without any background in social science, who head departments and advise ministers in Britain.

These differences in national receptivity to social science are evident in the history of governmental commissions this century. Apart from the influence of the Webbs, American commissions incorporated a much greater social science component at a much earlier date than did comparable British commissions. The Chicago Commission on Race Relations (1922) and the Wickersham Crime Commission (Wickersham Report, 1931) are landmarks in the history of applied social science which it took until the 1960s for Britain to emulate. The Robbins Committee (1963) on Higher Education, which cost £128,000, was one of the first Royal Commissions in recent times to have a large research budget and use social science in its deliberations. Is there a thirty-year time lag in Britain following America in this respect?

There are many examples of commissions in which social science has featured prominently on both sides of the Atlantic, but what conditions foster the most effective contribution of social science? Commissions tackle public issues with a significant social science component, to which inquiry is thought to have something to contribute.

One of the reasons why commissions' recommendations are accepted as authoritative is because they are reached in accord with the public's conception of how decisions should be made. One element of this public ideal for legitimate decision-making is that there be extensive factual inquiry supporting the conclusions reached. (Wolanin, 1975, p. 98)

This view is endorsed by Derthick. 'Commission reports must be judged as works of social science because commissions have been asked to do social scientists' work . . . [T]hey have emerged as a prominent instrument of social analysis' (1971, p. 623). A more systematic discussion of the contribution of social science will now be attempted. Its tentativeness should be emphasised, particularly the attempt to generalise about the *genus* commission on the basis of rather disparate empirical evidence. Often one seems caught between ideographic case-studies and very broad and somewhat speculative generalisations. Nevertheless the latter have some interest.

The Structure of Commissions and How They Operate

The effectiveness of social science is clearly conditioned by the structure and methods of working of commissions. Each commission has a chairman and members, a secretariat and possibly a staff to assist the members and to do research. Consultants may also be employed. The character and orientation of the chairman clearly plays a very important role in the extent to which social science is brought in. On the President's Commission on Obscenity and Pornography, 1968–71, the chairman (a lawyer) was interested in the *empirical* conditions assumed by various types of legislation, pressed for research at the expense of other activities, such as public relations, and was influenced in the conclusions he drew by the results of research. 'He read every article, research proposal, and report. He even labored on some of the questionnaires' (Larsen, 1975, p. 24). The Robbins Committee mounted a major research programme under the influence of its chairman, a distinguished academic economist. Such keen interest on the part of the chairman is not common, but it makes the point that he or she influences the use made of social science by the commission. The fact that so many commissions are chaired by lawyers (in Britain by judges) places the relationship between legal and social science approaches to problems at the centre of discussion, a point which recurs again and again in the following analysis.

Commissions are composed of the chairman plus the members, who are appointed for various reasons to represent various constituencies, fill different roles and provide a mixed and wide-ranging perspective on the problem at issue. Various typologies of commission members have been proposed, such as expert, layman, party man, official and interested party (Wheare, 1955), or expert, representative of an interest, fuse-box, advocate of a particular philosophy, consensus builder, or genial host (Donnison, 1980, pp. 15–17). Members are not all of a kind, and only a few of them, if any, will have any detailed knowledge of social science. From that point of view they are lay people, whatever role they fill on the committee. Any social scientist on the commission, and social scientists on its staff or from outside, must therefore always be aware that they are talking to and writing for those not having background academic knowledge in their subject.

British and American commissions differ markedly in their administrative support. Royal Commissions typically have a small secretariat of administrative personnel who are civil servants seconded to work for the commission by its sponsoring department. They are generalists, usually with degrees in the humanities, and are likely to lack knowledge of the social sciences. Their expertise lies in running the government machine, skills which they apply to the affairs of the commission. There will be only two or three such staff, with clerical and secretarial support, to look after the commission. This contrasts markedly with the American practice of appointing lawyers to run the commission. Usually they are headed by an executive director, who in turn hires a staff to work under him. Thus the Kerner Commission had a *senior* staff of twenty-six, and a further eighty-nine support staff (Kerner Report, 1968, pp. xix–xx). The National Commission on the Causes and Prevention of Violence had a *senior* staff of twenty-seven, while one task force alone (that headed by Jerome Skolnick) had thirty-three staff, plus consultants (Violence Commission, 1970, pp. xix, 258–9; Skolnick, 1970).

An essential distinction must be made between administrative and research staffs. Royal Commissions on occasion do have their own research staff who are additional to the secretariat. Practice varies; sometimes there is only one research director who co-ordinates the work of outside consultants (see Kilroy-Silk, 1973, p. 58), sometimes he or she heads a small research team (Sharpe, 1980), more rarely a larger body of researchers is assembled (Flowerdew, 1980; Bulmer, 1980a). The secretariat itself remains small and usually the combined staff including researchers will be fewer than ten. Presidential Commission staffs include both administrators and researchers, though the executive director is usually a lawyer practising in Washington or working in some capacity for the federal government. Many specialist posts are established by Presidential Commissions. The Kerner Commission's staff included, for example, directors of investigations, congressional relations, program operations, research services and information, and a general counsel with three assistants. Some American commissions also hire a professional writing staff. Research staff may consist of a research director and a number of supporting staff; or a research director who then draws on the services of outside academic consultants. Several US commissions have also created task forces, headed by a social scientist either alone or jointly with a lawyer, to investigate particular problems in depth. These task forces have also employed their own staff and consultants. Thus both on the administrative and research sides Presidential Commissions, compared to Royal Commissions, are likely to have much larger staffs. This reflects both differences in the political systems of the two countries, already referred to, and the more salient part played by social science in public policy in America. It does not follow, however, that Presidential Commissions are necessarily any more effective, for reasons which will be discussed shortly.

Commissions are set up to inquire and advise. How do they set about inquiry? The answers to this question are relevant both to the types of evidence collected and to who actually does any of the research which the commission undertakes. As noted earlier, the main forms of evidence sought by commissions, partly explicable by their public character and dominance by lay persons, has been to invite written and oral evidence and to make visits of inspection or inquiry. The receipt of written evidence is a necessary but manageable part of their work. Visits of inspection or inquiry may or may not yield useful insights in the short time usually available for them. One British researcher has suggested that they mainly fulfil latent functions of integrating the membership and providing opportunities for relaxation in congenial surroundings (Tunstall, 1980, pp. 137–8), though this is probably over-cynical as a generalisation. The most time-consuming activity is the receipt of oral evidence and the holding of public hearings. Here the influence of legal practice on the work of commissions is clear. The cross-examination of witnesses is basic legal procedure and it forms a most salient part of the work of commissions. Members of Royal Commissions are likely to be familiar with it if they have legal backgrounds, as are members and staff of Presidential Commissions. Yet it is the one activity which most serves to reduce the potential contribution of social science to the work of commissions.

The inadequacy of public hearings was first pointed out fifty years ago by the Webbs.

> Of all recognised sources of information, oral 'evidence' . . . has proved to be the least profitable. Considering the time spent in listening to it, or even in rapidly reading and analysing these interminable questions and answers – still more, the money spent over them – the yield of fact is absurdly small. (Webb and Webb, 1932, p. 142)

They argued that in these hearings, unlike a court of justice, the spoken word was not superior to the written word. Commissioners in the main were not expert lawyers or practised social investigators, skilled in taking evidence. (Though even if they were, havoc could result. Charles Booth once spent five hours of the time of the Royal Commission on the Poor Law eliciting detailed information about Poor Law unions in South Wales using 'the method of the interview', to the infuriation of the other members; see B. Webb, 1948, pp. 335–6.) Moreover, commissions lacked intelligent procedure in the selection of witnesses and in their questioning, members being more concerned to score points than to establish the truth.

These reservations about the value of oral evidence continue to be expressed. Several members of recent British Royal Commissions have considered hearings a waste of time, principally because many of those who give evidence elaborate positions they are already known to hold. The distinguished criminologist L. Radzinowicz considered that the Royal Commission on the Penal System, 1964–6, wasted its time in cross-examination of witnesses and that the evidence given was pitifully weak and often inaccurate (Hood, 1974, p. 387). Marvin Wolfgang and James Short argued unsuccessfully that the National Commission on the Causes and Prevention of Violence should not hold hearings, as these were likely to be unproductive and time-consuming. They were overruled but Short reports that 'none of the participating social scientists with whom I have talked about the matter have expressed satisfaction with the hearings' mode of inquiry' (1975, p. 81). The staff lawyers, on the other hand, strongly favoured the procedure. On occasion hearings become public spectacles. The Commission on Obscenity and Pornography held few hearings, and these late in its work, but they achieved national prominence because one witness threw a cheese-cake at the unfortunate Otto Larsen, who had questioned him persistently (Larsen, 1975, pp. 35–7), thereby supporting Skolnick's contention about the Violence Commission that:

> hearings are a form of theater. Conclusions must be presented to evoke an emotional response in both the Commissioners and the wider television audience. In this respect, the planners of the hearings can be likened to the author and director of a play with strategy substituting for plot. (1970, p. 36)

British practice is less flamboyant and hearings (like Parliamentary proceedings) are not televised. In both cases the limitations of the method detract from the potential influence of social science.

Commissions do, however, also use social science and social science research methods. How do they do so? One consideration is who they get to do the research. Is research conducted by members of the commission themselves? Or does the commission employ its own staff to carry out research? Or does it contract research to in-house government research bodies (such as the Bureau of the Census or OPCS Social Survey Division) or to research organisations outside government? Or does it employ research consultants, usually academics acting in a private capacity? All these methods have been used, often in combination. In Britain social scientist members of commissions have played a key research role, such as Norman Hunt on the Fulton Committee on the Civil Service (Chapman, 1973, pp. 17–20) and Roy Parker on the Seebohm Committee on the Personal Social Services (Hall, 1980, pp. 78–82). The appointment of a director of research on the staff is not unusual; appointment of a large research staff is. Outside bodies are frequently called upon to do factual inquiries, for example, social surveys, as for the Maud Commission on Local Government (Sharpe, 1980, pp. 26–7) or the Younger Committee on Privacy (Rhodes, 1980, pp. 110ff.). Consultants are often used, though on a less elaborate scale than by Presidential Commissions.

Fewer members of Presidential Commissions are themselves social scientists but they are much more likely to appoint social scientists to their staff. Indeed the scale on which research is organised reflects both the much greater professionalism of American social science and the nature of the federal and continental political system within which it operates. The 'best' experts are brought in from wherever they happen to be, task forces are established, if need be, on the other side of the continent and if their co-director of research is away for a year in England, they just put in a direct telephone line between his Cambridge apartment and the Commission's offices in Washington, DC (Short, 1975, p. 67). Consultants are also used on a large scale much more widely than in Britain, reflecting the greater American faith in the social science 'expert'.

Another factor conditioning the effectiveness of social science influence is the nature of the task given to the commission. Some famous commissions, most notably the Warren Commission, have been set up to establish what happened at a particular critical moment. When rioting and police violence occurred at the Chicago Democratic Convention in 1968 the Violence Commission set up a task force that produced the Walker Report (1968), a detailed study of the events that happened there. As the Kerner Commission showed, however, a thorough analysis of what happened also requires consideration of why it happened and what sorts of policies might prevent it happening again. Derthick has argued that commissions are not qualified to tackle these broader questions. They should confine themselves to questions like 'what happened at Kent State?', rather than 'what causes campus unrest?' In that, however, she is in a minority. Provided the focus of the commission's work is fairly broad, social science will be likely to have a role to play.

Social science research, however, as is shown in Chapter 7, is not unitary. It may be used by commissions for fact-finding, political ammunition, causal analysis, or conceptualisation, or may form part of the interactive process of policy formulation. The enlightenment model suggests that social science can function at a rather general level to provide the intellectual conditions for social problem-solving. An 'effective' contribution by social science to a commission's work may therefore take various forms, depending on what is meant by social science.

The Use of Social Science

Can one draw up a balance sheet of factors favouring, and hindering, the use of social science by commissions? Several points clearly favour the use of social science expertise. Commissions are set up to investigate a problem and their members are keen to draw on available knowledge. In some circumstances there may be considerable gaps in available knowledge and also an absence of members of the public wishing to give evidence. In the case of the Younger Committee on Privacy in Britain such a situation was instrumental in leading the commission to undertake its own research, a survey of public attitudes to privacy. The more usual situation is an already well-researched field, where the emphasis is more upon drawing together and synthesising existing knowledge for the benefit of commission members.

The composition of the commission is likely to influence the extent to which social science is used. Where there are one or more 'expert' members, whose views carry weight, large-scale research and investigation is made more likely. The Roskill Commission on the Third London Airport (Flowerdew, 1980), though chaired by a judge, had among its members a leading urban planner, a transport consultant, an expert in aircraft design and an academic economist. It is likely that this led to the establishment of the commission's own research team of twenty-three staff, the first British Commission to employ a really substantial in-house research team. Similarly, the fact that the Royal Commission on the Distribution of Income and Wealth set up an elaborate statistical and research organisation, with at its peak a staff of over thirty, was not unconnected with the fact that three out of the original nine commissioners were academic social scientists with special expertise in the study of income and wealth. The research orientation of the Presidential Commission on Obscenity and Pornography owed something to the predominance of academics or ex-academics among its membership, as well as to the interests of the chairman already mentioned.

The degree of expertise among commission members will also affect the way in which social science research findings filter through to the deliberations of the commission. In extreme cases, like the Royal Commission on the Distribution of Income and Wealth, commissioners may be actively involved in advising staff on the design of research and problems of interpreting results (Bulmer, 1980a, p. 168). At the other extreme, if members lack expertise, research (if it is undertaken) is delegated to staff who are then required to present the results to members in a non-technical fashion. There is evidence that academic social scientist members may play a key role on commissions both in influencing the research undertaken and more particularly in interpreting the results to their fellow commissioners. This was clearly the case on the Donovan Royal Commission on Trades Unions and Employers' Associations where Hugh Clegg, an academic specialist in industrial relations, suggested that the commission undertake research and later argued for a particular analysis of Britain's industrial relations problems using the research evidence in support. The research director, W. E. J. McCarthy, was a close associate of his from Oxford and the industrial relations research consultants used were closely associated with their positions. 'Clegg acted as the Father, McCarthy as John the Baptist and the other researchers as their disciples' (Kilroy-Silk, 1973, p. 58).

Arguably this sort of influence is stronger in Britain, where the legitimacy of social science is less well recognised. The attitude is found in official circles and among public figures that social science can contribute little of value to solving practical problems in broad areas of government policy-making. In British law, too, there is little receptivity to the introduction of social criteria in the manner of Brandeis or Frankfurter. Therefore the influence of social scientist members of commissions in persuading their lay colleagues of the value of social science may be critical. This is less likely to be the case in the United States, where the legitimacy of social science and its potential contribution to policy-making is more widely recognised.

Social scientist members and staff can also play an important educative role. All commissions spend a considerable period of time getting to grips with the area they are studying. Where issues are at all technical this is facilitated by social scientists being part of the commission. On the Commission on Population Growth most of the members were not experts in demography and needed to be educated in the subject.

This took the form of circulating reading material, bringing in experts to lecture on different topics, and presentations by individual staff members. The members worked hard and contributed a significant portion of their time to homework and meetings. Later in the process, research that had been commissioned was made the topic of presentation. (Westhoff, 1975, pp. 49–50)

In some cases there is clear evidence that social science research directly influenced the way that commissioners reached recommendations. In the case of obscenity and pornography, the Presidential Commission took account of research findings in drawing up its policy proposals. 'On the surface, at least, effect studies by social scientists had a powerful, if not an overwhelming, impact on the commissioners when they finally made their policy recommendations' (Larsen, 1975, p. 26). Opinion on the commission shifted as a result of being presented with the results of research which showed that the effects of exposure to erotic material did not lead to anti-social behaviour. The chairman, too, changed his view of he subject. As Larsen points out, social science can only be used so far. However compelling the evidence about effects and how people feel about it, the level of intervention to recommend for policy (in terms of free publication v. censorship) involves considering principles and competing interests as well as simply the results of research. Even in this case with clear-cut research results, the influence of social science only extended so far.

Obstacles to the Effective Use of Social Science

The factors favouring the contribution of social science have to be weighed against the influences hindering its effective use. Though it is comforting to find examples of good use, the literature is full of the frustration and resignation of social scientists brought in to advise commissions, whose experience has made them feel that they were less effective than they might have been. Realism is a more appropriate posture than self-congratulation, and the discussion will now examine at some length barriers to the effective use of social science by commissions.

The single greatest obstacle to the use of social science is time, 'the discordant pacing of empirical social inquiry and of decision-making' (Merton, 1975, p. 163). Accounts by social science participants in the work of commissions stress this point above all others. Commissions work quickly and under pressure. If they want to draw on social science or undertake their own research they need rapid results. The average duration of Royal Commissions since 1945 has been two and a half years (Cartwright, 1975, p. 190) and of Presidential Commissions just under one year (Wolanin, 1975, p. 100). If research is to influence conclusions and recommendations it must be ready well before the final stage to feed into the commission's deliberations. Yet social scientists work to long time scales and cannot necessarily adjust their schedules to fit in with short-term demands. James Short, for example, recounts how the Violence Commission set up task forces but how slow the process was of recruiting and bringing on board senior social scientists, owing to their other, prior, commitments. By contrast the young lawyers who staffed the commission were there and prepared to work hard under pressure.

They were accustomed to the quick gathering and assimilation of concrete facts and then used in advocacy, in contrast to the [social scientists'] more deliberative academic style of research and preference for abstract theoretical formulations in the search for knowledge. (Short, 1975, p. 71)

The actual experience of time constraints on commissions is variable. Sometimes major pieces of research only appear after the commission has reported. This was the case with a major survey of civil servants undertaken for the Fulton Committee on the Civil Service of 1964–8. Sometimes research is commissioned quickly and published while the commission is still deliberating, in advance of its report, as in the case of the Royal Commission on the National Health Service, 1976–9 (Farrell, 1980, pp. 13–14).

How rapidly research can be started depends upon recruiting staff and consultants quickly at the outset. This can pose difficulties. Westhoff (1975) and Ohlin (1975) have emphasised how the time of year can hinder effective recruitment. Seeking to recruit American research staff between May and October, a commission is likely to run into the problem that academics are committed for the next academic year and cannot easily shift to a Washington post at short notice, in contrast to the much more mobile lawyers. In the case of the Commission on Population Growth, recruiting staff took one-eighth of the commission's life, and in the end much of the research had to be contracted out at 'levels of honoraria that were attractive by academic standards in order to attract such people and to induce them to produce on a fairly short time-schedule' (Westhoff, 1975, p. 48). Both the Population and Violence Commissions recruited research staff from elsewhere in government service, because they were more readily available than academics. Academic researchers were used principally to do contract research and as consultants.

The timing and staff recruitment problems also affect what 'research' commissions are able to draw on. By and large, commissions find it easier to draw on existing research than to mount new original work.

The deliberate pace of social research is incompatible with the urgency and haste under which recent commissions have operated. Under pressures of time, acceptability of findings and limitations of theory and methodology, the contributions of social scientists are reduced to . . . synthesising existing research and theory and preparing it for presentation. (Lipsky and Olson, 1977, p. 197)

Donnison has emphasised how the scope for more original and fundamental inquiries on behalf of a commission is very limited, due to time constraints (1980, p. 11). Even where the commission's research draws on existing theory and fact by exploiting existing knowledge, pressure of deadlines may prevent adequate effort being put in by consultants. On the President's Commission on Law Enforcement many consultants

> produced hasty reports that failed to identify issues clearly or failed to organise facts and theories in response to them. Almost invariably, there was a great reluctance to make policy recommendations. Most of the reports contained summaries of the literature and occasionally, ideological polemics. In other reports, analysis proceeded at too high a level of abstraction. (Ohlin, 1975, p. 115)

Most of these failings were due to conflicts between consultants' own teaching and research work, and what they had undertaken to do for the commission in a short time span.

Lipsky and Olson argue, on the basis of their analysis of the Kerner Commission, that the conduct of original research is undertaken by commissions not because it will feed directly into the commission's work, but because it 'may contribute to public understanding through subsequent publication' (1977, p. 197), after the commissioners have reached their conclusions. Thus studies produced for Kerner such as that by Fogelson and Hill refuting the riffraff theory of riot participation made important contributions to general understanding but were largely irrelevant to the commission's deliberations. It is recognised at the outset that such research may be 'late', but nevertheless it is thought worth conducting.

A further obstacle to the conduct of research may be lack of adequate resources. To do 'in-house' research or engage contractors will require funding. This funding may not be readily available. Particularly in the case of Presidential Commissions, large amounts of the time of executive and research directors may be spent in negotiations in Washington to secure sufficient funding for their activities (see Dean, 1969, pp. 107–9). Ever since the Chicago Commission on Race Relations in 1919 this has been a problem, though it is not invariably so. As with directors of large research institutes, much of the time of senior staff may have to be directed away from research management to liaison with funding agencies and efforts to keep the whole enterprise financially viable (see Short, 1975, p. 78). Funding is less of a problem for British Royal Commissions, since their closeness to sponsoring departments usually means that the department can either make funds available for research, or in certain cases undertake some of the research through its own internal research organisation. The Government Social Survey, which has done a good deal of research for Royal Commissions, has its own budget and may finance certain surveys without requiring a contribution from the commission. The chairman or secretary are therefore not expected to play the role of entrepreneur.

To what extent are commissions handicapped by having to work within a fixed time schedule of short duration? Time of itself may in fact be less important than the underlying predispositions of academics and researchers which pressures of time bring to the surface. Several experienced commentators have pointed to the very real conflicts which may arise between social scientists and policy-makers, deriving from their different outlooks. On the part of social scientists there may be awareness of the relative indeterminacy of social science findings, a strong need to enter qualifications and reservations about any conclusions reached, awareness of values and ideological bias and possible suspicion of the higher reaches of government (Sharpe, 1978, pp. 76–80). On commissions, research staff

> are generally interested in particular aspects of the committee's work, in teasing out particular problems and discovering the truth about them. Often they are less concerned than the committee – sometimes scarcely concerned at all – about the final recommendations to be made. They are most unlikely to have a grasp of all features of the situation which the committee must consider before framing its recommendations. (Donnison, 1980, p. 11)

Short states, comparing the role of lawyers and social scientists, that 'basic differences in perspective often characterised task force operation' (1975, p. 74). Ohlin observes that

> the sociologists serving as consultants to the commission were reluctant to specify the logical implications of their analyses in the form of action recommendations for the Commission. When they did try to do this, the recommendations were often more influenced by personal ideological conviction than by appropriately organised facts and theories as arguments. (1975, p. 110)

Lord McGregor concludes an exchange with Jeremy Tunstall, a research consultant to the Royal Commission on the Press, 1974–7, which he chaired, by observing that 'his central disagreement with the Commission turns on differences of view about policy matters. Yet he seems unable to accept that the Commission, having heard what he had to say, simply disagreed with him' (1980, p. 156). Time pressures of themselves reflect more fundamental differences in outlook between academic social scientists and policy practitioners, which members of commissions inevitably become.

Obstacles and difficulties in the use of social science also arise in the workings of commissions apart from time-scale problems. The general political culture, for example, may either devalue the contribution of social science or push it further back in the priorities of the commission. The way in which this happens can be through the influence of the staff of the commission, whose composition and orientation need examining. Here contrasts between Britain and America are perhaps most apparent. British commissions are run by generalist administrators from the civil service without special social science expertise, and with an exceptionally strong code of political neutrality which prevents them from identifying with any party political position. There is still an attitude found in official circles in Britain that social science can contribute little of value to solving practical problems in broad areas of general policy-making. This is diminishing, particularly as the wide use of research by Royal Commissions establishes precedents which later committees may follow in drawing on social science. But the central role played by the civil service secretariat may help or hinder the use of social science crucially. The secretary, for example, may prepare summaries of research findings for circulation to members. How well he understands them (and how intelligible they are) may greatly influence their reception.

The Influence of Lawyers

In the United States the staffs of commissions are dominated by public service lawyers (Kraft, 1969). Short, for example, describes the process of recruitment, which for lawyers is far easier than for social scientists. The lawyers

> came from influential law firms throughout the country and from a variety of government agencies. Most were young, bright, confident; and they know their way around Washington. Their recruitment was a relatively simple matter of contact by telephone between the director (or his delegate) and personal acquaintances in the firms and agencies whence they came. (1975, p. 65)

Few, moreover, had special relevant legal experience in criminal or poverty law. They were generalists whose value was seen to lie in adapting legal skills to the work of the commission. Not only did lawyers dominate the executive staff, but fifteen of the twenty-five task force directors were lawyers.

The explanation for the dominance of lawyers lies in their place in the American political system and in characteristics of their occupation. They are more readily available for immediate public service, and this perpetuates a tradition of public service within the guild. 'Lawyers also experience something of role-congruence between the requirements of their occupational roles and the demands of such *ad hoc* units as national commissions' (Merton, 1975, p. 165). The important contrasts with social scientists lie in the intellectual perspectives, styles of work and conceptions of evidence held by lawyers. Lawyers prefer sworn eye-witness testimony, sociologists favour systematic data collection, surveys and quantitative analysis of results. For the lawyer, evidence is presented and evaluated simultaneously, in the hearing, whereas for the social scientist there is an elaborate system of data analysis and report-writing, often incorporating peer review before publication, which makes the process of reaching conclusions much more long drawn-out.

It is hardly accidental that commissions' staff are so dominated by lawyers. Apart from their availability, and the fact that senior staff who are lawyers will tend to hire junior staff who are lawyers, two characteristics are of particular importance. Lawyers are generalists who work in a problem-solving context requiring the accommodation of the interests and perspectives of clients and colleagues. These skills may be particularly advantageous at the early stages of a commission's work when issues are weakly defined and direction uncertain. Secondly, lawyers have considerable experience of working under pressure for clients regardless of personal interests. When preparing the final report,

> the most important qualities are the ability to work all day and night, to absorb endless criticism without taking personal affront and to synthesise sentiments of commissioners or anticipate and then articulate their positions on various issues. (Lipsky and Olson, 1977, p. 166).

These qualities tend to be possessed by lawyers and are not at a premium among social scientists.

The lack of effectiveness of social science may therefore arise more from the structural situation of the staff than from antipathy to social science as such. This is shown by the experience of task forces for the Violence Commission with joint social scientist-lawyer heads.

> The lawyer's approach to problems was generally preferred by the Commissioners, who felt compelled to marshall facts quickly in order to reach plausible, if not entirely acceptable conclusions and make recommendations . . . The formal specification of equal decision-making power between lawyers and social scientists were undermined by the informal norms, values and communication networks that existed among the staff lawyers and between the lawyers and some of the Commissioners. Additionally, most academicians are not prepared to function effectively in the

Washington bureaucracy where these same norms, values and communication networks prevail. (Short, 1975, p. 72)

The relative positions of social scientists and generalists on the staff of commissions may be explored further by examining how both relate to commission members. Both Royal and Presidential Commissions tend to have weighty legal representation, as shown in the preference of judges to chair Royal Commissions, or in the numbers of lawyers who sit on Presidential Commissions, and the additional likelihood that political members will have a legal background. Thus a third of the Commission on Pornography had law degrees (Larsen, 1975, p. 21), while fifteen of the nineteen members of the Law Enforcement Commission were lawyers. While there is thus likely to be a predisposition in favour of legal modes of thinking among commissioners, there is much less likely to be receptivity to social science approaches. In Britain A. R. Prest has recounted how difficult he found it to communicate fundamental principles of economics, through concepts such as 'cost' and 'externality', on a commission considering civil liability. Algebra provoked reactions of horror and compound interest was beyond most people's comprehension. To put across social science effectively, 'what is needed is a persuasive tongue and a willingness both to repeat the same points *ad nauseam* and to rebut insubstantive objections with patience and tolerance' (Prest, 1980, pp. 182–4).

Whereas generalist administrators or lawyers are likely to be in tune with the ways of thinking of the majority of commissioners, social scientists are not. Research workers for commissions, if of high enough calibre, have views of their own, well-established working methods and public reputations. They are not a neutral element providing technical help.

> From time to time they will find the committee's outlook and methods irritating, and some committee members will be equally irritated by the researchers. Their contribution and the way it is used will depend heavily on members of the committee – often academics – who are familiar with research in relevant fields. These members can make, or break, the link between research workers and the main body of the committee. (Donnison, 1980, pp. 11–12)

Similar observations are made of American commissions.

> [T]he conceptual, research and interpretive effort involved . . . is formidable. It takes concerted effort to convince commissioners, let alone policy-makers, that policy is not necessarily synonymous with law, or that social control can mean anything other than law enforcement. (Larsen, 1975, p. 17)

Tradition, government sponsorship and backgrounds of commissioners make for a heavy commitment to the legal approach.

Sometimes these difficulties may result in outright conflict. It has been suggested that 'the relationship between the commission and the staff is usually one of mutual contempt' (Drew, 1965, p. 48). As a generalisation this is highly debatable. Nevertheless, there are striking instances of mutual misunderstanding. A British case-study of the Royal Commission on the Press (Tunstall, 1980, and McGregor, 1980) shows evidence of different perspectives on the problem, different conceptions of what the commission should have been doing, different assumptions about the role of social science, and differences of view about how social science should have been incorporated into the final report. Despite the fact that the commission produced an impressive body of research (much more so than other British commissions on the mass media), nevertheless the chairman and one of the research consultants took very different views of what was done and what was achieved.

The Dynamics of Commissioners and Staff

The internal politics of commissions do clearly on occasion affect the influence exercised by social science. The clearest example of this is provided by the Kerner Commission when in the middle of its work a substantial proportion of the staff, including research workers, were dismissed at short notice. There were various factors contributing to these events, including financial difficulties, but one of the most important was disappointment among the executive staff at the quality of the research produced.

> In some respects staff weaknesses or failures must be blamed for these disappointments, but unrealistic executive staff expectations and their changing conceptions of the purposes of documents presented to the commission also played a part. [For example,] 'quick and dirty' preliminary surveys of riot cities proved inadequate as comprehensive statements, and their shortcomings had to be obscured to get them into acceptable form. (Lipsky and Olson, 1977, p. 191).

Particular controversy centred on an analytic essay by commission social scientists examining riot causation. It was a loose, imaginative, document attempting to make sense of confusing events and suggest categories for future analysis. Though the executive staff had originally asked for it, it was judged too sweeping and too far from a legal brief to be acceptable. It was too speculative and not sufficiently documented. 'To ask commissioners to put their signatures to such a

document would be folly. To present the document for their consideration would seriously impair confidence in the staff' (Lipsky and Olson,
1977, p. 186). Instead, the executive staff's rejection of the document
precipitated internal crisis and outside criticism when dismissals were
instituted.

Sweeping generalisations about the internal workings of commissions are particularly likely to be wide of the mark. Neither a picture of
deep cleavages between staff and commissioners, nor that of a cosy
conspiracy among all concerned to arrive at predetermined results, is
near to the general state of affairs. It may be true that lawyers are more
predisposed to advocacy, marshalling evidence in support of a particular case, while social scientists are more likely to look at all sides of a
question and to want to generate new data (Short, 1975, p. 74). In the
actual workings of commissions, however, these differences tend to
get softened in the sheer hard work involved and the development
of a common commitment to reach a final report and achieve some impact. This tendency for commissions to seek consensus was discussed
earlier, but it also bears on their internal organisation.

> The atmosphere of Commission activity is difficult to approximate
> or imagine . . . We worked incredibly long hours . . . While all of
> this activity seemed to occur more-or-less continuously in a frenetic
> mélange, it was not unstructured. Staff contact with the Commis-
> sioners . . . was handled through the executive director . . . Re-
> search directors were the chief mediators between the task forces
> and senior staff, though there was much direct contact among all
> parties . . . [T]here was an active social life, – among Commis-
> sioners, between Commissioners and staff, and within the staff.
> (Short, 1975, pp. 78–9)

A good deal of the time of the research directors, and indeed of more
junior research staff, may be spent on matters not directly related to
research or report preparation. For example, on Royal Commissions
the research director may be encouraged to attend hearings of witnesses in order to be available to answer questions, though his or her
time would be better spent elsewhere on research matters. These
pressures bear on the chairman, too. The reminiscences of the chairman of the Royal Commission on the Poor Laws, 1906–9, on which
Beatrice Webb sat, record that it 'was by far the heaviest business in
which I was ever engaged . . . The task of keeping [the members]
together was very tiring and at times impossible' (Hamilton, 1922, p.
329). In the end Majority and Minority Reports were produced.

In this social process informal groups may arise which cut across the
conventional boundaries of the commission. Ohlin on the Law
Observance Commission observed the emergence of small informal

groups, or cliques, among members and staff, holding broadly similar but non-specific ideological positions. The existence of these groups was recognised by the chairman and executive director, and the divisions were kept firmly under control. At the same time such differences actually performed an integrative function from the point of view of the objectives of the commission. The chairman and executive director

> maintained constant pressure to keep the recommendations closely tied to factually-supported premises or to theoretical views which should be shared in common. At the same time, these informal ideological factions generated strong motivation to produce persuasive factual and theoretical support for the arguments and recommendations proposed to the full Commission. (Ohlin, 1975, p. 111)

The formation of subcommittees or task forces may also help to achieve a similar objective. Though conflict often exists, it may be functional for the workings of the commission (see Coser, 1956). A full account of how commissions operate cannot be confined to analysis of the different roles played by commissioners and staff, administrative or research. The dynamics of their interaction have to be considered, and the sense of purpose and group morale which an *ad hoc* commission generates appreciated.

Evidence and Theory

Several further factors may inhibit the use of social science by commissions. One is the views of different members of a commission about the value of different types of evidence. An extreme instance of this is provided by the Royal Commission on the Penal System, 1964–6, which was set up to make a fundamental reappraisal of national policy. One of the members, criminologist Leon Radzinowicz, was increasingly dissatisfied with the methods of working of the commission, which relied principally on written and oral evidence. 'To elicit the experience and views of the usual list of organisations and of various meritorious individuals and weigh them up in an hour or two's discussion from time to time is not enough' (quoted in Hood, 1974, p. 386). He favoured a much more research-based inquiry. Eventually he led the resignations of a minority of the members of the commission, resulting in its disbandment. The resigning members took the view that the taking of oral evidence about penal philosophy was getting nowhere and was a waste of time.

There are indeed powerful pressures which lead to this reliance on oral evidence. British commissions, Andrew Shonfield has argued, taking a simplistic view of their investigatory role, tend to be the victims of the pragmatic fallacy. His view was quoted earlier on page 32. The opposite tendency, immersion in social science theory, is one that leads to difficulties, some of which have already been discussed. The presentation of social science theory may not be well received by commissioners or executive staff. What Lipsky and Olson term the 'paprika role', spicing investigative activities with social science findings and wisdom like a chef sprinkling paprika on a dish (1977, p. 182) can backfire. There are, however, more deep-seated objections which improved communication and more receptive commissioners will not necessarily overcome (see Wolanin, 1975, p. 103). They include the question of whether commissions are suitable bodies to tackle complex theoretical issues. The extreme view is that

> commissions are poor instruments for a particular purpose – explaining complicated social phenomena, which requires a high order of scientific competence. Committees are probably poor instruments for conducting scientific inquiry under any circumstances, and when the circumstances include the President's sponsorship, the close attention of the press, an atmosphere of crisis, and a subject matter inherently very difficult, they are poorer still. (Derthick, 1971, p. 635)

An early example of such difficulties was the Wickersham Commission of 1931 (Wickersham Report, 1931). Having commissioned a number of pioneering studies of the causes of crime, including studies of juvenile delinquency causation by Shaw and McKay and a study of the ethnic origins of Chicago criminals by W. F. Ogburn, it declined to pronounce upon the scientific evidence, to favour one theory rather than another. Nearly fifty years later the Royal Commission on the Distribution of Income and Wealth, strongly committed to research and with impressive results behind it, examined the incidence of poverty. Having received written and oral evidence on its causes, including cross-examination of leading social scientists on hereditary and environmental factors in human differences, it concluded that

> questions of causation are notoriously difficult to answer in the economic and social fields . . . The present state of knowledge does not point with certainty to any single explanation as to why some families and individuals have lower incomes than others. (Bulmer, 1980a, p. 170)

The chairman quite explicitly justified this position. Its task could not embrace getting involved in a vast field, requiring lengthy study, which was a side issue to the distribution of income and wealth. Another member of the commission drew a sharp distinction between factual and theoretical inquiry.

> The unanimity of the Commission on its presentation of its factual materials has been reached only after long discussion, and its *Reports* are the more valuable for that reason. But this experience makes me doubtful whether panels of persons of different social and political attitude and conviction can form an effective instrument of inquiry and report in questions not of fact but of social causality. (Sir Henry Phelps-Brown, quoted in Bulmer, 1980a, p. 172)

The problems of communication and understanding of complex ideas and theoretical principles can also arise in the presentation of evidence and the explanation of methodology. One British commission, the Seebohm Committee on Personal Social Services, made little use of social research. One piece of research which it did commission, however, had little impact because not only were the results inconclusive but they were technically presented and difficult to interpret. The secretary could not summarise them and members were no more successful (Hall, 1980, p. 79). These difficulties, of course, arise more generally in making social science relevant to policy. As Cohen and Garrett (1975) have noted, more research does not necessarily mean clearer-cut answers to questions. It may in fact mean *less* clear-cut answers, more complex results and a greater effort needed to interpret these results. Social science research presented to commissions is an acid test of relevance and intelligibility since staff and commission members expect material to be relevant and to be stated in such a form that the lay person can understand it.

A more general comment still on the role of social science in the work of commissions is to ask whether the most basic questions which commissions face are susceptible to answer by social science techniques. Are matters on which commissions deliberate not ultimately matters of judgement on the principles which should guide policy? The Commission on Obscenity and Pornography was criticised for relying too exclusively on social science research.

> In the cases of [the commissions on] violence and obscenity, it is unlikely that social science can either show harmful effects or prove that there are no harmful effects. It is unlikely, in short, that considerations of utility or disutility can be governing. These are moral issues and ultimately all judgements about the acceptability of restrictions on various media will have to rest on political and philosophical considerations. (Wilson, 1971, p. 61)

Westhoff considers that in the case of the Commission on Population Growth research

> probably had little effect on the philosophic spirit of the report. The same competing frames of reference would have been advanced and probably resolved in the same way because they were essentially different views of the world, largely outside the jurisdiction of scientific evaluation. Much of the rhetoric . . . would [also] have been the same. (1975, p. 54)

(Nevertheless, research did influence some of the basic conclusions about the effects of population growth, and policy recommendations.) Commissions on moral and penal questions are perhaps more likely to make recommendations resting ultimately on philosophical principles, whereas commissions on subjects like social unrest, government organisation, income and wealth, or the location of an airport may give more weight to social-science-based evidence.

The Political Context

What is certainly true, however, is that commissions, in reaching conclusions and making recommendations, take a great deal of account of the political context in which they operate.

> Collectively – that is for the commission *qua* organisation – it becomes more important to arrive at agreement than to arrive at the fullest and most accurate explanation of events; and more important to win acceptance for what is said than to assume that what is said is the closest approximation to the truth. (Derthick, 1971, p. 629)

The emphasis upon achieving consensus among the members of the commission reflects the equation between unanimity and likely political effectiveness. A commission which produces two or more reports is less likely to be listened to carefully than one which produces a single report. The pressures to unanimity are reinforced by the socialisation and collective experience of their members, and their *esprit de corps*, but the overriding aim is based on an assessment of the political disadvantages of dissension.

Achieving consensus without the need to present minority reports is therefore likely to be a major objective of the commission's chairman and of its secretary or executive director (cf. Wolanin, 1975, pp. 120, 152–3, 180). On the Law Enforcement Commission, for example,

> the process of communication among commission and staff members was designed to forestall the development of sharply conflicting positions and to achieve a compromise position wherever possible.

> The chairman showed considerable ingenuity and talent in his capacity to search out and negotiate compromise positions when serious conflicts developed. (Ohlin, 1975, p. 105).

The desire to achieve consensus may act as a constraint upon the expression of differing perspectives and their exploration through research.

A particular danger is the liability of commissions to intellectual capture and the structuring of inquiry from the outset in particular directions. The 'capture' may be political. Derthick (1971) maintains that commissions are primarily political instruments and that the Kerner Report, for example, became 'the orthodox liberal textbook' for a whole range of social issues beyond race relations. Or the 'capture' may, more insidiously, be intellectual. In Britain the Donovan Commission on Trades Unions mounted an impressive research programme, but one carried out within a specific orientation to industrial relations problems.

> The authors [of the research] constituted a small inbred group sharing a similar frame of reference, what has been called the 'new Oxford group'. Most of the authors of the papers were known to be against the introduction of the law into industrial relations and most of the papers argued against it. The authors were 'fact-grubbers'. What they provided was an impressive array of facts and little in the way of attempts to link cause and effect and generalise from them. They summarised each other's work and quoted each other with approval. (Kilroy-Silk, 1973, p. 58)

Acland has suggested that despite its apparent reliance upon objective research, the influential Plowden Committee used research as a device for 'stage-management', to frame and strengthen the conclusions of the liberal educationists who had most weight in the committee. It provided the setting and the scenery for an action (the commission's report) which was distinct from the research but which was framed by it (Acland, 1980, p. 53).

In the end, a commission's work, whatever the extent that it is social-science-based, will result in a report, with recommendations, which is published. Does it have any effect? Do the recommendations get implemented? Though experience is very variable, it is here perhaps that cynicism about the usefulness of commissions is most marked. As Lord Rothschild put it: 'was the sweat worth while?' Elisabeth Drew (1968) has suggested, tongue-in-cheek, five strategies for governments to deal with reports: (1) hide for as long as possible and then throw it over the White House fence; (2) postpone or play down its release; (3) dissociate from or denounce the report; (4) hope the public's interest in the report has waned; or (5) ignore it. She reflects the feeling among commissioners and observes that all too often the report falls on stony ground.

A dramatic example of this was the social-science-based Commission on Obscenity and Pornography, whose report was rejected by Congress as 'irresponsible' and 'degrading' and by President Nixon as 'morally bankrupt' (Larsen, 1975, p. 9). In both cases the word 'unacceptable' would be a more accurate description. The commission had more input than any previous one from sociologists, yet was judged almost entirely unacceptable when published. Its effect was not wholly negative (Larsen, 1975, pp. 39–40), but it was in effect rejected out of hand by those to whom it was principally addressed. Daniel Bell has recounted a very similar experience with the report of the Technology Commission, which the White House issued in an underhand fashion and in effect buried, because it was regarded as too controversial (1966, pp. 4–5). Publication of reports of British Royal Commissions cannot be delayed by political interference, but their recommendations face the same hurdle as those of Presidential Commissions: political acceptance.

Commissions do have great impact, far more than an individual social scientist or journalist. 'Commission reports, whatever their analytic strictures, defects or omissions, come to have a special standing within the *political* community' (Skolnick, 1970, p. 38). 'Facts' presenting a harshly critical appraisal of a social institution by a journalist or social scientist would be labelled muck-raking. The same or similar facts presented by a commission would be seen as a series of startling and respectable social findings. This impact, however, is a general and rather diffuse one, which will not necessarily persuade politicians and officials to press for the report's implementation, nor persuade governments to act (cf. Wolanin, 1975, pp. 145–54).

The many obstacles to the effectiveness of Royal Commissions and Presidential Commissions should not surprise the student of contemporary politics. Theories of the policy-making process such as Lindblom's disjointed incrementalism and partisan mutual adjustment stress the interactive nature of national policy-making. It can be argued that commissions are created to try to break the log jam which so often builds up, but it should come as no surprise that when a commission reports it runs into the same problems which beset advocates of change before it came into existence. Indeed, the effects of many commissions, in the short run, seem to be more disjointed than incremental – that is, they do *not* lead directly to policy change, and the members of the commission and those who observe its work become cynical and disillusioned about its effects.

This, however, is to miss a very important point. The Royal Commission on the Poor Law, 1906–9, had no immediate effect. Indeed in the short run it was largely a waste of effort, other than as a means of educating the public about the poor and giving some support to collectivist ideas which were growing in popularity at the time. Yet in the longer term the Minority Report, of which Beatrice Webb was the main author, anticipated many of the features of the system of welfare provision and support that became established in Britain in the middle of the twentieth century. Its effect was a long-range one, diffuse and difficult to pin down. Yet it is now recognised to have been an important landmark about social welfare in the history of British social policy. So it is with many of the subjects on which commissions report, particularly on moral issues such as censorship, obscenity, gambling, homosexuality, and so on.

Conclusion

In judging whether social science contributes effectively to the work of commissions, therefore, one also needs to take a long view. Those who hold that social science research has a pre-eminent role to play in leading commissions toward recommendations which would be implemented quickly tend to use an engineering model of the relationship between social science and social action (Janowitz, 1970, pp. 243–59). The social scientist is seen as analogous to a doctor or engineer. A problem is presented and the social scientist identifies the knowledge that is missing, seeks means to gather some or all of this knowledge, analyses the results and interprets the results to make them relevant to the problem posed initially. Policy implementation follows. The approach to applied research has had a number of advocates (for example, Zetterberg, 1962; Lazarsfeld and Reitz, 1975) but it has also been severely criticised (for example, Lindblom and Cohen, 1979).

An alternative approach, the enlightenment model, suggests that the impact of social science upon social policy is more diffuse, and that there is a less sharp distinction between basic and applied research.

> The sociologist recognises that he is part of the social process and not outside of it. The advocates of the enlightenment model reject the view that sociological knowledge produces definitive answers on which policy and professional practice can be based. Sociology is but one aspect of the social sciences, and the social sciences themselves but one type of knowledge required for policy. (Janowitz, 1972, p.4)

Social scientists as diverse as F. Znaniecki (1940), W. F. Ogburn (1964) and Harold Lasswell (1951) have tended to take this view of the application of social knowledge. An allied approach, to see social science as a means of conceptualisation (Weiss, 1977a, pp. 15–16), emphasises its importance as providing a way of looking at society, of thinking about issues, of defining and redefining 'problems' and assisting policy-makers to cope with the world.

The experience of the use (and non-use) of social science research by commissions fits in much better with the enlightenment than with the engineering model. The influence of sociology and other social sciences lies less in being of direct use than in providing a general perspective upon the problems and issues with which particular commissions are concerned. Commissions use social science research in a variety of ways – for providing authoritative facts, in permitting causal analysis, in facilitating conceptualisation – but above all in contributing to the interactive process out of which policy emerges.

6
The Institutional Context of Social Research

Governmental commissions provide an instructive case-study of the uses which can be made of social research because their short time scale and concentration of effort on policy issues make the interactive process of inquiry and recommendation clearer. Most social research, however, including some of that carried out by commissions, is done elsewhere. The aim of this chapter is to describe some of these other contexts and to discuss the extent to which context determines the nature of the research done. When talking of 'applied' research or 'useful' research, one is referring to different conceptions of research (as discussed in Chapter 2) and to different locations for that research to be carried out in.

In Chapter 1 the nineteenth-century origins of applied social research were discussed and twentieth-century development in Britain up to 1945 outlined. Up to 1914 the pattern owed much to reforming public servants who encouraged social inquiry; the important role of both private individuals of means and voluntary associations which they formed; the significance of communication among a small elite drawn from the professional middle class; and the absence from the scene of universities, which were not centres for applied social research until well into the twentieth century.

For most of the pioneer social investigators discussed in Chapter 1, social inquiry was either a leisure-time activity or a full-time activity supported by private wealth (as in the case of Beatrice Webb). Those in the forefront of social research were amateurs, ministers of religion, physicians, civil servants and businessmen who were primarily interested in social reform. There was no specialisation or professionalisation in social research and, before the First World War, no avenues for training and learning the skills of social research, since social science had no base in the universities. Therefore no one thought of himself as a social researcher.

During the twentieth century this situation has completely altered. Two general developments in particular have been of the utmost importance; the growth of government and the establishment of social science in universities. The extent of research in the 1980s as a large-scale activity carried on by central and local government, commercial market research firms, independent research organisations and universities and polytechnics bears witness to the very considerable changes which have taken place.

The Growth of Government

Partly as a result of the social research and political activities of socially minded individuals earlier this century, the scope of social provision by government has greatly increased. Particularly intense legislative action occurred in the periods 1906–14 and 1945–50. As a result, central government 'social' departments such as education, health and social security and employment now account for a high proportion of central government expenditure, channel resources to the majority of the population in one form or another and employ hundreds of thousands of staff. By 1972 social security, health and personal social services, education and housing accounted for half of total public expenditure. The 1971 Census recorded that two million people were employed in the social services, including a high proportion of the country's highly qualified manpower. The *impact* of social and economic policies upon individuals and groups also became of interest. Were social services reaching those for whom they were intended? What were the unintended consequences of particular measures? Government has, therefore, become progressively more interested in social research as a guide to social policy.

Parallel with the growth of government has been the institutionalisation of social science in British universities. This may be dated to the foundation in 1895 (by Sidney and Beatrice Webb and a group of associates) of the London School of Economics and Political Science. This college of London University, devoted exclusively to the study of the social sciences, provided continuity and a focus for organised research. For two generations, until the 1960s, it was the dominant centre for postgraduate education in British social science. The college originally concentrated on economics, political studies and statistics, but other social sciences such as sociology, social administration and social psychology have gradually increased in importance.

By the Second World War growth had been modest and outside LSE the number of social scientists was small. Universities had, however, become centres of research. Many interwar surveys of social conditions, including the repeat of Booth's survey in London, were carried out from a university base. The growth of the social sciences was stimulated by the Clapham Report (1946) which recommended increased government support for the social sciences in the universities.

Even with the Clapham resources postwar development was slow and the size of the social science community small.

The largest expansion occurred in the middle and late 1960s, following the report of the Committee on Higher Education chaired by Lord Robbins, an LSE economist. This recommended substantial expansion of higher education as a whole, both in student and staff numbers and by the creation of new institutions (Robbins Committee, 1963). The large expansion which followed in higher education in general and the social sciences in particular reflected not just the internal preoccupations of higher education, but demands for social science and social research from policy-makers outside. (For a general review of postwar developments, see Cherns and Perry, 1976.) A very important consequence of this expansion for social policy and social research has been that the influential social policy-thinkers of the later twentieth century, such as Richard Titmuss, T. H. Marshall, Peter Townsend, Brian Abel-Smith, A. H. Halsey, and others, have almost all been university professors. There are one or two exceptions, such as the educationalist Michael Young, founder of the Institute of Community Studies in Bethnal Green, but the contemporary counterparts of Booth and Beatrice Webb are likely to be found in a university.

The Organisation of Social Research

One consequence of the trend to greater government involvement in social research has been a major increase in the scale of social research which central government itself carries out. One thread of continuity between the nineteenth and twentieth centuries has been provided by the General Register Office, set up in 1837 and from 1841 responsible for carrying out the decennial census of population, as well as for the registration of births, marriages and deaths, and the vital statistics thereof. Though much of its work has been sheer data collection and storage, it has been an important pioneer of demographic work and of socio-medical research.

Large-scale government social research is much more recent. Concern about a falling population in the 1930s gave some encouragement to demography. Then social changes during the Second World War gave a push to applied psychology, economics, social statistics and survey research. The Government Statistical Service was established in 1946, its growth illustrating the increasing demands for data which are made by government policy-makers. Statistics inside government are organised and co-ordinated through the small central statistical office (part of the Cabinet Office, under the Prime Minister), with specialist statistical divisions in each main government department. The Office of Population, Censuses and Surveys (which now incorporates the General Register Office) performs specialised data collection functions for population and medical statistics, the census and social surveys (Redfern, 1976). In the ten years between 1965 and 1975 the number of professional statisticians employed in government increased from about 200 to over 500, and the numbers working on social topics, within this total, increased at a faster rate. This is one of the most formidable concentrations of social research manpower (backed up by 6,000 administrative staff) anywhere in the country.

Though the Government Statistical Service exists primarily to serve ministers and civil servants, increasing resources have been devoted in recent years to making government statistics more widely and attractively available. The publications *Social Trends* (annual) and *Population Trends* (quarterly) are models of their kind for the collection together and presentation of quantitative data on social conditions. It is a far cry from the days of Chadwick and Farr, or indeed from the time of Booth and Bowley.

Other developments have given social science a rather greater role in government. Several departments (for example, DHSS, DoE, the Home Office and the Department of Employment) have established their own small social research units, carrying out research on subjects of departmental interest. The development of quangos (quasi-non-governmental organisations), on the margin of government but semi-autonomous, has also encouraged social research to some extent. Bodies like the Manpower Services Commission, the Equal Opportunities Commission, the Commission for Racial Equality, and others, have developed a research capability.

One more specific development, partly within government and partly outside it, has been very important. Bowley's development of random sampling, discussed in Chapter 1, was first taken up in the United States in market research and public opinion polling. In Britain the first major development was the establishment during the Second World War of the Government Social Survey, within the Central Office of Information, partly to carry out surveys of the morale of the population. After the war its main work became the carrying out of factual inquiries into social questions on behalf of other government departments. Today it is part of OPCS as the Social Survey Division. Its work embraces a wide range of topics, mainly involving the measurement of objective social conditions. Its characteristic strengths are very high standards of technical competence in survey work and non-involvement in public opinion polling work and other politically contentious issues.

Parallel to the work of the Government Social Survey, but distinct from it, has been the growth of market research and public opinion polling using social survey methods. Market research is mainly research for commercial firms into the acceptability of their consumer products or services. Public opinion polling questions members of the public for their voting intentions, their opinions about political leaders and their attitudes to the political and social opinions of the day (see Marsh, 1982, ch. 6). Such research uses similar techniques and methods of research to the Government Social Survey but in practice the results are rather different. The typical product of the non-governmental research sector is an opinion poll published in the *Daily Telegraph* or *Daily Mail*, or a survey of people's preferences for butter, or foreign travel. The typical product of the Government Social Survey is less sensational, but more important for policy. Probably the most important work that they do is to carry out large-scale continuous social surveys, such as the Family Expenditure Survey (FES) and the General Household Survey (GHS). For the GHS, for example, all adults in approximately 15,000 households are interviewed every year and the information they give is used to analyse a wide range of social conditions, particularly in employment, housing, education and health. The GHS is the main source of objective evidence that we have of the state of health (morbidity) of the population of Britain, as discussed in Chapter 4.

In addition to the universities, central government and the market research sector, social research is increasingly important in local authorities, bigger authorities in particular often employing quite large social research staff, particularly on population, planning and social services subjects. So too are independent, non-commercial, research organisations, which are growing rapidly and both do research of their own and carry out contract research for government and academics. The oldest among them are Political and Economic Planning (PEP), founded in the 1930s and now part of the Policy Studies Institute (PSI), which concentrates on surveys of social conditions and economic and planning problems, the National Institute for Economic and Social Research (in fact almost exclusively concerned with economic research), and the Tavistock Institute, which has played a leading role in psychiatry and social psychology. More recent are the Institute of Community Studies in Bethnal Green, the Centre for Environmental Studies and Social and Community Planning Research, an independent non-profit social survey organisation. Several of these bodies have over the years carried out research which has had a major impact on social policy. For example, PEP has carried out surveys of race relations in 1967 and 1974 which influenced legislation on race relations introduced shortly after they were published. The Tavistock Institute has played a major role in developing consultancy with industrial firms. Some of the ideas germinated there played a part in the 1974 reorganisation of the NHS. The Institute of Community Studies under Michael Young has carried out the famous studies of family life in East London (especially Bethnal Green and Woodford) and is also the home of the Institute of Social Studies in Medical Care, where Ann Cartwright has done several important pieces of research into the workings of medical services.

An indication of the distribution of research organisations by type in 1972 (the latest date for which comprehensive data are available) is provided in Table 6.1. This shows that although over half of social research organisations are located in universities and polytechnics, many of those sited in teaching departments are small in size. The larger research organisations employing sizeable staffs are found in central government and in commercial and independent non-commercial research organisations, and then in the research council and university research units. University and polytechnic teaching departments typically have a small number of research staff; some have no research staff at all. These organisations are heavily concentrated in London and the South East. Over four-fifths of commercial and non-profit research enterprises are located there, as are two-thirds of government research teams. Even among universities, one-quarter of university research units were in Greater London. The reasons are clear. In London, research organisations are near to government, business, the media, the various pressure groups and associations and the largest concentration of academic manpower. In 1979 three-

Table 6.1 *Organisations Doing Social Science Research in the United Kingdom in 1972*

Type of organisation	Number of organisations	As percentage of all organisations	Average number of research staff per organisation
University ⎱ teaching	443	38	3
Polytechnic ⎰ department	88	8	3
University research units	160	14	7
Research Council units	29	2	8
Central government	70	6	11
Local government	216	19	5
Independent non-commercial research organisations	42	4	9
Commercial research firms	56	5	10
Professional associations/ charities	52	4	—
	1,156	100	

Source: Cherns and Perry, 1976, pp. 79 and 86.

quarters of the 700 members of the Social Research Association lived in London or the South East (SRA, 1979).

The Financing of Social Research

How research is financed obviously bears some relation to where it is carried out, but not entirely so. For the British government in particular does not directly finance social research and social science to the extent that it could. Indirect routes are often preferred. Looking back at the history of government support for social science, two official reports, in 1946 and 1965, were particularly significant. The Clapham Committee of 1946 recommended increased government support for the social sciences. This was implemented and the money was channelled through universities. The Heyworth Committee in 1965 also recommended greatly increased government spending on social science and as a result of its recommendations the Social Science Research Council (SSRC) was set up in 1965. The SSRC, like other research councils such as the older Medical Research Council, Science Research Council and Agricultural Research Council, is financed from taxation by the Department of Education and Science. The Council itself, however, is composed mainly of university teachers of social science. Its funds, therefore, are to a considerable extent distributed according to what the social science community judges worthwhile, rather than according to what the government directs. Slightly less than half its budget of £17m. in 1979/80 was spent on postgraduate training, more than half on social science research projects. The proportion spent on research has since increased.

A clarification of channels and types of expenditure upon social research will now be attempted. A diagrammatic representation of a rough kind is shown in Figure 6.1. It is very difficult to give figures of actual expenditure for the different sources, but an attempt is made to show orders of magnitude.

Central government is the principal source of support for social research and social science, which it finances in various ways. Directly, government funds its own internal ('in-house') research, the work of the Government Statistical Service and OPCS, including OPCS Social Survey Division. This expenditure is large and has grown. It also supports social research directly through funding quangos which carry out research and through payment for the staff of Royal Commissions and departmental committees. This expenditure is relatively large. In addition to this research carried out within the orbit of government, it directly commissions research from outside government, either from universities or from independent research bodies. This is relatively small, but growing. DHSS, for example, spends several million pounds per year on this type of research.

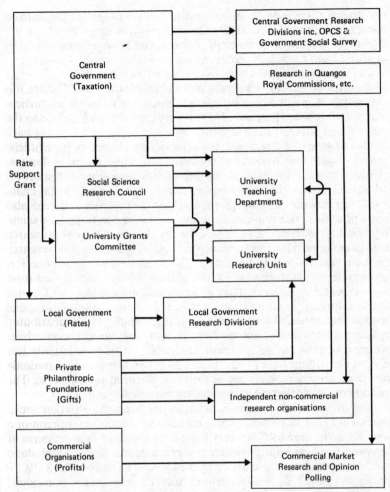

Figure 6.1 *Sources of finance for social science and social research in Britain today.*

An even more important contribution by government is its indirect funding of social science through the University Grants Committee (UGC) and the Social Science Research Council (SSRC) (see below). Although government determines the size of their annual grants, it does not control (though it may influence) how they are spent. The UGC budget is very large, but only a tiny proportion is spent directly on social research. The SSRC budget is relatively large.

Local government social research is financed from the rates and from the rate support grant. Almost all local government social research is carried on 'in-house' under control of the local authority concerned. Expenditure is still relatively small, but grew rapidly in the late 1970s. In the private sector, commercial firms sponsor research financed from corporate profits. Some very large firms have their own market research organisations but most rely on the services of specialist research firms for market research and opinion polling. Though the expenditures involved are very large, almost all research has a commercial subject and purpose. There is very little social research done in the commercial sector at present.

The finances of universities and polytechnics are organised differently but the main source of finance is from government in the end. (Universities are increasingly having to rely on income from fees in addition.) Under the dual support system operating in Britain, the UGC finances the building, plant, teaching staff salaries and overhead costs of universities, but does not provide funds earmarked for social science research. Even so, the UGC is the most important single source of support for social science in Britain. Moreover, the majority of the country's social scientists work as teachers of their subject in universities or polytechnics. As part of their job they are also required to do research, which often has to be fitted in in vacations.

More formal, organised, research in universities, whether projects with a budget employing staff and using resources or independent research units within universities, have to be funded from other sources, such as central government, SSRC, or the foundations, and cannot be paid for out of UGC funds. In general, research in universities is secondary to teaching in terms of financial priorities, so that outside sources of research support are particularly important.

One of the most important of these has been the SSRC. With a budget of £17m. in 1978/9 devoted exclusively to social science training and research, the SSRC is a very important source of finance, particularly so since it pays for grants for postgraduates and for research staff, neither of which can be financed by the UGC. The work of the SSRC is partly organised by subject committees (in economics, sociology, politics, and so on) and partly by boards which identify areas which are thought to need developing. In addition the SSRC finances several research units of its own, notably on industrial relations, ethnic relations and socio-legal studies. Almost all of the SSRC's budget is directed to universities and polytechnics.

Apart from government and the SSRC, an additional significant source of research money for applied social research comes from the large private philanthropic foundations set up in the past by great industrialists to make some of their wealth available for the public good. These foundations are run by independent trustees and are non-profit-making bodies which are completely separate from the firms with which they were originally associated, except that they usually still own large stocks of shares in the firms, the gift of which was the means by which the founders set up the foundation (Whitaker, 1979). The best-known British foundations are the Nuffield Foundation, set up by Lord Nuffield, the maker of Morris cars; the Rowntree Trusts, set up by the cocoa manufacturer, Joseph Rowntree, father of Seebohm Rowntree; and the Leverhulme Trust, set up by Lord Leverhulme, founder of Unilever. There are others. In total expenditure the trusts do not dispense very large amounts of money (several million pounds per year – small by comparison with central government), but they are selective in whom they support, and look for good results often from established social scientists. In addition, some trusts support institutions; the Nuffield Foundation supports research bodies in the medical field, one of the Rowntree Trusts now partly finances the Policy Studies Institute (into which PEP was merged).

The foregoing sketch of the present British system of research support is imprecise just because research is of different kinds and supported from different directions. Some rather more precise estimates for expenditure on social research in different locations are available for 1976–7. These are shown in Tables 6.2 and 6.3.

Table 6.2   *Estimates of Amount Spent on British Social Research, 1976–7*

	£m.	%
Universities (from all sources including share of UGC funds)	24·173	48
Government departments ('in-house')	12·306	24
SSRC research units	1·330	3
Independent institutes (from all sources)	6·713	13
Other*	6·259	12
	50·781	100

Note: *This is a minimum estimate.
Source: report by Mrs A. K. Jackson of the Cabinet Office to the SSRC (quoted in SRA, 1980, p. 3).

Nearly half of expenditure on social research is directed to universities; one-eighth to independent institutes; and approximately one-quarter 'in-house' within government departments. A breakdown of universities' direct expenditure on research shows that approximately one-third of it comes from the SSRC, two-fifths from central government, and only 6 per cent from private foundations. There are thus a variety of different sources, reflecting the divergent paths in Figure 6.1.

Table 6.3   *Sources of Direct Funding of Social Research in Universities and Independent Institutes, 1976–7*

	Universities £m.	%	Institutes £m.	%
Government departments (excluding UGC)	4·463	40	3·251	48
SSRC	3·548	32	0·512	8
UK charitable foundations	0·713	6	0·467	7
Other	2·407	22	2·499	37
Total (excluding UGC)	11·131	100	6·729	100

Source: report by Mrs A. K. Jackson of the Cabinet Office to the SSRC (quoted in SRA, 1980, p. 3).

The Effect of Context on Type of Research

One would expect that the location of research would influence the type of research carried out. Universities are more committed to independent scholarship, abstract learning and the development of their constituent academic disciplines. 'In-house' government research divisions are more directly concerned with policy issues, with 'relevance' and with practical usefulness. This view of the effect of context on applied research is summarised in Table 6.4.

If one looks at research organisations serving particular clients – market research, central government research divisions and local government research – this relationship is clearest. These organisations are commissioned to produce research that is directly relevant to

Table 6.4   *Different Types of Research Organisation*

	User organisations	University departments	Special institutes
Source of problem	specific client needs	needs of theory and method	general 'field' needs
Level of problem	concrete	abstract	generic
Activity mix	research/ service	research/ teaching	research/ application
Disciplinary mix	multiple	single	interrelated

Source: Trist, 1970, p. 783.

their clients' needs, with the requirements of policy-makers in the foreground. To take the example of local government, if research is financed it is expected to be directly relevant to the policy and management functions of the authority which it serves.

> The ratepayers in a local authority area who pay for research want, not knowledge for its own sake (this they leave to the universities and other similar centres for pure research) but better local government. They want the local authority to seek ways of fulfilling its statutory functions to the satisfaction of the community and in the most cost-effective way. Provided that it can be clearly seen to be directed to better decision-taking and therefore to better management, they will be willing to accept that research might be needed to cover an extremely wide field. (Benjamin, 1973, p. 19)

Useful evidence about variations in the problem-orientation, audience and character of social research in different British research organisations is available from a survey carried out in 1972 by Norman Perry. Table 6.5 shows the major audience for which the results of social science research projects were intended in the UK in 1972. A consistently high proportion – more than four-fifths in each case – of research work in market research and central and local government was intended for policy and decision-makers. More than half of projects in independent institutes had a similar audience, as did about one-third of projects in university teaching departments and research units. As would be expected, a proportion – about one-third – of projects in universities were aimed primarily at fellow researchers in similar fields. The independent institutes stood out in that one-fifth of their projects were aimed at informed public opinion.

The variations between research settings can be explored further by looking at the main focus of particular projects. This is shown in Table 6.6. Three-quarters of market research and local government research was primarily descriptive and information-gathering, with a strong bias to the empiricism criticised in Chapter 2. Surprisingly, however, for other kinds of research organisation (including central government) the proportion of projects falling in this category varied between 56–61 per cent; three-fifths of projects were descriptive or information-gathering in nature. There are of course limitations to the definitive conclusions which can be drawn from these data, since the categorisation of projects is rather a blunt one. Nevertheless it suggests a rather substantial modification of the typology set out in Table 6.4. It is by no means clear that university research is primarily oriented to the needs of theory and method, and abstract in character. Table 6.6 shows that only one-fifth of university research was focused mainly on theory testing and development and another one-eighth of projects on

Table 6.5 *The Major Audience for Which the Results of Social Science Research Projects Were Intended in the UK*

Types of organisation	Researchers in similar fields	Other professionals	Policy or decision-makers	Informed public opinion	Other	Total	Number of projects
	Percentage of projects						N
University/polytechnic department	34	17	38	4	7	100	655
University research unit	36	20	34	5	5	100	429
Research Council and other government-affiliated	33	23	37	1	6	100	84
Independent research organisation	10	11	55	20	4	100	132
Central government division	7	8	82	1	1	100	153
Local government department	2	10	86	—	2	100	205
Market research agency	3	4	83	5	5	100	172
Overall	24	15	51	5	5	100	1,830

Source: Perry, 1976, p. 165.

Table 6.6 Main Focus of Research Projects in the Social Sciences

Types of organisation	Theory testing and development	Descriptive and information-gathering	Methodological or technique testing	Policy-oriented evaluation research	Other	Total	Number of projects N
	Percentage of projects						
University/polytechnic department	21	59	12	2	6	100	647
University research unit	20	57	13	3	7	100	395
Research Council and other government-affiliated	25	61	13	1	—	100	84
Independent research organisation	13	61	10	4	12	100	126
Central government division	10	56	18	6	10	100	152
Local government department	4	76	11	5	4	100	204
Market research agency	9	76	4	3	8	100	166
Overall	16	62	12	3	7	100	1,774

Source: Perry, 1976, p. 168.

methodology or technique testing – a total of only one-third on theory and method compared to three-fifths on description and information-gathering. University departments seem to be not nearly so 'academic' as sociological theories of science would predict.

The Effect of Government Support for Social Science

The explanation for this lies in part in the growth of government support for social science research discussed earlier and the dependence of universities on government for about two-fifths of their research funds (Figure 6.1 and Table 6.3). Developments in central government funding of social science research therefore bear looking at more closely. Before the late 1960s direct government funding of social research (outside the UGC and SSRC arrangements), was slight and concentrated mainly on 'in-house' bodies like the Government Social Survey, which prior to 1967 was part of the Central Office of Information. (It then had three years' autonomy before being merged into the new OPCS in 1970.) As government funding expanded in the late 1960s and early 1970s a variety of arrangements for allocating resources, mostly quite informal, were developed in the different Whitehall departments. In some departments single individuals had autonomy in allocating quite large sums of money to social research. In a few departments – notably the Home Office and DoE – 'in-house' research divisions were expanded to meet some of the demands for research and information from policy-makers (SRA, 1980).

A major change occurred in the philosophy and organisation of social research following the Rothschild Report of 1971, briefly discussed in Chapter 2. Applied research, according to Rothschild, has a practical application as its objective. The customer (usually a government department) says what is wanted, the contractor (usually an applied researcher) does the research and the customer pays. Rothschild's argument was for a closer linking of government research expenditure to policy objectives, using a version of the engineering model of applied research. He said nothing specifically about social research, and it is doubtful whether he intended his analysis to apply to social research, but in practice government set up machinery which did cover direct funding of social research projects.

The White Paper (HMSO, 1972) which accepted his recommendations also anticipated that departments would set up rather more formal arrangements for commissioning research. This they did, and both the machinery established and the customer/contractor principle which Rothschild enunciated came to cover direct funding of social research by central government. Machinery for consulting policy divisions on their needs was established. Research management to deal with external applications, look after the evaluation process and negotiate contracts became formalised, notably in divisions within DHSS and DoE. In a few government social research units (such as the Home Office Research Unit and the Department of Employment research division) research managers also themselves conducted research. In departments like DHSS and DoE with very large research budgets and many projects (only a minority of which are concerned with social research), formalised committee structures involving administrators in policy divisions, research managers and (in DHSS) outside academic experts have been set up. In the Home Office and the Departments of Employment and Education and Science, where there is little non-social-science research, arrangements are more informal.

Departments differ in the extent to which they carry out research 'in-house' or contract it to outside bodies. The functions of research managers include liaising with the outside research community, negotiating with applicants for grants and ensuring that possible projects are adequately evaluated. Three modes of support for social research may be distinguished.

(1) Support for 'in-house' units, such as the Home Office Research Unit, the DoE (former) Sociological Research Branch (housing research) and the Transport and Road Research Laboratory, and DHSS social research branch (wound up in 1980). OPCS Social Survey Division is a special case in that it has its own budget but carries out research for other government departments which ask it to do so for them. (Currently the scale of this support is shrinking, see HMSO, 1981.)

(2) Support for an outside research unit or research institute, doing policy-related research but located entirely outside government, usually in a university. Examples of this include the Home Office support for the Cambridge Institute of Criminology or DHSS support for a variety of units (many of them medical or socio-medical) including the Personal Social Services Research Unit at the University of Kent. Support takes the form of programme grants, usually for a number of years, so that the longer-term continuation of a line of research can be guaranteed.

(3) Support for outside research through *ad hoc* grants to outside researchers located in universities or independent institutes. The department may either respond to outside applications or seek out possible applicants. A variant of the latter – very widely practised in the United States – is to invite tenders for advertised research tasks. Research managers and the formal committee structures are used to process and evaluate such proposals prior to decisions on support being taken.

The evolution of this structure of government support for social research – which is quite distinct from the SSRC-supported system –

places considerable power in the hands of departments to influence the direction taken by social research. Although in the past some major initiatives have been channelled via the SSRC – notably the DHSS-financed 'transmitted deprivation' research stemming from an interest of Sir Keith Joseph when Secretary of State – the present trend is for departments to keep control of research funding in their own hands. The evolution of this system also explains in part why such a large proportion of research in universities is directed to policy-makers, and descriptive and information-gathering in orientation. There is some variation by academic subject. Overall, two-fifths of social science teachers in Perry's survey saw policy-makers as the main intended audience for their research. The proportion in management, law, criminology, economics and geography was one-half or more. In planning, sociology and social administration it was about two-fifths, in education one-quarter and in psychology and politics fewer than one-sixth (Perry, 1976, p. 166). This reflects to some extent the disciplines to which government research support is directed, to some extent the 'usefulness' of particular disciplines in policy-making.

The Weaknesses of Applied Social Research in Britain

In some respects government control over research which it supports is slight and many wide-ranging innovative programmes have been funded with official support. The EPA and CDP action research projects, for example (Bulmer, 1978, pp. 137–200), were funded by the Department of Education and Science and Home Office respectively and were hardly cast within the mould of the engineering model of applied research. Some government-financed research units in universities do not differ greatly from comparable units supported by the SSRC. Some departments, notably the Department of Employment, take a wide-ranging interest in research within their field and play an important interpretive role in making policy-makers aware of relevant academic research on employment matters (for one example see Brannen, 1975).

The drawbacks of government support of a direct kind need also to be kept in mind. The requirement that research should be related to an identified policy concern of a department serves to bind social research increasingly to *current* interests of *specific* departments (SRA, 1980, p. 4). It thus becomes more difficult to develop research which deals with a problem that cuts across departmental boundaries (such as children, or the elderly), or which seeks information on a long-term basis, for example, longitudinal studies such as the National Children's Bureau 1958 cohort study (Davie *et al.*, 1972). The policy of the Conservative government elected in 1979, with a strong commitment to reducing government expenditure, was to enforce an increasingly stringent criterion of 'usefulness', so that even basic fact-gathering inquiries of OPCS Social Survey Division, such as the General Household Survey, came under threat (see HMSO, 1981).

More generally, the reliance on government for support bolsters an approach to applied research in terms of the engineering model of application, when the relevance of this model to the social sciences is far from clear. The pull in this direction, and in the direction of empiricist research, is quite strong from government, and one which the social sciences in universities are not well placed to resist. There is even evidence that the SSRC itself is under increasing pressure from government to demonstrate the policy-relevance of work that it supports, and the five designated research centres announced in 1980 are all in fields with strong applied interests.

However, the forces pushing social researchers toward an inappropriate engineering model are not all on the side of government. They also reflect certain characteristics of the social research community in Britain which, by comparison with the United States, render it less independent and more susceptible to outside influences. Though research is a basic commitment of universities, there is marked ambivalence among British social scientists, particularly in disciplines such as sociology and political science, about the merits of large-scale, organised, social research with a strong quantitative element. A result is that a great deal of academic research in those subjects is on a small scale, without any infrastructure in support, and involving at most two or three people (including research students). The situation is somewhat different in subjects like economics and geography, where there are more large-scale programmes, but even there these do not involve the majority of staff or graduate students. In the field of research methodology – notably survey research – the British scene has been remarkable for the absence of any university-based survey research centre until the setting up in 1980 of the Social and Community Planning Research (SCPR) – City University Survey Methods Centre.

This situation has had various consequences for the education and training of social science graduate students. Without the background in required course work characteristic of North American postgraduate studies, few British postgraduates in sociology or political science departments receive an adequate training in research methodology. (For the situation in one discipline see *Sociology*, 1981.) Recruitment to posts in social research in government, the commercial sector and the independent research sector, therefore, tends to draw primarily not from social science graduates but rather from graduates in any discipline who can learn how to do research on the job. This is one reason among others for the relatively weak links between academic social science and the non-academic research sphere. The gap which divides academic from non-academic social research in

Britain is a serious one, which helps to perpetuate inappropriate models of the utilisation of research. So long, for example, as social survey research is thought to be primarily a fact-finding and descriptive activity (rather than a scientific strategy with an analytic purpose – see Marsh, 1982), then simplistic models of research 'use' will continue to hold sway.

Deficiencies in graduate education and training in universities, and the failure to institutionalise large-scale social science research in academic settings, are only part of the problem. In the period of expansion of the social sciences in the decade after 1965 the extensive opportunities for employment in higher education attracted many of the better social science graduates at the expense of the non-academic research sector. The latter is in any case greatly handicapped by its fragmentation and divided state. 'Social science' is not a profession (or semi-profession) like university teacher, social worker, or actuary. This is reflected both in the inadequacy of existing professional training (which should be provided by universities) and in occu-pational fragmentation between and within different sectors. In the civil service, for example, there is still no coherent occupational or career structure for social scientists other than economists (Bulmer, 1978, pp. 38–9). In universities, research posts still tend to be seen as stepping stones to a teaching career and there are difficult problems in trying to create long-term prospects for those more committed to research than to teaching (see Illsley, 1980, pp. 170–5). In a climate of retrenchment and expenditure cuts, research is one of the first areas to suffer.

Social research in Britain, although it has expanded considerably during the last fifteen years both in the academic and non-academic sectors, is not as solidly established as in some other countries such as the United States. Graduate education is weak, university support for large-scale research ambivalent, many commercial, non-profit and government research units are remote from the academic world and see little value in promoting contact with universities. Some university departments – notably those in sociology – evince little interest in, and show a good deal of antipathy to, both large-scale research and policy research. An uncertain economic situation may lead to damaging cuts in support both for social research organisations and for academic social science. The full potential for using social science is not being realised because these deficiencies are allied to models of research utilisation which (in their empiricist version) relegate social science to a subordinate technical role, or (in the engineering model) pushes the social sciences into a straitjacket which does not fit them at all well. The appropriateness of different models is considered further in Chapter 7. The present chapter concludes with a British case-study of applied research and its organisation.

Local Authority Research: an Example

The case-study concerns a particular example of local authority research in Britain. Since in many respects this study reveals ignorance, low technical standards and inadequate staff it should be said quite explicitly that it is *not* representative of British applied social research, which is generally well conducted, to high levels of technical competence, by experienced and qualified staff. The case-study is included here because it does illustrate some of the problems – of quality, design, organisation and application – which can develop when social research is not adequately funded and institutionalised.

The 1970 Chronically Sick and Disabled Persons Act, put forward by Alfred Morris, MP, as a Private Member's Bill, provided in section 1 that local authorities should inform themselves of the number of chronically sick and disabled people in their area. This requirement came into operation in October 1971 and the DHSS advised local authorities, in Circular 45/71, that 100 per cent identification and registration should be their goal although sample surveys might be an acceptable alternative on grounds of cost. Local authority social service departments were thus statutorily required to carry out a social investigation of the number of handicapped people living in their area. In 1973 M. J. Brown and R. Bowl of the University of Birmingham obtained a grant from the DHSS to study how and with what success local authorities had set about doing this. This case-study is based upon their report (Brown and Bowl, 1976; Bowl, 1976), which in turn was based on a questionnaire survey of all local authorities supplemented by personal interviews with staff from 165 authorities.

The main findings of interest concern how the survey of disability was conducted across the country. Prior to this time the OPCS social survey division had conducted the national sample survey cited in Chapter 4 (Harris *et al.*, 1971), and a guide for local authorities as to how to carry out sample surveys of the handicapped had been issued (Harris and Head, 1971). Brown and Bowl's findings show a very high degree of variability in the quality of the research conducted by local authorities. In view of the fact that these results relate to the early 1970s and to local authority social service departments, they indicate very serious lacunae in provision for applied social research in one local government service field.

Although departmental research staff were involved in studies made by 45 per cent of the local authorities surveyed by Brown and Bowl, in an equal proportion of local authorities there were no research personnel *at all* to conduct the study. It was therefore carried out by staff lacking knowledge about basic principles of social research. Research staff supervised only one-quarter of the studies carried out and wrote only one-fifth of the reports. There was little attempt to use outside specialist help (though where it was used, studies were of a higher quality), reliance in the main being placed upon other staff of the social services department.

Brown and Bowl evaluated the studies in terms of a simple set of criteria, essentially involving a judgement about how well each study covered different stages of the research process (as outlined, for example, at the beginning of Chapter 3). Extreme variability was apparent. One-third of the studies were considered excellent or good but over two-fifths were judged mediocre or poor. Half of the studies did not define 'handicap'. Over a third of the problem formulations were inadequate, as were almost half of the research designs. Over half the reports were poorly presented, and a third were less than ten pages in length. Almost two-thirds of the reports had four frequency tables or less (a quarter had none) and over a half had four or less cross-tabulation tables (a quarter had none).

Some of these defects were glaring. Whereas half the authorities defined 'handicap' either following the method used in the national survey or using criteria of their own, half had no definition. In essence, in these surveys it was left to the respondent to determine himself or herself what 'chronically sick' or 'disabled' meant. In the light of the discussion of physical handicap in Chapter 4 such a failure is extraordinary, and likely to produce results of little value.

Other major defects included heavy reliance upon volunteers for the distribution of the first-stage postal questionnaire, which was distributed in many cases by schoolchildren and in some cases by private firms, including those responsible for milk deliveries and 'free' newspapers. Where personal interviews were conducted, half were carried out by volunteers who had received slight training and had no previous experience of social research interviewing (such practices would ruin the reputation of any social survey research organisation).

The failure to analyse the results of the research was clearly associated with the absence of research staff. Where there were no research staff it was much more likely that no attempt had been made to analyse the results.

There was considerable variation in the proportion of handicapped people identified in different local authorities, varying from less than 1 per cent in some areas to over 7 per cent in others. (The Harris national survey suggested a national figure for impairment of about 6½ per cent.) Though one would expect to find considerable geographical variability (see the discussion of health in Chapter 4), the fluctuations between authorities in the proportion identified as handicapped were far greater than one would expect on this basis. Brown and Bowl reasonably concluded that these variations reflected variability in the quality of the surveys carried out. And indeed one of the strongest relationships discovered was between whether a definition of 'handicap' was used in the study and the proportion of handicapped persons identified. Over nine out of ten of the studies which found less than 1 per cent impaired in that local authority area did not define the terms, whereas those using the definitions of the national survey formed the great bulk of the surveys which showed 6 per cent or more impaired in the community. The authors justifiably conclude:

> The surveys report enormously varied proportions of the total populations to be disabled. This must reflect differences in definition and quality of study as well as 'real' geographical differences. The proportions were generally lower than those found in the National Study (Harris *et al.*, 1971) and the local surveys add little to it as a means of estimating numbers of chronically sick or disabled people in the country except confusion. (Brown and Bowl, 1976, p. 2)

This depressing case-study is untypical and somewhat extreme. Research capability in social work in Britain is particularly weak and in the light of this the results of Brown and Bowl's study are rather unsurprising. But the case demonstrates very clearly the relationship between methodological input and research results. In this case, quite literally, the more carefully the research was conducted, the higher the proportion of the population who were identified as handicapped. It is nearly incredible that a major research exercise of this kind could proceed when in half the cases no attempt was made to define the key term. Some of the difficulties arose, of course, from the attempt to make a 100 per cent survey. Sample surveys, used by some authorities, were generally better conducted and produced more meaningful results. The experience also shows that well-conducted sample surveys are superior to poorly conducted attempts at 100 per cent enumeration.

Conclusion

The situation described in the case-study is the result of attempting to conduct research without proper preparation, without proper staffing and without insistence upon professional standards. Even though the case is untypical of standards in survey research organisations, in situations where research is undertaken by those who are not properly trained (for example, some academics) the results can be unsatisfactory (see Harrop, 1980). Professionalisation is often criticised as a thinly veiled form of self-interest on the part of higher non-manual occupations. It is, however, also a way of ensuring that work of requisite quality is carried out. The organisational diversity of British social research, coupled with inadequacies in graduate research training provided in universities, render the need for some form of professional organisation urgent. The Market Research Society already exists for the commercial sector. The newer Social Research Association links social researchers in a variety of different contexts. A number of other smaller organisations exist. Organisational fragmentation coupled with occupational fragmentation poses problems which are difficult to overcome and hinder the effective use of social researchers' skills.

7

Patterns of Influence

This final chapter returns to some of the more general issues raised in the latter part of Chapter 2. It will be apparent, from Chapter 5 particularly, that the author regards the enlightenment model as more plausible than the engineering model in examining the relationship between research and policy.

> Social science provides an angle of vision, a focus for looking at the world. It is a source of illumination on the rich details and tangled interrelationships in that world. Whatever else it may or may not do, it serves a global function of enlightenment. (Weiss, 1977a, p. 17)

Despite the persuasiveness of the enlightenment model, however, it remains at a very broad level of generality. How, in practice, does social science come to influence policy-making? How is opinion illuminated? What sorts of social research and social science are most effective in having some effect upon the policies of governments and firms?

Varieties of Applied Social Research

Applied social science and applied social research are not homogeneous. This is one of the most important points to appreciate about them. Policy-makers and opinion-makers expect many things from social science, often different in nature. Social scientists themselves pursue different objectives when undertaking applied research. The character of different disciplines and different methodologies sets limits to the uses and usefulness of particular inquiries.

Moreover, there is a very wide range of views about the extent to which the social sciences *should* be useful. There are those in the academic world who ask why the social sciences should be expected to be useful at all. We do not expect the academic study of mathematics, or history, or English literature, to be of direct practical usefulness. Why expect that of sociology or political science? The task of the social scientist is to seek understanding of the world through a combination of theoretical and empirical inquiry of a 'basic' or 'pure' kind. At the other extreme is the practical man or woman who asks, in highly instrumental terms, why social science should be supported at all unless it produces results which are of direct and demonstrable practical usefulness in the development of policy and in practical affairs. Most of those involved in applied social science occupy a position some way between these two extremes, but these extremes do exist, they are not ideal types. Proponents of the 'pure' view are to be found, for example, in universities and are particularly likely to be located in departments of political science or sociology. Proponents of the 'instrumental' view are to be found among members and supporters of the British Conservative government elected in 1979 (see Wilmott, 1980, p. 2) and of the Reagan administration which took office in the United States in 1981.

There is room for both basic and applied social science research, and the former is of longer-term importance for the health of the constituent disciplines. As suggested at the very beginning, however, a dichotomy between basic and applied research is relatively unhelpful, just as is a polarisation between 'pure theory' and 'applied empiricism'. Theory needs to be confronted with empirical evidence in basic research. Evidence needs to be informed by theory and interpreted in the light of it in policy research. Modern versions neither of mediaeval scholasticism ('how many angels can dance on the head of a pin?') nor of Samuel Smilesian hard common sense ('does asking people questions about social matters create more wealth?') correspond to the reality of the place of the social sciences and social research in contemporary society. As Chapter 1 shows, even in Victorian times major empirical social inquiries were carried out. In the latter half of the present century the academic social sciences have been institutionalised and have grown. A major element in both traditions has been to serve as an aid in policy-making and to influence events.

It is probably appropriate to think that there is more than one tradition because of the long-standing distance between social *research* and social *science*, stressed at a number of points in this book. This distance persists today. There is a very wide gap between the general methodological approach to inquiry of members of the Government Statistical Service or staff of commercial market research firms and that of many academic social scientists. Just as in the nineteenth century empiricism held powerful sway, so it still dominates the practice in certain organisations doing applied research. Moreover it is not unknown in academic circles, particularly in social administration. It is necessary to try to be more precise about what is meant by 'applied research'. What follows is an effort to get behind simple antinomies between social research and social science, or saying that the context determines (rather than merely influences) the type of work done, to try to understand the intellectual basis of different conceptions of research application in order to be able to analyse more clearly its possible influence.

Six Types of Influence

'Research' is not a unitary term. It may refer, in the manner discussed earlier, to the collection of data pure and simple, gathering 'the facts'. It may refer, secondly, to the interpretation and understanding of 'the facts' in some kind of broader framework. Much historical research is of this type and many social sciences have taken over this mode of analysis – for example, political science (for example, Headey, 1974; Heclo and Wildavsky, 1974), sociology (for example, Crouch, 1977; Halsey, 1978), or social policy (for example, Valentine, 1967; Blaxter, 1976a). In each case the research starts from a factual basis but places the facts within an analytic framework drawing on the concepts and theories of different social sciences. Or, thirdly, 'research' may refer to causal analysis, the search for the determinants of social conditions, independent and dependent variables, and the identification of factors that produce changes in the world. There are many examples – in education the work of J. W. B. Douglas (1964), Christopher Jencks *et al.* (1972) and Michael Rutter *et al.* (1979); in political behaviour the work of Butler and Stokes (1969); in delinquency research the work of Hirschi and Selvin (1967) and West (1973); in the study of poverty the work of Layard *et al.* (1978) and Townsend (1979). Characteristic of this type of analysis is the search for underlying structure and the determinants of behaviour in a more precise and deterministic way than in the second mode of interpretation and understanding.

If 'research' can be classified by type, it may also be classified in terms of its purpose. Three broad objectives for which applied social research is used may be distinguished. The first is research as intelligence and monitoring, the collection of demographic, economic and social data which are then available to be drawn upon by the policy-maker. The decennial census is the paradigmatic case, but much of the activity of government statisticians compiling data from administrative sources is also of this type. Usually, though not invariably, such data are sought in quantitative form, giving them more accessibility and authority in the eyes of policy-makers.

The second broad purpose is what may be termed 'strategic analysis' (Dainton Report, 1971, pp. 3–4; Donnison, 1978, p. 51). Stategic applied research is grounded in an academic discipline, or disciplines, but firmly oriented toward a problem which has arisen in society. It is considerably wider-ranging than intelligence and monitoring, drawing on more general bodies of ideas. Its purpose is to illuminate a problem in such a way as to permit action to be taken to change the situation revealed. An excellent example of such strategic analysis, applied to a major national problem, is Gunnar Myrdal's (1944) classic study of American race relations, *An American Dilemma*, which combines detailed empirical analysis within a general framework with explicit prescriptive recommendations.

The third distinct purpose served by social research is what may be called 'scientific control'. The natural sciences or medicine serve as a model here. In the control of the spread of disease, for example, science has been used as a means of extending our knowledge of the factors producing sickness to control the incidence of ill-health. The discovery and application of penicillin is but one instance. Macro-economic modelling is a way of simulating the behaviour of the national economy in order to study its behaviour and predict the effects of changes in one part of the system given changes in another part of the system. A powerful underlying assumption of the engineering model of applied social research is that given adequate scientific knowledge of the problem being examined, it should in principle be possible to expose the forces at work through applied research in order to enable the policy-maker to intervene in some way to achieve change.

Three types of analysis, and three broad purposes of applied social research, have been distinguished. These categories are not the most comprehensive that could be developed, but they serve to make important distinctions that enable us to appreciate the diversity of work which is carried on under the name of 'applied social research'. This variety is represented in Figure 7.1, which classifies six different kinds of research according to purpose and type of analysis. This is also an attempt to refine further the distinction between the engineering and enlightenment models discussed earlier.

(1)   *Authoritative Facts*

Applied social research as the production of data has been discussed earlier. One influential version of this role, expounded, for example, by Lord Diamond (Bulmer, 1980a, pp. 162–3) and Benjamin (1973), is that the task of the research is to produce reliable and valid (quantitative) evidence on the basis of which policy-makers can reach decisions. The work of the Government Statistical Service is of this type, to produce comprehensive and authoritative economic and social data for administrators in central government to use in the formulation of policy and the tendering of advice to ministers. Such advice is supposed to be politically neutral and the evidence on which it is based above criticism. Applied research as the production of authoritative facts encompasses not only administratively derived statistics, vital registration data and the census but also a good deal of government social survey research. The large continuous surveys such as the Family Expenditure Survey, General Household Survey and Labour

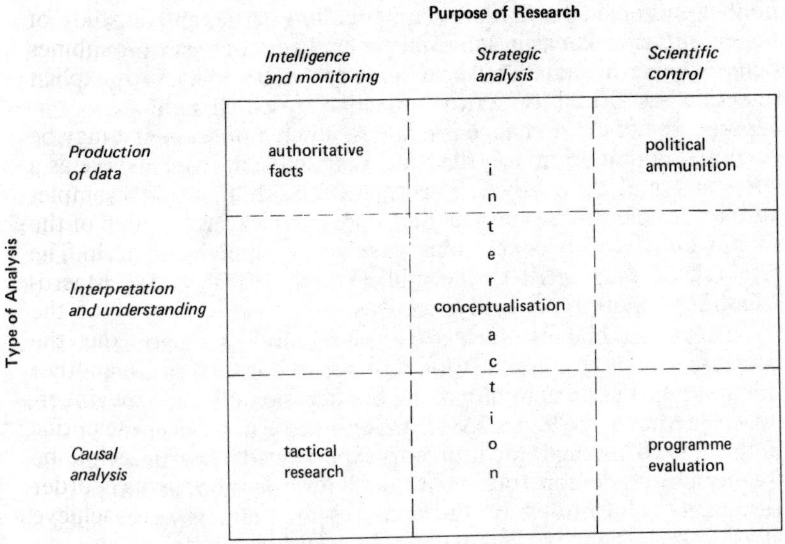
Purpose of Research
Intelligence and monitoring
Strategic analysis
Scientific control
Type of Analysis
Production of data
Interpretation and understanding
Causal analysis
authoritative facts
political ammunition
interaction
conceptualisation
tactical research
programme evaluation

Figure 7.1 *A classification of kinds of applied social research.*

Force Survey (Hakim, 1982, ch. 7) are designed to produce comprehensive factual information on certain topics of direct usefulness to policy-makers. Data on household expenditures from the Family Expenditure Survey, for example, is used in the calculation of weights to apply to different items in the retail price index (*DE Gazette*, 1975).

The limitations of such an empiricist approach to applied social research have been discussed in the second chapter. The consequences of the adoption of such a definition are at least two-fold. Intellectually it confines 'research' to the production of data (albeit of a methodologically respectable quality), exemplifying the 'bucket' theory of the mind. One may note that in natural science such a view of 'research' as the accumulation of factual data has no respectability whatever and is, indeed, regarded as the antithesis of scientific inquiry, in the sense that 'the facts' alone tell one nothing (see Medawar, 1969). Organisationally such a concept of 'research' relegates those who produce such data to the position of subordinate technicians. This point has been developed further in Chapter 6 but it is a major one for the position and influence of applied social research.

(2) *Political Ammunition*

A different though related view of applied research is to see it as providing data which will enable a degree of scientific control of a problem to be achieved. Such use of the findings of social research as political ammunition recognises that policy is formulated within a political system in which there are contending parties and interests. No policy initiative is easily undertaken, and research can provide evidence which will enable those pursuing particular policies to give them scientific respectability. With 'objective' research findings in their support, the case for change is made so much more cogent. Research becomes ammunition for the side that finds its conclusions most congenial and supportive. 'Partisans brandish the evidence in an attempt to neutralise opponents, convince waverers, and bolster supporters. Even if conclusions have to be ripped out of context, research becomes grist to the mill' (Weiss, 1977a, p. 14). It lends scientific support to political objectives.

At its most blatant, such a use of research is demonstrated by pressure groups who commission research to bolster a case which they are arguing. Public opinion polling has occasionally been used in this way (see Marsh, 1979, pp. 268–88). Survey research can easily be used in this way to highlight the problems experienced by particular minority groups and demonstrate their 'need' for attention, action or extra resources. (Unfortunately, the same research almost never suggests any criteria by which policy-makers should weigh 'needs' or adjudicate between worthy competing interest groups.) Or research may be used in political polemics in such a way as to add force to the case which is being argued. Michael Harrington's (1962) rediscovery of poverty in the United States is an excellent example of this use of social science findings.

The use of research as political ammunition is, however, frequently more veiled, and by one means or another given an apparent air of legitimation. The Fabian style of applied research, discussed earlier, is a case in point. The work is nowadays conducted by academics from a university base. The scientific credentials of the work are generally sounder and the political use made of findings much more sophisticated. Nevertheless research data is clearly seen as a political weapon. The part played by Richard Titmuss, Brian Abel-Smith and Peter Townsend in the discovery of poverty in Britain in the late 1950s and early 1960s forced the issue back into the political arena.

> They were convinced that myths about the generosity of the Welfare State had blinkered discussion of social policy, and in the late 1950s they set out to gather the evidence with which to challenge the comfortable assumptions of the day. Their research was explicitly political; they were setting out to reshape policy-makers' interpretation of their environment. (Banting, 1979, pp. 69–70)

Policy-makers, too, may frequently make use of research as political ammunition if it serves their purpose to do so. The evidence for this in

Britain is less easily available because of official secrecy, but in the United States there are numerous cases. 'Many a battle-scarred research veteran ascribes to government agencies only the most self-serving uses of research for justification and agency aggrandisement' (Weiss, 1977a, p. 15).

The setting up of Royal Commissions, discussed in Chapter 5, may in certain circumstances be a way of marshalling political ammunition, partly research-based, for policy change in an area in which governments are unwilling to initiate policy without such independent support. As Lord McGregor has observed:

> Sometimes, official Committees of Inquiry, like the Committee on One-Parent Families [Finer Committee, 1974], are appointed in part as a result of the range and vitality of research in the areas covered by their terms of reference. Such committees are likely to have at least several members expert in different parts of their remit, and they may start work with a clear notion of what their policy choices are and along what lines their main recommendations will run. Their chief task will be to draw together and deploy existing knowledge in such a way as to present the politically influential public with the most compelling supporting arguments for their conclusions. (McGregor, 1980, p. 154)

It is to be expected that applied social research carried out on politically sensitive issues is likely to be used by different parties to the political process. Carol Weiss argues (1977a, p. 15) that this is not improper. Just because sides have been taken is not a reason to discount the effects of research. If an issue is still open, research can add strength to the side which the evidence supports. It gives those who use it confidence, removes lingering doubts and provides an edge in the continuing debate. This is all very well, but an empiricist conception of research as providing political ammunition devalues social science just as much as social research defined as the production of authoritative facts. At worst, it leads to

> attempts to settle public issues by reference to crude ad hoc generalisations. So 'right-wing' facts are refuted by 'left-wing' facts and vice versa, and in the argument which ensues nothing becomes clear except the value-biasses which the authors seek desperately to conceal. (Rex, 1961, p. vii)

The Fabian influence, in particular, dies hard in Britain, but it is a quite inadequate conception of the role of applied social research.

(3)   *Tactical Research*

If the two previous types of research are empiricist, tactical research is based on the engineering model – indeed it is the example *par excellence* of research as problem-solving. By tactical research is meant the social science (and its application and development) needed by governments and industry to further their immediate executive or commercial functions (see Dainton Report, 1971, p. 3). The results of such research are designed to solve practical, operational problems faced by policy-makers. Usually the research is carried out to a specification provided by the policy-maker, who is interested in the answer to a highly specific set of questions concerned with his operating procedures and practices.

In describing what he calls a 'scholarly consultation', Zetterberg tells how he was called upon by a museum to advise it how to increase audience response to museum activities. His analysis of the problem involved an exploratory investigation, studying the response of the public, examining the place of the museum in the artistic reward system, looking at art in relation to social stratification, and developing a theory of art and the circulation of political and economic elites. He then presented his sociological interpretation to the gallery officials and in due course formulated practical advice as to how they might act to increase their audience. Despite the specific nature of the problem it was analysed within an explicit theoretic framework drawn from sociology (Zetterberg, 1962, pp. 135–78).

The sorts of issues tackled by 'in-house' government or industrial research units are frequently of a 'tactical' kind, concerned with a particular client group, service delivery, or an organisational problem to do with the administration of a service. For example, some studies of problems of handicapped groups such as the blind and the deaf may be classed as tactical research, or studies of the advantages of queueing systems in social security offices, or studies of the internal organisation of local authority social service departments. A good deal of industrial sociology carried out within firms is of a tactical kind. Klein usefully discusses a number of cases, for example, the reorganisation of an oil company depot at London Airport in charge of refuelling aircraft, in order to achieve both greater efficiency and higher job satisfaction among the staff (1976, pp. 81–95).

Such tactical research differs from the production of authoritative facts in that it embodies an analytic framework and an attempt to analyse the causes of (narrowly delimited) phenomena in order to make recommendations for intervention. Commonly the intellectual basis for such an analysis – in industrial studies, for instance – lies in either psychological or sociological theories of the middle range. But the objectives of such tactical research tend toward intelligence and monitoring rather than scientific control. Research of this kind is seen more as an extension of the intelligence function of statisticians than a major application of social science as a means of social control. It is useful, but not earth-shattering, again casting the social scientist rather in the role of the technician, although with some claims to independent disciplinary expertise recognised.

(4)   *Programme Evaluation*
The aims and claims of what may be called programme evaluation are much greater, indeed this is the engineering model in full flower. The term 'programme evaluation' is used to refer to a variety of types of research design, variously called action research, evaluation research, social experimentation and project appraisal. Programme evaluation combines a rigorous scientific analysis of causality with the purpose of achieving scientific control. This is the most scientistic conception of applied social research, the 'hard' end of applied social science.

It has several distinguishing characteristics. First, it tends to be the type of applied social research with the most rigorous research design, based upon the logic of the experiment (see Stouffer, 1950). Indeed, many studies of this type actually employ experimental designs or approximations to such designs called 'quasi-experiments' (Cook and Campbell, 1979). Secondly, the use of such designs is intended to enable precise measurements to be made of the effects of independent upon dependent variables, with the emphasis on controlling the situation in which these effects are observed. This is linked to a third characteristic, that the research is designed to observe and report on changes actually occurring in the world, either as a result of policy intervention (whose effects it is the task of the research to study) or as a result of changes built into the design of the research (that is, the research itself actually involves social intervention on a small scale in order to study its effects).

Evaluation research typically has a five-stage structure. (*a*) Find out the goals of the (limited) policy being evaluated; (*b*) translate the goals into measurable indicators of goal achievement; (*c*) collect data on these indicators for the study participants who have been exposed to the programme; (*d*) collect similar data on an equivalent group that has not been exposed to the programme; (*e*) compare the results for the experimental and control groups in relation to the goals set. This design is very similar to the classic experiment, though there are problems in approximating this in the real world.

One type of evaluative research seeks to exploit natural situations or policy initiatives as they occur, to use people in receipt of the product of the policy as the experimental subjects for study and to match them with a comparable control group. There are a number of examples of experimental or quasi-experimental evaluations of this kind from the field of education, particularly in the United States, incorporating quite sophisticated research designs.

The most impressive examples of social research intervention are the American negative income tax experiments carried out since 1968 to investigate the effects of different levels of welfare payments upon work incentive and other social characteristics. This has involved very large expenditure and actual research intervention, whereby the researchers have paid cash benefits to experimental subjects who formed part of a complex research design involving experimental (paid) and control (not paid) subjects. In the New Jersey negative income tax experiment (the earliest), there were a total of twenty-seven treatment groups, including one control group and eight experimental groups in each of the three income strata, the eight experimental groups being differentiated both in terms of their income guarantee levels and the rate of reduction applied when their income exceeded the guarantee level (Kershaw, 1972; Kershaw and Fair, 1976). No social policy programme evaluation research on a large scale of a comparable nature has been carried out in Britain, though there are rigorous limited studies (for example, Cornish and Clarke, 1975).

(5) Interaction

The enlightenment model of research does not assume that scientific control is possible through applied social science. It emphasises the greater openness of the process of influence and more diffuse effects of social scientific inquiry. One pattern of influence which is congruent with such a view (though not strictly speaking a 'type' of social research) is what may be termed 'interaction'. It has been spelled out most clearly in Britain by David Donnison and in the United States by Charles Lindblom and David Cohen. Its main characteristic is a broadly strategic purpose, ranging across a variety of different types of analysis.

Seeing research as 'interaction' focuses primarily upon the political and social context in which research is used. Those engaged in developing policy communicate with many different sources of information, advice and pressure – administrators, politicians, practitioners, planners, journalists, clients, interest groups and social scientists, among others. All these participants are pooling their efforts and knowledge in an attempt to tackle a particular problem. They engage in mutual consultations and discussion, or produce evidence relative to the policy in question. But 'the process is not one of linear order from research to decision but a disorderly set of interconnections and back-and-forthness that defies neat diagrams' (Weiss, 1977a, p. 14). Research is thus only one part of a complicated process that also uses experience, political know-how, practical technologies, pressure and judgement to arrive at policy decisions.

Donnison (1978, pp. 52–4) discusses the example of British housing legislation in the mid-1960s aimed at controlling the level of rents of privately rented accommodation. He emphasises the role of four parties in the discussions which led up to legislation – politicians, administrators, social researchers, and those professionals who commanded the technological means to implement policy (in this case, the mechanism for regulating and fixing rents). He describes the nature of the discussions which went on between them, the to-ing and fro-ing involved, the importance of research findings of the right kind being available at the right time, and the way in which a solution gradually emerged. In this case the solution to a policy problem was worked out among experts, without great involvement of pressure groups and the public, but even among experts the findings of social research were merely one input among many. There were underlying models of the regulatory process being used, one a market view of the problem, the other a social service view. Housing research provided a test of these models, but even that was not definitive since the other experts involved had their own views about the theoretical merits of each. Banting has provided an extended account of this legislation which complements that of Donnison (a participant). He emphasises that although party politics raised the issue of regulation originally, expertise shaped the response. Party ideology and pressure group influence played a small part in influencing a solution worked out among specialists. But in that process social scientists interacted with the other participants to arrive at the solution (Banting, 1979, pp. 14–65).

How far can this case be generalised to decision-making within the British political system? Certainly the Fabian doctrine of 'permeation' of the political structure by influencing both politicians and administrators fits with such a model of interaction. Social networks which link leading social scientists to policy-makers have clearly been important in social science influencing policy. The 'close-knit world of interlocking networks and institutions clustered in the single, overwhelmingly dominant centre of London' (Sharpe, 1975, p. 28) is the setting for interaction. When a social democratic government of the left or centre is in power the voice of social scientists tends to be heard, and this influence has led social scientists to believe that this is an effective model of research utilisation.

In its British version, however, it has serious weaknesses. It depends on politicians and administrators being willing to listen and on the legitimation of social science as having something to contribute. When leading politicians and leading academics have close personal ties this appears not to be a problem; when politicians are unsympathetic it not only breaks the ties but threatens all social science through guilt by association. The political tinge of much social science in Britain is also associated with a lack of technically informed criticism of the results of research.

> British sociology lacks that plurality of openly competing institutions which, in Popper's terms, ensures that work of integrity is done even by scientists who lack integrity . . . In this country any research worker who comes up with vaguely progressive conclusions is likely to get an uncritical hearing, however rubbishy his work. (Hope, 1978, pp. 260–1)

It may be argued, however, that the interactive model is a convincing one even in situations where social scientists are less politically committed and where they contribute to the policy-making process more in the role of scientists. The model underlying Lindblom and Cohen's critique of much professional social inquiry is one of decision-making as discrete, incremental, partisan mutual adjustment in which many factors play a part. To claim, as the engineering model does, a special status for social science is unwarranted and illegitimate. What is required is an interactive model of the problem-solving process in its widest sense, including political, market, philosophical and other elements (Lindblom and Cohen, 1979, p. 32). This is a legitimate point to make about the process by which policy-decisions are reached. It is not, however, necessarily the case that the role of social science research is as limited as they appear to believe. This role depends upon what research can contribute; it does not depend simply on showing that the policy process is a complex one. That contribution remains a variable one, depending on the model espoused by the researcher.

(6) Conceptualisation
An alternative view of applied research highlights its characteristics as a tool of interpretation and understanding for strategic analysis. In this view social science provides a way of looking at and approaching policy problems. Social science can influence the ways in which society defines phenomena as 'problems' or can revise the ways in which issues are thought about.

> Thus social research may sensitise decision-makers to new issues and turn what were non-problems into policy problems (a current controversial example is 'white flight'). In turn, it may convert existing social problems into non-problems (e.g. marijuana use). It may drastically revise the way that a society thinks about issues (e.g. acceptable rates of unemployment), the facets of the issue that are viewed as susceptible to alteration, and the alternative measures it considers. Global reorientation of this sort is not likely to be the outcome of a single study on even one specific line of enquiry. But

over time and with the accumulation of evidence, such use can have far-reaching implications. (Weiss, 1977a, p. 16)

Social science research may exercise its most important influence through affecting the general frameworks that policy-makers employ to look at issues, the implicit theories that they use. This links up with the more general argument of Janowitz about the enlightenment functions of research, that the results of social science become widely diffused in the longer term and percolate into general cultures. The effects of the sociological and psychological study of race relations, for example, has over a period of half a century helped to transform the way in which race problems are regarded. Similarly in educational research sociological perspectives have had an important impact in bringing about a shift from a genetic to an environmental perspective.

Empirical evidence from studies of research utilisation support this interpretation of the use of research. Nathan Caplan's (1976) research on federal government officials in Washington shows that the orienting function of research is of pre-eminent importance. Carol Weiss and Michael Bucuvalas, in a study of 155 federal state and local policy-makers in the mental health field, found that the most important use made of research was to help structure people's perceptions of social reality:

> officials are engaged by the concepts of social science, which contribute to their understanding of the nature of social problems, the range of possible options for addressing problems, and the context in which remedies must be applied. In new program areas, where officials lack firsthand experience, such orienting perspectives are particularly valuable. They use research ideas, too, to rethink old program assumptions and as scaffolding for building new formulations. (Weiss, 1980b, p. 396)

The evidence for this conclusion is presented in a recent monograph (Weiss, 1980a) which shows effectively that the engineering model bears little relation to how policy-makers at different levels in government make use of social research. Two-thirds of policy-makers acknowledged that social science influenced them. They were unable to find, however, very many instances of actual studies read which led to a change in attitude or a different perspective upon a policy issue. Weiss's interpretation of this phenomenon agrees with that of Nathan Caplan. Ideas that policy-makers obtain and attribute to the social sciences – for example, that attitudes tend to follow behaviour rather than govern behaviour – are integrated into their entire perspective upon a problem. If a respondent is requested to cite instances of making direct use of social science studies, it is as if he or she is being asked to atomise his or her conception of social reality, taking knowledge out of its context: a context without which the knowledge would not have been retained in the first place (Caplan *et al.*, 1975, pp. 18–19).

> Those social scientists who expect research to be authoritative enough to *determine* policy choices are giving insufficient weight to the many and varied sources from which people derive their understandings and policy preferences . . . People in official positions often do not catalogue research separately in their minds. They interpret it as they read it in the light of their other knowledge, and they *merge* it with all the information and generalisations in their stock. Therefore they find it difficult to identify the contribution that one study, or even a group of studies, has made to their actions. (Weiss, 1980a, p. 161)

Research and Values in the Policy-Making Process

Another major finding of Weiss's study was that government officials in the mental health field did not see themselves as making decisions. Questions about use of particular pieces of social science research implies there is a clear-cut *output* in the form of discrete decisions. But the work of officials, as they portrayed it, was much more to recommend, advise, confer, develop plans, write guidelines, report, assist, meet, argue, or consult than reach decisions. This reflects dispersion of responsibility and participation of multiple actors in decision-making, division of authority between federal, state and local levels, and the gradual and amorphous process by means of which many decisions emerge. Clearly there may be an element of self-deception in these responses, but it seems more likely that they provide an important insight into the nature of decision-making in many parts of contemporary government. Academic studies of decision-making tend to focus upon major political issues which are highly controversial. But much ordinary bureaucratic work is not of this kind, and Weiss's data are probably an accurate reflection of the nature of the policy-making process as it is perceived by many participants.

This finding fits, too, with Lindblom and Cohen's (1979) attack on what they see as the over-authoritative claims made on behalf of professional social inquiry. A further criticism which can be levelled specifically at the view of research as providing political ammunition is that policy is not determined directly by the publication of research results showing that something needs (or does not need) to be done. How policy evolves is a much more drawn-out, complex and interactive process, in which research has a part to play but not necessarily one of direct and immediate influence.

A different line of argument is to emphasise the importance of value-choice in determining which policies are pursued. The use made of research, it is then argued, depends on how congruent the results are with particular normative positions. In a sense this is a view that research can be used as ammunition provided it backs up the right causes. More sophisticated versions emphasise the extent to which particular social science frameworks embody value assumptions, and hence influence the way in which social problems are perceived (see Rule, 1978).

I have considerable sympathy with an emphasis on the role of values in policy research and have discussed this elsewhere (Bulmer, 1978, pp. 22–7). I agree with the argument that many of the choices faced in policy-making and policy research are ultimately of a moral kind.

> There is no central, abiding, over-arching principle that can fill the gaps in understanding, resolve the quandaries of action, order the conflicts of human purposes or resolve the conflicting interpretations of action that competing frameworks pose . . . I am inclined to take the view that these dilemmas are desirable, because they pose moral choices and hence permit a debate about moral purposes. If there were no dilemmas in social action, then there would be no opportunity for meaningful moral discourse on human affairs. (Rein, 1976, p. 259)

Nevertheless, the value-laden character of social science can undoubtedly be exaggerated, to the point where all differences of view are seen as a matter of taste and no standards are admitted for judging the rightness or wrongness of particular analyses. Such extreme relativism is partly a consequence of an excessive devotion to the sociology of knowledge – in the British context exaggerated by the weight given in undergraduate sociology courses to the issue of 'objectivity'. There are indeed major issues to be considered here (see Weber, 1949; Myrdal, 1958; Riley, 1974), but the net result of raising them often seems to be to instil a disbelief in the possibility of objective scientific inquiry and to lead to various forms of shallow relativism.

Another case of value-intrusion into research is provided by the subject of British social administration, discussed briefly in Chapter 1, which has no precise analogue in some other countries such as the United States or Canada. Social administration is not distinguished by a coherent body of theory, though it does make use of a set of distinctive concepts which include 'need', 'welfare' and 'citizenship'. Its peculiar blend of empirical data and philosophy thrives at the expense of theory – too much is prescribed and too little is explained, values intrude too forcefully. One critic cogently suggests that:

in British social policy and administration, we begin with fact-finding and end in moral rhetoric, still lacking those explanatory theories that might show the process as a whole and reveal the relations of the separate problems to one another. (Pinker, 1971, p. 12)

Where explanation is attempted, the line of influence tends to be from normative theory to explanatory theory, rather than in the reverse direction (Pinker, 1981, p. 9). Interest in the role of theory for the study of social policy is growing but needs to be married more firmly than it has been to date with empirical inquiry conceived of as something more than merely the accumulation of facts.

Conclusion

If a conclusion is required let it be one about what social science can hope to contribute to policy. Social science is likely to contribute most by blending its theoretical insights with empirical inquiry, by cultivating the interpretation and understanding of the world through a judicious mixture of the concrete and the abstract. In British social science at the present time there is too much of one or the other. In sociology abstraction runs rampant.

> Many early and even some contemporary social scientists appear to consider a conceptual analysis of society as if it were a substitute for research. The survival of the tradition of the social philosopher has retarded the development of sociological research. (Burgess, 1945, p. 475)

In social administration there is a strong tradition of empiricist investigation, linked to a powerful normative orientation in favour of social justice, with relatively little attention to theory and explanation.

The most effective contributions of social science to policy have been made in areas where the problem tackled was narrowly enough defined so that both theory and evidence could be brought to bear on the subject, whether it was health, illness, unemployment, disability, poverty, race relations, housing, or whatever. A generation ago T. H. Marshall observed that while the general or theoretical sociologist may become a slave to his concepts, the passionately empirical investigator may become a slave to his methods. Stepping-stones into the middle distance (Marshall, 1946, p. 22), or what R. K. Merton calls 'theories of the middle range' (1957, pp. 9–10), offer a middle way between a vague and abstract philosophy and pure description. Nor need social scientists be ashamed about wishing to be useful. There are real advantages in relating research to current issues. It provides stimulation and purpose, and is less likely to lead to haphazard inquiries. Moreover, facilities are available on a wider scale through co-operation with public authorities.

> Much of the data now needed can be collected only by public authorities, and when the needs of the moment urge them to action, social scientists can reap the benefit. At the same time, co-operative or parallel studies by social scientists may greatly increase the value of official inquiries. (Marshall, 1946, p. 23)

Social scientists have a particularly important role to play in trying to enrich policy research, in giving more body to the thin empiricist inquiries which often pass for 'research' in government and the private sector, and in showing the relevance of middle-range theory to many of the problems faced by policy-makers. This requires effort on their part, an adjustment to the world of policy and a recognition of their own limitations.

In the realm of policy the case for broader-based research needs to be continually argued. Research of a strategic kind, occupying the middle ground between basic social science research and research addressed to specific practical questions of a short-term kind, is needed and must be grounded in theory. Social science research can be the foundation for broad-based advice, not just discrete one-off studies.

> [R]esearch commissioned by government should include a fairly sizeable proportion which is specified in broad terms, is concerned with processes rather than immediate issues, and is the subject of continuing discussion between researchers and those in government – and, for that matter, those outside it who are interested in the policy debate. (Wilmott, 1980, p. 7; see also Blume, 1979, pp. 333–4)

The modes of influence through conceptualisation and interaction, discussed earlier in this chapter, show that this is how research is actually used in practice. The way in which policy research is framed and specified therefore needs to be in accord with that use. A stronger and more robust applied social research requires both infusions of social science and a recognition by policy-makers that broader perspectives can and do aid them in their task. If this can be achieved, social policy research may be made more effective and its potential for social usefulness realised more adequately in the future than in the past.

References

Abel-Smith, B., and Townsend, P. (1965), *The Poor and the Poorest* (London: Bell).

Abrams, M. (1951), *Social Surveys and Social Action* (London: Heinemann).

Abrams, P. (1968), *The Origins of British Sociology 1834–1914* (Chicago: University of Chicago Press).

Acland, H. (1980), 'Research as stage management: the case of the Plowden Committee', in Bulmer (1980b), pp. 34–57.

Ainsworth, M. D. (1962), 'The effects of maternal deprivation: a review of findings and controversy in the context of research strategy', in *Deprivation of Maternal Care: A Reassessment of Its Effects* (Geneva: World Health Organisation).

Anderson, P. (1968), 'Components of the national culture', *New Left Review*, vol. 50, pp. 3–57.

Annan, N. (1955), 'The intellectual aristocracy', in J. H. Plumb (ed.), *Studies in Social History: A Tribute to G. M. Trevelyan* (London: Longman), pp. 241–87.

Annan, N. (1959), *The Curious Strength of Positivism in English Social Thought*, L. T. Hobhouse Memorial Trust Lecture No. 28, 1958 (London: Oxford University Press).

Askham, J. (1975), *Fertility and Deprivation: A Study of Differential Fertility Amongst Working-Class Families in Aberdeen* (Cambridge: Cambridge University Press).

Bakke, E. W. (1933), *The Unemployed Man* (London: Nisbet).

Banfield, E. C. (1970), *The Unheavenly City: The Nature and Future of Our Urban Crisis* (Boston, Mass.: Little, Brown).

Banting, K. (1979), *Poverty, Politics and Policy* (London: Macmillan).

Barnes, J. (1975), *Educational Priority 3: Curriculum Innovation in London EPAs* (London: HMSO).

Bebbington, A. C., and Davies, B. (1980), 'Territorial need indicators: a new approach', *Journal of Social Policy*, vol. 9, pp. 145–68 and 433–62.

Bell, D. (1966), 'Government by Commission', *The Public Interest*, vol. 3 (Spring), pp. 3–9.

Benjamin, B. (1973), 'Research strategies in social service departments of local authorities in Great Britain', *Journal of Social Policy*, vol. 2, pp. 13–26.

Berthoud, R. (1976), *The Disadvantages of Inequality: A Study of Social Deprivation* (London: Macdonald & Jarvis).

Blackburn, R., and Mann, M. (1979), *The Working Class in the Labour Market* (London: Macmillan).

Blackstone, T. V., Gales, K., Hadley, R., and Lewis, W. (1970), *Students in Conflict: LSE in 1967* (London: Weidenfeld & Nicolson).

Blaug, M. (1963), 'The myth of the old Poor Law and the making of the New', *Journal of Economic History*, vol. 23, pp. 151–84.

Blaug, M. (1964), 'The Poor Law re-examined', *Journal of Economic History*, vol. 24, pp. 229–45.

Blaxter, M. (1976a), *The Meaning of Disability* (London: Heinemann).

Blaxter, M. (1976b), 'Social class and health inequalities', in Carter and Peel (1976), pp. 111–25.

Blaxter, M. (1981), *The Health of the Children* (London: Heinemann).

Blume, S. S. (1979), 'Policy studies and social policy in Britain', *Journal of Social Policy*, vol. 8, pp. 311–34.

Blume, S. S. (1980), 'Explanation and Social Policy: "the" problem of social inequalities in health', Department of Social Science, London School of Economics, mimeo.

Booth, C. (1889–1903), *Life and Labour of the People in London*, 17 vols (London: Macmillan).

Bowl, R. (1976), 'A survey of surveys', *New Society*, 28 October, p. 195.

Bowlby, J. (1951), *Maternal Care and Mental Health* (Geneva: World Health Organisation).

Bowley, A. L. (1915), *Livelihood and Poverty* (London: Bell).

Bowley, A. L., and Hogg, M. H. (1925), *Has Poverty Diminished?* (London: P. S. King).

Boyd Orr, J. (1936), *Food, Health and Income: Report on a Survey of the Adequacy of Diet in Relation to Income* (London: Macmillan).

Brannen, P. (ed.) (1975), *Entering the World of Work: Some Sociological Perspectives* (London: HMSO for Department of Employment).

Briggs, A. (1961), *A Study of the Work of Seebohm Rowntree* (London: Longman).

Brotherston, J. (1976), 'Inequality: is it inevitable?', in Carter and Peel (1976), pp. 73–104.

Brown, G. W. (1976), 'Social causes of disease', in D. Tuckett (ed.), *An Introduction to Medical Sociology* (London: Tavistock), pp. 291–333.

Brown, G. W., NiBhrokhain, M. N., and Harris, T. (1975), 'Social class and psychiatric disturbance among women in urban population', *Sociology*, vol. 9, pp. 225–54.

Brown, G. W., and Harris, T. (1978), *The Social Origins of Depression* (London: Tavistock).

Brown, M. J., and Bowl, R. (1976), 'Study of local authority chronic sick and disabled persons surveys', Social Services Unit, University of Birmingham, mimeo.

Bulmer, M. (ed.) (1977), *Mining and Social Change: Durham County in the Twentieth Century* (London: Croom Helm).

Bulmer, M. (ed.) (1978), *Social Policy Research* (London: Macmillan).

Bulmer, M. (1979), 'Concepts in the analysis of qualitative data', *Sociological Review*, vol. 27, pp. 651–77.

Bulmer, M. (1980a), 'The Royal Commission on the Distribution of Income and Wealth', in Bulmer (1980b), pp. 158–179.

Bulmer, M. (ed.) (1980b), *Social Research and Royal Commissions* (London: Allen & Unwin).

Bulmer, M. (1981a), 'Quantification and Chicago social science: a neglected tradition', *Journal of the History of the Behavioural Sciences*, vol. 17, no. 3, pp. 312–31.

Bulmer, M. (1981b), 'Charles S. Johnson, Robert E. Park, and the research methods of the Chicago Commission on Race Relations, 1919–22', *Ethnic and Racial Studies*, vol. 4, pp. 289–306.

Burgess, E. W. (1945), 'Sociological research methods', *American Journal of Sociology*, vol. 50, pp. 474–82.

Butler, D., and Stokes, D. (1969), *Political Change in Britain* (London: Macmillan).

Byrne, D., Williamson, W., and Fletcher, B. (1975), *The Poverty of Education* (London: Martin Robertson).

Caine, S. (1963), *The History of the Foundation of the London School of Economics and Political Science* (London: London School of Economics and Bell).

Caplan, N., Morrison, A., and Stambaugh, R. J. (1975), *The Use of Social Science Knowledge in Policy Decisions at the National Level: A Report to Respondents* (Ann Arbor, Michigan: Centre for Research on Utilisation of Scientific Knowledge, Institute for Social Research, University of Michigan).

Caplan, N. (1976), 'Social research and national policy: who gets used, by whom, for what purpose, and with what effects?' *International Social Science Journal*, vol. 28, pp. 187–94.

Carley, M. (1981), *Social Measurement and Social Indicators* (London: Allen & Unwin).

Carter, C. O., and Peel, J. (eds) (1976), *Equalities and Inequalities in Health* (London: Academic Press).

Cartwright, T. J. (1975), *Royal Commissions and Departmental Committees in Britain* (London: Hodder & Stoughton).

Casler, L. (1961), *Maternal Deprivation: A Critical Review of the Literature* (London: Monographs of the Society for Research in Child Development, No. 26).

Chapman, R. A. (ed.) (1973), *The Role of Commissions in Policy-Making* (London: Allen & Unwin).

Checkland, S., and Checkland, E. (1974), *The Poor Law Report of 1834* (Harmondsworth: Penguin).

Cherns, A., and Perry, N. (1976), 'The development and structure of social science research in Britain', in Crawford and Perry (1976), pp. 61–90.

Chicago Commission on Race Relations (1922), *The Negro in Chicago* (Chicago: University of Chicago Press).

Clapham Report (1946), *Report of the Committee on the Provision for Social and Economic Research*, Cmd 6868 (London: HMSO).

Clark, G. N. (1948), *Science and Social Welfare in the Age of Newton* (London: Oxford University Press).

Clarke, A. M., and Clarke, A. D. B. (1976), *Early Experience: Myth and Evidence* (London: Open Books).

Cleveland, H. (1964), 'Inquiry into presidential inquirers', in D. B. Johnson and J. L. Walker (eds), *The Dynamics of the American Presidency* (New York: Wiley), pp. 291–4.

Clokie, H. M., and Robinson, J. W. (1937), *Royal Commissions of Inquiry* (Stanford, Calif.: Stanford University Press).

Coates, B. E., Johnston, R. J., and Knox, P. L. (1977), *Geography and Inequality* (London: Oxford University Press).

Coffield, F., Robinson, P., and Sarsby, J. (1981), *A Cycle of Deprivation? A Case Study of Four Families* (London: Heinemann).

Cohen, D. K., and Garrett, M. S. (1975), 'Reforming educational policy with applied social research', *Harvard Educational Review*, vol. 45, pp. 17–43.

Cole, S. (1972), 'Continuity and institutionalisation in science', in A. Oberschall (ed.), *The Establishment of Empirical Sociology* (New York: Harper & Row), pp. 73–129.

Coleman, J. S. (1972), *Policy Research in the Social Sciences* (Morristown, NJ: General Learning Systems).

Coleman, J. S., Campbell, E. Q., Hobson, C. J., McPartland, J., Mood, A., Wingfield, F. D., and York, R. L. (1966), *Equality of Educational Opportunity* (Washington, DC: Office of Education, US Department of Health, Education and Welfare).

Cook, T. D., and Campbell, D. T. (1979), *Quasi-Experimentation: Design and Analysis Issues for Field Settings* (Chicago: Rand McNally).

Cornish, D. E., and Clarke, R. V. G. (1975), *Residential Treatment and its Effects on Delinquency*, Home Office Research Unit Studies, No. 32 (London: HMSO).

Corrigan, P. (1982), *State Formation and Moral Regulation in Nineteenth Century Britain* (London: Macmillan).

Coser, L. A. (1956), *The Functions of Social Conflict* (New York: The Free Press).

Crawford, E., and Perry, N. (eds) (1976), *Demands for Social Knowledge: The Role of Research Organisations* (London: Sage).

Cronin, T. E., and Greenberg, S. D. (eds) (1969), *The Presidential Advisory System* (New York: Harper & Row).

Crouch, C. (1977), *Class Conflict and the Industrial Relations Crisis* (London: Heinemann).

Cullen, M. J. (1975), *The Statistical Movement in Early Victorian Britain: The Foundations of Empirical Social Research* (Hassocks: Harvester Press).

Dahrendorf, R. (1980), *Life Chances: Approaches to Social and Political Theory* (London: Weidenfeld & Nicolson).

Dainton Report (1971), 'The future of the research council system', in *A Framework for Government Research and Development*, Cmnd 4184 (London: HMSO).

Daniel, W. W. (1968), *Racial Discrimination in England* (Harmondsworth: Penguin).

Davie, R., Butler, N., and Goldstein, H. (1972), *From Birth to Seven: A Report of the National Child Development Study* (London: Longman).

Davies, B. (1968), *Social Needs and Resources in Local Services* (London: Michael Joseph).

Davis, A., McIntosh, N., and Williams, J. (1977), *The Management of Deprivation: Final Report of the Southwark Community Development Project* (London: Polytechnic of the South Bank).

DE Gazette (1975), 'The unstatistical reader's guide to the Retail Price Index', *Department of Employment Gazette* (October), pp. 971–8.

Dean, A. L. (1969), 'Ad hoc commissions for policy formulation?', in Cronin and Greenberg (1969), pp. 101–16.

Derthick, M. (1971), 'On commissionship – Presidential variety', Public Policy, vol. 19, pp. 623–38.

DHSS (1980), 'Inequalities in health: report of a research working group', Department of Health and Social Security, mimeo.

Dibelius, W. (1930), England (London: Cape).

Dicey, A. V. (1905), Lectures on the Relation between Law and Public Opinion in Britain during the Nineteenth Century (London: Macmillan).

Donnison, D. V., Cockburn, C., and Corlett, T. (1961), Housing since the Rent Act (London: Bell).

Donnison, D. V. (1973), 'The development of social administration', in W. D. Birrell, P. A. R. Hillyard, A. S. Murie and D. J. D. Roche (eds), Social Administration: Readings in Applied Social Science (Harmondsworth: Penguin), pp. 28–41.

Donnison, D. V. (1978), 'Research for policy', in Bulmer (1978), pp. 44–66.

Donnison, D. (1980), 'Committees and committeemen', in Bulmer (1980b), pp. 9–17.

Douglas, J. W. B. (1964), The Home and the School (London: McGibbon & Kee).

Drew, E. (1968), 'On giving oneself a hotfoot: government by commission', The Atlantic, vol. 221 (May), pp. 45–9.

Dror, Y. (1971), Design for Policy Sciences (New York: Elsevier).

Eckland, B., and Kent, D. P. (1968), 'Socialisation and social structure', in Perspectives on Human Deprivation: Biological, Psychological and Sociological (Washington DC: Department of Health, Education and Welfare).

Edwards, J. (1978), 'Social indicators, urban deprivation and positive discrimination', in Bulmer (1978), pp. 215–27.

Faris, R. E. L. (1970), Chicago Sociology 1920–32 (Chicago: University of Chicago Press).

Farr, W. (1885), Vital Statistics (London: Sanitary Institute; repr. Metuchen, NJ: Scarecrow Press, 1975).

Farrell, C. (1980), 'The Royal Commission on the National Health Service', Policy and Politics, vol. 8, pp. 189–203.

Finer, S. E. (1952), The Life and Times of Sir Edwin Chadwick (London: Methuen).

Finer Committee (1974), Report of the Committee on One-Parent Families, Cmnd 5629 (London: HMSO).

Floud, J. E., A. H. Halsey, and F. M. Martin (1956), Social Class and Educational Opportunity (London: Heinemann).

Flowerdew, A. D. J. (1980), 'A commission and a cost-benefit study', in Bulmer (1980b), pp. 85–109.

Ford, P. (1934), Work and Wealth in a Modern Port (London: Allen & Unwin).

Foster, C., Jackman, R., and Perlman, M. (1980), Local Government Finance in a Unitary State (London: Allen & Unwin).

Fried, A., and Elman, R. (1971), Charles Booth's London (Harmondsworth: Penguin).

General Household Survey (1971–   ) *Reports* (London: HMSO for OPCS Social Survey Division).

Gittus, E. (1976), 'Deprived areas and social planning', in D. T. Herbert and R. J. Johnson (eds) *Social Areas in Cities II: Spatial Perspectives on Problems and Policies* (Chichester: Wiley), pp. 209–33.

Glass, D. V. (1950), 'The application of social research', *British Journal of Sociology*, vol. 1, pp. 17–30.

Glass, D. V. (1973), *Numbering the People* (Farnborough: Saxon House).

Glennerster, H., and Hoyle, E. (1972), 'Educational research and educational policy', *Journal of Social Policy*, vol. 1, pp. 193–212.

Gordon, M. (1973), 'The social survey movement and sociology in the United States', *Social Problems*, vol. 21, pp. 284–98.

Gosnell, H. F. (1934), 'British Royal Commissions of Inquiry', *Political Science Quarterly*, vol. 49, pp. 84–118.

Gouldner, A. W. (1954), *Patterns of Industrial Bureaucracy* (New York: The Free Press).

Greer, S. (1969), *The Logic of Social Inquiry* (Chicago: Aldine).

Hakim, C. (1982), *Secondary Analysis in Social Research* (London: Allen & Unwin).

Hall, P. (1980), 'The Seebohm Committee and the under-use of research', in Bulmer (1980b), pp. 67–84.

Halsey, A. H. (1972), *Educational Priority* (London: HMSO).

Halsey, A. H. (1978), *Change in British Society* (Oxford: Oxford University Press).

Hamilton, Lord George (1922), *Parliamentary Reminiscences and Reflections 1886–1906* (London: Murray).

Hanser, C. J. (1965), *Guide to Decision: the Royal Commission* (Totowa, NJ: Bedminster Press).

Harrington, M. (1962), *The Other America: Poverty in the United States* (Harmondsworth: Penguin).

Harris, A. I., with E. Cox and C. R. W. Smith (1971), *Handicapped and Impaired in Great Britain* (London: HMSO for OPCS Social Survey Division).

Harris, A. I., and Head, E. (1971), *Sample Surveys in Local Authority Areas with Particular Reference to the Handicapped and Elderly: A Guide Commissioned by DHSS* (London: OPCS).

Harrop, M. (1980), 'Social research and market research', *Sociology*, vol. 14, pp. 277–81.

Hart, N. (1978), 'Health and inequality', Department of Sociology, University of Essex, Colchester, mimeo; and London: Macmillan, forthcoming.

Hawthorn, G., and Carter, H. (1977), 'The concept of deprivation', Social and Political Sciences Committee, University of Cambridge, for DHSS/SSRC Transmitted Deprivation Programme, mimeo.

Headey, B. (1974), *British Cabinet Ministers* (London: Allen & Unwin).

Heclo, H., and Wildavsky, A. (1974), *The Private Government of Public Money* (London: Macmillan).

Hennock, E. P. (1976), 'Poverty and social theory in England: the experience of the 1880s', *Social History*, vol. 1, pp. 67–91.

Herbert, A. P. (1961), 'Anything but action? A study of the uses and abuses of committees of inquiry', in R. Harris (ed.), *Radical Reaction* (London: Hutchinson for the Institute of Economic Affairs), pp. 251–302.

Heyworth Report (1965), *Report of the Committee on Social Studies*, Cmnd 2660 (London: HMSO).

Hindess, B. (1977), *Philosophy and Methodology of the Social Sciences* (Hassocks: Harvester Press).

Hirschi, T., and Selvin, H. (1967), *Delinquency Research: An Appraisal of Analytic Methods* (reissued 1973 in paperback under the title *Principles of Survey Analysis*) (New York: The Free Press).

HMSO (1972), *A Framework for Government Research and Development*, Cmnd 5046 (London: HMSO).

HMSO (1981), *Government Statistical Services*, Cmnd 8236 (London: HMSO).

Holtermann, S. (1975), 'Areas of urban deprivation in Great Britain: an analysis of 1971 Census data', *Social Trends*, vol. 6, pp. 33–47.

Hood, R. (1974), 'Criminology and penal change: a case study of the nature and impact of some recent advice to government', in R. Hood (ed.), *Crime, Criminology and Public Policy* (London: Heinemann), pp. 375–90.

Hope, K. (1978), 'Indicators of the state of society', in Bulmer (1978), pp. 244–67.

Hutt, A. (1933), *The Condition of the Working Class in Britain* (London: Martin Lawrence).

Illsley, R. (1980), *Professional or Public Health: Sociology in Health and Medicine* (London: Nuffield Provincial Hospitals Trust: 1980 Rock Carling Fellowship).

Janowitz, M. (1970), *Political Conflict* (Chicago: Quadrangle Books).

Janowitz, M. (1972), *Sociological Models and Social Policy* (Morristown, NJ: General Learning Systems).

Jencks, C., Smith, M., Acland, H., Bane, M. J., Cohen, D., Gintis, H., Heyns, B., and Michelson, S. (1972), *Inequality* (Harmondsworth: Penguin).

Jones, D. C. (ed.) (1934), *The Social Survey of Merseyside*, 3 vols (Liverpool: Liverpool University Press).

Jones, D. C. (1948), *Social Surveys* (London: Hutchinson).

Jones, E., and Eyles, J. (1977), *An Introduction to Social Geography* (London: Oxford University Press).

Kahn, H. (1964), *Repercussions of Redundancy* (London: Allen & Unwin).

Karl, B. E. (1969), 'Presidential planning and social science research: Mr Hoover's experts', *Perspectives in American History*, vol. 3, pp. 347–409.

Keating, P. (ed.) (1976), *Into Unknown England 1866–1913: Selections from the Social Explorers* (London: Fontana).

Kerner Report (1968), *Report of the National Advisory Commission on Civil Disorders* (Washington, DC: Government Printing Office).

Kershaw, D. T. (1972), 'A negative income-tax experiment', *Scientific American*, vol. 227, no. 4 (October), pp. 19–25.

Kershaw, D. T., and Fair, J. (1976), *The New Jersey Income-Maintenance Experiment I: Operations, Surveys and Administration* (New York: Academic Press).

Keynes, J. M. (1936), *The General Theory of Employment, Interest and Money* (London: Macmillan).

Kilroy-Silk, R. (1973), 'The Donovan Royal Commission on Trade Unions', in Chapman (1973), pp. 42–80.

Klein, L. (1976), *A Social Scientist in Industry* (London: Gower Press).

Knorr, K. D. (1977), 'Policy-makers' use of social science knowledge: symbolic or instrumental?', in Weiss (1977b), pp. 165–82.

Komarovsky, M. (ed.) (1975), *Sociology and Public Policy: the Case of the Presidential Commissions* (New York: Elsevier).

Kosa, J., and Zola, J. K. (eds) (1976), *Poverty and Health: A Sociological Analysis* (Cambridge, Mass.: Harvard University Press).

Kraft, J. (1969), 'The Washington Lawyers', in Cronin and Greenberg (1969), pp. 150–5.

Lambert, J. (1963), *Sir John Simon, 1816–1904, and English Social Administration* (London: McGibbon & Kee).

Larsen, O. N. (1975), 'The Commission on Obscenity and Pornography: form, function and failure', in Komarovsky (1975), pp. 9–41.

Lasswell, H. (1951), 'The policy orientation', in D. Lerner and H. Lasswell (eds), *The Policy Sciences* (Stanford, Calif.: Stanford University Press), pp. 3–15.

Lawless, P. (1979), *Urban Deprivation and Government Initiative* (London: Faber).

Layard, R. (ed.) (1972), *Cost-Benefit Analysis* (Harmondsworth: Penguin).

Layard, R., Piachaud, D., and Stewart, M. (1978), *The Causes of Poverty: A Background Paper to Report No. 6*, RCDIW Background Paper No. 5 (London: HMSO).

Lazarsfeld, P. F., and Reitz, J. G. (1975), *An Introduction to Applied Sociology* (New York: Elsevier).

Leacock, E. B. (1971), *The Culture of Poverty: A Critique* (New York: Simon & Schuster).

Lecuyer, B., and Oberschall, A. (1968), 'Sociology: the early history of empirical social research', in D. Sills (ed.), *International Encyclopaedia of the Social Sciences* (New York: Macmillan).

Leete, R., and Fox, J. (1977), 'Registrar General's social class: origins and use'. *Population Trends*, no. 8, pp. 1–7.

Lewis, O. (1966), *La Vida: A Puerto Rican Family in the Culture of Poverty – San Juan and New York* (New York: Random House).

Lindblom, C. E., and Cohen, D. K. (1979), *Usable Knowledge: Social Science and Social Problem Solving* (New Haven, Conn.: Yale University Press).

Lipsky, M., and Olson, D. J. (1977), *Commission Politics: The Processing of Racial Crisis in America* (Rutgers, NJ: Transaction Books).

Little, A. N., and Mabey, C. (1972), 'An index for designation of educational priority areas', in A. Shonfield and S. Shaw (eds), *Social Indicators and Social Policy* (London: Heinemann), pp. 67–93.

MacDonagh, O. (1977), *Early Victorian Government* (London: Weidenfeld & Nicolson).

McGregor, O. R. (1957), 'Social research and social policy in the nineteenth century', *British Journal of Sociology*, vol. 8, pp. 146–57.

McGregor, O. R. (1980), 'The Royal Commission on the Press, 1974–7: a note', in Bulmer (1980b), pp. 150–7.

McIntyre, A. (1972), 'Is a comparative science of politics possible?' in P. Laslett *et al.* (eds), *Philosophy, Politics and Society – Fourth Series* (Oxford: Blackwell), pp. 8–26.

MacRae, D. (1976), *The Social Functions of Social Science* (New Haven, Conn.: Yale University Press).

McVicar, J. (1979), *McVicar, by Himself* (London: Arrow Books).

Manfield, H. C. (1968), 'Commissions, Government', in D. L. Sills (ed.), *International Encyclopaedia of the Social Sciences*, Vol. 3, pp. 13–18.

Mann, M. (1973), *Workers on the Move* (Cambridge: Cambridge University Press).

Marsh, C. (1979), 'Opinion polls – social science or political manoeuvre?', in J. Irvine, I. Miles and J. Evans (eds), *Demystifying Social Statistics* (London: Pluto Press), pp. 268–88.

Marsh, C. (1982), *The Survey Method* (London: Allen & Unwin).

Marshall, T. H. (1946), 'Sociology at the Crossroads', inaugural lecture at the London School of Economics, repr. in T. H. Marshall, *Class, Citizenship and Social Development* (Chicago: University of Chicago Press, 1977), pp. 3–25.

Martin, R., and Fryer, R. (1973), *Redundancy and Paternalist Capitalism* (London: Allen & Unwin).

Marx, K. (1959), *Capital* (Moscow: Foreign Languages Publishing House); first published in 1867

Massam, B. (1975), *Location and Space in Social Administration* (London: Edward Arnold).

Mayhew, H. (1861), *London Labour and the London Poor*, 2 vols (London: Griffin Bohn).

Medawar, P. (1969), *Induction and Intuition in Scientific Thought* (London: Methuen).

Merton, R. K. (1957), *Social Theory and Social Structure* (Glencoe, Ill.: The Free Press).

Merton, R. K. (1975), 'Social knowledge and public policy: sociological perspectives on four presidential commissions', in Komarovsky (1975), pp. 153–77.

Mess, H. A. (1928), *Industrial Tyneside: A Social Survey* (London: Ernest Benn).

Moser, C. (1978), 'Social indicators: systems, methods, problems', in Bulmer (1978), pp. 203–14.

Moser, C. A., and Kalton, G. (1971), *Survey Methods in Social Investigation* (London: Heinemann).

Myrdal, G. (1944), *An American Dilemma* (New York: Harper & Row).

Myrdal, G. (1958), *Value in Social Theory* (London: Routledge & Kegan Paul).

Ogburn, W. F. (1964), *W. F. Ogburn on Culture and Social Change* (Chicago: University of Chicago Press).

Ohlin, L. E. (1975), 'The President's Commission on Law Enforcement and the Administration of Justice', in Komarovsky (1975), pp. 93–115.

Payne, G., Dingwall, R., Payne, J., and Carter, M. (1981), *Sociology and*

Social Research (London: Routledge & Kegan Paul).

Perry, N. (1976), 'Research settings in the social sciences: a re-examination', in Crawford and Perry (1976), pp. 137–90.

Pfautz, H. (ed.) (1967), *Charles Booth on The City: Physical Pattern and Social Structure* (Chicago: University of Chicago Press).

Pilgrim Trust (1938), *Men Out of Work* (Cambridge: Cambridge University Press).

Pinker, R. A. (1971), *Social Theory and Social Policy* (London: Heinemann).

Pinker, R. A. (1981), 'Introduction', in T. H. Marshall, *The Right to Welfare and Other Essays* (London: Heinemann), pp. 1–28.

Platt, A. (ed.) (1971), *The Politics of Riot Commissions 1917–1970* (New York: Macmillan).

Plowden Committee (1967), *Children and Their Primary Schools*, 2 vols, (London: HMSO); see also Acland (1980).

Popper, F. (1970), *The President's Commissions* (New York: Twentieth Century Fund).

Popper, K. R. (1961), *The Logic of Scientific Discovery* (London: Hutchinson).

Popper, K. R. (1972), *Objective Knowledge* (Oxford: Clarendon Press).

President's Research Committee on Social Trends (1933), *Recent Social Trends in the United States* (New York: McGraw-Hill). W. F. Ogburn was director of research.

Prest, A. R. (1980), 'Royal Commission reporting', in Bulmer (1980b), pp. 180–8.

Rainwater, L. (1968), 'The lower class: health, illness and medical institutions', in I. Deutscher and E. J. Thomson (eds), *Among the Poor* (New York: Basic Books).

RAWP (1976), *Sharing Resources for Health in England: Report of the Resource Allocation Working Party* (RAWP) (London: HMSO).

RCDIW (1974–80), *Royal Commission on the Distribution of Income and Wealth: Reports* (London: HMSO); see also Bulmer (1980a).

Redfern, P. (1976), 'Office of Population Censuses and Surveys', *Population Trends*, vol. 4, pp. 21–3.

Registrar-General (1977), *Decennial Supplement: Occupational Mortality 1970–72* (London: HMSO).

Reid, I. (1977), *Social Class Differences in Britain* (London: Open Books).

Rein, M. (1969), 'Social class and the health service', *New Society*, vol. 14, no. 807 (20 November).

Rein, M. (1976), *Social Science and Public Policy* (Harmondsworth: Penguin).

Rex, J. (1961), *Key Problems in Sociological Theory* (London: Routledge).

Rhodes, G. (1975), *Committees of Inquiry* (London: Allen & Unwin).

Rhodes, G. (1980), 'The Younger Committee and research', in Bulmer (1980b), pp. 110–21.

Riley, G. (1974), *Values, Objectivity and the Social Sciences* (Reading, Mass.: Addison-Wesley).

Robbins Committee (1963), *Higher Education*, Cmnd 2154 (London: HMSO).

Robinson, W. S. (1950), 'Ecological correlations and the behaviour of individuals', *American Sociological Review*, vol. 15, pp. 351–7.

Rossi, P., Wright, J. D., and Wright, S. R. (1978), 'The theory and practice of applied social research', *Evaluation Quarterly*, vol. 2, pp. 171–91.

Rothschild, Lord (1971), 'The organisation and management of government R and D', in *A Framework for Government Research and Development*, Cmnd 4184 (London: HMSO).

Rowntree, B. S. (1901), *Poverty: A Study of Town Life* (London: Macmillan).

Rowntree, B. S. (1941), *Poverty and Progress: A Second Social Survey of York* (London: Longman).

Rowntree, B. S. (1951), *English Life and Leisure* (London: Longman).

Rule, J. (1978), *Insight and Social Betterment: A Preface to Applied Social Science* (New York: Oxford University Press).

Runciman, W. G. (1966), *Relative Deprivation and Social Justice* (London: Routledge & Kegan Paul).

Rutter, M. (1972), *Maternal Deprivation Reassessed* ((Harmondsworth: Penguin).

Rutter, M., and Madge, J. (1976), *Cycles of Disadvantage* (London: Heinemann).

Rutter, M. (1977), 'Research into prevention of psychosocial disorders in childhood', in J. Barnes and N. Connelly (eds), *Social Care Research* (London: Bedford Square Press), pp. 104–17.

Rutter, M., Maughan, B., Mortimer, P., Ouston J., and Smith, A. (1979), *Fifteen Thousand Hours: Secondary Schools and Their Effects on Children* (London: Open Books).

Sainsbury, S. (1970), *Registered as Disabled* (London: Bell).

Sainsbury, S. (1973), *Measuring Disability* (London: Bell).

Sharpe, L. J. (1975), 'The social scientist and policy-making', *Policy and Politics*, vol. 4, no. 4, pp. 3–27.

Sharpe, L. J. (1978), 'The social scientist and policy-making in Britain and America: a comparison', in Bulmer (1978), pp. 302–12.

Sharpe, L. J. (1980), 'Research and the Redcliffe-Maud Commission', in Bulmer (1980b), pp. 18–33.

Shils, E. (1961), 'The calling of sociology', in T. Parsons, E. Shils, K. D. Naegele and J. R. Pitts (eds) *Theories of Society* (New York: The Free Press), pp. 1405–48.

Shonfield, A. (1980), 'In the course of investigation', in Bulmer (1980b), pp. 58–66.

Short, J. F., Jr (1975), 'The National Commission on the Causes and Prevention of Violence: the contributions of sociology and sociologists', in Komarovsky (1975), pp. 61–91.

Short, J. F., Jr (ed.) (1978), *Delinquency, Crime and Society* (Chicago: University of Chicago Press).

Simey, T. S., and Simey, M. B. (1960), *Charles Booth, Social Scientist* (London: Oxford University Press).

Simon, E. D., and Inman, J. (1935), *The Rebuilding of Manchester* (London: Longman).

Skolnick, J. H. (1970), 'Violence Commission Violence', *Transaction*, vol. 7 (October), pp. 32–8.

Smith, Sir H. L. (ed.) (1930–35), *The New Survey of London Life and Labour*, 9 vols (London: P. S. King).

Sociology (1981), special issue, *The Teaching of Research Methodology*, vol. 15, no. 4.

SRA (1979), *Social Research Association Register of Members* (London: Social Research Association).

SRA (1980), *Terms and Conditions of Social Research Funding in Britain: Report of the Working Group* (London: Social Research Association).

Stevenson, J. (1977), *Social Conditions in Britain between the Wars* (Harmondsworth: Penguin).

Stinchcombe, A. (1970), review of Blackstone *et al.* (1970), *British Journal of Sociology*, vol. 21, pp. 455–8.

Stouffer, S. A. (1950), 'Some observations on study design', *American Journal of Sociology*, vol. 55, pp. 355–61.

Suchman, E. (1967), 'Appraisal and implications for theoretical development', *Millbank Memorial Fund Quarterly*, vol. 45, no. 2, pt 2, pp. 109–13.

Sulzner, G. T. (1971), 'The policy process and the uses of National Government Study Commissions', *Western Political Quarterly*, vol. 24, pp. 438–48.

Susser, M. (1973), *Causal Thinking in the Health Sciences* (New York: Oxford University Press).

Susser, M., and Adelstein, A. (1975), 'Introduction', in W. Farr, *Vital Statistics* (Metuchen, NJ: Scarecrow Press), pp. iii–xiv; first published in 1885.

Thomas, H. (ed.) (1959), *The Establishment* (London: Blond).

Thompson, E. P. (1978), *The Poverty of Theory* (London: Merlin).

Titmuss, R. M. (1938), *Poverty and Population* (London: Macmillan).

Town, S. (1978), 'Action research and social policy: some recent British experience', in Bulmer (1978), pp. 160–85.

Townsend, P. (1954), 'Measuring poverty', in *British Journal of Sociology*, vol. 5, pp. 130–7.

Townsend, P. (1962), 'The meaning of poverty', in *British Journal of Sociology*, vol. 13, pp. 210–27.

Townsend, P. (1976), 'The difficulties of policies based on the concept of area deprivation', Barnett Shine Foundation Lecture, Department of Economics, Queen Mary College, London.

Townsend, P. (1979), *Poverty in the United Kingdom* (London: Allen Lane).

Trist, E. (1970), 'Social research institutions: types, structures, scale', *International Social Science Journal*, vol. 22, pp. 301–24.

Tudor Hart, J. (1975), 'The inverse care law', in C. Cox and A. Mead (eds), *A Sociology of Medical Practice* (London: Collier Macmillan), pp. 189–206.

Tunstall, J. (1980), 'The Royal Commission on the Press, 1974–7', in Bulmer (1980b), pp. 122–49.

Valentine, C. A. (1967), *Culture and Poverty* (Chicago: University of Chicago Press).

Vernon, R. V., and Mansergh, N. (eds) (1940), *Advisory Bodies* (London: Allen & Unwin).

Violence Commission (1970), *To Establish Justice, To Ensure Domestic Tranquility: The Final Report of the National Commission on the Causes and Prevention of Violence* (Washington, DC: Government Printing Office).

Walker Report (1968), *Rights in Conflict: A Report to the National Commission on the Causes and Prevention of Violence* (New York: Dutton).

Warner, M. (1979), 'The Webbs', in T. Raison and P. Barker (eds), *The Founding Fathers of Social Science* (London: Scolar Press), pp. 174–84.

Waskow, A. I. (1967), *From Race Riot to Sit In: 1919 and the 1960s* (Garden City, NY: Doubleday).

Webb, S., and Webb, B. (1932), *Methods of Social Study* (London: Longman).

Webb, B. (1938), *My Apprenticeship* (Harmondsworth: Penguin).

Webb, B. (1948), *Our Partnership* (London: Longman).

Weber, M. (1949), *On the Methodology of the Social Sciences* (Glencoe, Ill.: The Free Press).

Weiss, C. H. (1977a), 'Introduction', in Weiss (1977b), pp. 1–22.

Weiss, C. H. (ed.) (1977b), *Using Social Research in Public Policy Making* (Farnborough: Saxon House).

Weiss, C. H. (1980a), with M. Bucuvalas, *Social Science Research and Decision Making* (New York: Columbia University Press).

Weiss, C. H. (1980b), 'Knowledge creep and decision accretion', *Knowledge: Creation, Diffusion, Utilisation*, vol. 1, pp. 381–404.

Wells, A. F. (1935), *The Local Social Survey in Great Britain* (London: Allen & Unwin).

West, D. J. (1973), *Who Becomes Delinquent?* (London: Heinemann).

Westhoff, C. F. (1975), 'The Commission on Population Growth and the American Future: origins, operations and aftermath', in Komarovsky (1975), pp. 43–59.

Wheare, K. C. (1955), *Government by Committee* (Oxford: Clarendon Press).

Whitaker, B. (1979), *The Foundations: An Anatomy of Philanthropic Bodies* (Harmondsworth: Penguin).

Wickersham Report (1931), *Report on the Causes of Crime of the National Commission on Law Observance and Enforcement* (Washington, DC: Government Printing Office).

Wilmott, P. (1980), 'A view from the independent research institute', in M. Cross (ed.), *Social Research and Social Policy: Three Perspectives* (London: Social Research Association), pp. 1–13.

Wilson, J. Q. (1971), 'Violence, pornography and social science', *The Public Interest*, vol. 22 (Winter), pp. 45–61.

Wolanin, T. R. (1975), *Presidential Advisory Commissions: Truman to Nixon* (Madison, Wis.: University of Wisconsin Press).

Yeo, E. (1973), 'Mayhew as a social investigator', in E. P. Thompson and E. Yeo (eds), *The Unknown Mayhew* (Harmondsworth: Penguin), pp. 56–109.

Zetterberg, H. (1962), *Social Theory and Social Practice* (Totowa, NJ: Bedminster Press).

Znaniecki, F. (1940), *The Social Role of the Man of Knowledge* (New York: Columbia University Press).

Index